CRIPPLED IMMORTALS

Chris Murray is from Dublin. He has written dry, academic works about authors such as Samuel Taylor Coleridge and John Keats, and has been broadcast internationally as a musician. He lives in Melbourne, where he teaches literature at Monash University.

CRIPPLED IMMORTALS

CHRIS MURRAY

© Chris Murray 2018

First published 2018 by Arcadia
the general books imprint of
Australian Scholarly Publishing Ltd
7 Lt Lothian St Nth, North Melbourne, Vic 3051

Tel: 03 9329 6963 / Fax: 03 9329 5452
enquiry@scholarly.info / www.scholarly.info

ISBN 978-1-925801-34-7

Cover design Wayne Saunders

For Christopher and Kathleen Murray

CONTENTS

NOTE TO THE READER

The practitioners in this book speak the Chinese dialects of Mandarin, Hokkien Minnan and Cantonese at various times (for example, Chan See-meng refers to his primary art variously as *Wuzuquan* in Mandarin or *Ngor Chor* in Hokkien). For consistency, all Chinese terminology has been rendered here in *pinyin*, the standardized transcription method for Mandarin. Practitioners who speak English tend to refer to certain arts/ideas using the Chinese names (*Wuzuquan*, *Bagua*) but to translate others (Praying Mantis, the Five Elements). I cannot surmise a reason for this inconsistency but have stayed true to the speakers.

In reference to people and organisations, I have used the English forms by which they are best known: Chee Kim Thong (Hokkien) rather than Xu Jindong (Mandarin); Chin Woo Athletic Association (by which the group became famous worldwide) rather than Jingwu Mun (*pinyin*, devised much later). I have used 'Malaya' and 'Malaysia' respectively for periods before and after the foundation of Malaysia in 1963.

Most Han Chinese have three names in the order **surname**, <u>generational name</u>, *given name*, as in **Chee** <u>Kim</u> *Thong*. Brothers share a generational name, hence Chee Boon Teck, Chee Boon Leong etc. Sisters share a different generational name from their brothers. As an endearment, one may drop the generational name and use a gendered prefix instead, 'Ah' for a man and 'Ai' for a woman. Hence 'Ah-Thong,' 'Ai-Ling'. Those who also take an English name will place it before the Chinese sequence: Timothy Chan See-meng.

INFINITE ABYSS

Many commentators insist there's no truth to the story that Yang Luchan shaved off his eyebrows. For our teacher, though, the tale is too precious to challenge its veracity, or he thinks it's obtuse to apply the lens of historical fact to such a useful martial-arts parable.

'This Yang,' he will begin (*will begin*, for there are stories he loves to tell time and again). 'This Yang was keen to learn Chen Changxing's art. But when he went to see the master, Mr Chen did not accept him. You see, Yang made a mistake: he brought gold bars and a lot of expensive gifts to the master. When he saw these riches, Chen was disgusted. He said, "You think your money can *buy* my art?" He turned Yang away.

'Then, out of the blue, there appeared a strange man in the area. He was bald-headed, and he had no eyebrows. He would spend all evening sweeping leaves around Mr Chen's house. He did it for about a year.

'One day, another master visited Mr Chen to challenge him to fight. Unfortunately Mr Chen had diarrhoea. He couldn't even get out of bed, he was so weak. The stranger insisted, "I've waited ten years for this fight." Chen's students all kept quiet; none of them would accept the challenge. It was a great embarrassment for Chen and his school. But then the leaf-sweeper appeared and said, "Mr Chen, don't worry. I will represent you." And the leaf-sweeper fought off this assailant. Mr Chen said, "Hey, your technique is like mine!" The man knelt down and apologized. "It is me, Yang. I came to see you one year ago, but you turned me away." So Chen asked, "How did you learn my art?" Yang said, "Every night when you teach I'm out in the woods, sweeping leaves and watching you."

'Mr Chen called all of his students. In the old days, if you peeped and tried to learn, by tradition the master would kill you. One of these students knew Yang and said, "This guy comes from a good family. Please don't kill him. He's a good man, it's just that he's mad about learning martial arts." Chen answered, "I didn't say anything about killing him. You've all been with me for nearly ten years. This guy can learn my art in one year, but in ten years you can't. I'm going to accept him as my last disciple."'

Later, Yang taught at the Qing imperial court in Beijing, where he modified Chen's movements into a slow art suitable for opium addicts. He renamed the routine *Taijiquan*, 'Ultimate Fist'. This is the Yang-style *Taijiquan* that many Westerners know as 'Tai Chi'.

Most versions of the story have Chen ill when his challenger arrived, but not specifically with diarrhoea. The shaved eyebrows too appear to be our teacher's embellishment; it's usually said only that Yang disguised himself. To me, the rounded intervals in this telling – one year; ten years; ten years – illustrate that our master wants to direct us away from the notion that the anecdote is historically accurate, and towards the ideals it communicates. For such a short narrative, the encounter between Yang and Chen touches on many important aspects of martial-arts culture: the formal acceptance of disciples; the hangers-on who bask in the master's reflective glory, but who shy from a physical contest; the rare, dedicated aspirant upon whom the future of the art will turn; the etiquette by which a challenger must be accepted; dignity or 'face'; sincerity and humility; the integrity Chen displays when he refuses Yang's riches, but which portends the possible use of martial arts for financial gain.

We circle about such stories in our practice. Every stroke of martial arts has a precedent, a philosophical principle, and is attended upon by several kinds of narrative. No single form of communication is adequate to transmit the nuances of martial-arts technique. Take it for granted that there is silent demonstration of the movements and repeated practice. But alongside these we talk of history, legend, Chinese medicine and philosophy. The teacher might relate the crucial detail of a motion by an account of the person who made a particular error fifty years ago, or how the technique was applied in a confrontation, or the myth that gives the technique its name, a name that hints at the subtleties. Independent effort is vital for success in martial arts, but the ghosts of our predecessors surround us at all times.

For those of us who practice Chinese martial-arts – *gongfu* – seriously, the most important aspect of the Chen and Yang story, and the starting-point of this book, lies in Yang himself. He knew that the *gongfu* taught by Chen was not the same as the *gongfu* taught by some idiot down the street. There has never been a reliable method to document the principles of martial arts, nor a trustworthy system of accreditation for professed teachers. Westernized *gongfu* classes in particular are often just fitness sessions with Orientalist flourishes. The dedicated student knows that the only way to ensure accuracy of transmission is to find a great master, or at least a teacher who studies *under* a great master. And the devoted student has to be somewhat obsessive, maybe a little crazy. Hence disguise is not enough, in our master's version of the tale, but shaved eyebrows might indicate the requisite enthusiasm. Sometimes he elaborates that Yang also smeared mud all over his face to complete the disguise. For those who are most dedicated, *gongfu* exerts a magnetic attraction which I think defies rational explanation.

My own love of martial arts developed when I was a teenager, because of the new relationship it gave me with my physicality. I had spinal problems as a child – diagnosed much later as scoliosis – and didn't move well. Although I liked sports, I was endlessly frustrated by my inability to perform. Even in the late twentieth-century, Ireland was rather a Third World place. PE teachers gave me terrible grades, but no-one asked questions or speculated on causes.

Under a dedicated teacher, *gongfu* is like physiotherapy. When we practise martial arts, we see a movement, imitate it crudely, and thereafter we refine it constantly. Moreover, while physiotherapy is notoriously dull, who wouldn't want to execute crescent kicks and triple punches? What adolescence in Irish suburbs wouldn't be enriched by suggestions of a faraway world with martial-arts temples and warriors who lived by codes of honour? And what slight schoolboy wouldn't be enticed by the thought that bullies might be overcome by deftly applying the laws of physics? My earliest instructor told me I had a talent for improvement. As my *gongfu* advanced I became better at other sports. In idle games of football, friends asked whether I had practised ball control, but I knew it was the Shaolin footwork. Bullies decided I was too much trouble.

I progressed with my first *gongfu* teacher. After he relocated, I had mixed fortunes under other instructors, in a variety of Chinese martial-arts. At times I regressed. I speculated that some of these teachers withheld techniques. Years later I realized they comprehended too little *gongfu* to withhold anything, often dismissing my questions aggressively to conceal ignorance. I sought true *gongfu*, and believed such a thing existed. Yet the signal could be lost in the noises, not simply of poor tuition, but of capitalism. One chief instructor forbade his students from taking water to class. He declared our thirst a contemptible weakness; that is, until he announced a plan to sell water canteens emblazoned with the club's crest. His underlings insisted that their group upheld timeless custom. Meanwhile the head of school found ever-new means to gouge his pupils for money. He pushed the usual gradings and uniforms, and also such un-martial accessories as keyrings and car stickers. There were depressing politics too. Talented young teachers went unsupported by those further up the hierarchy. In their power struggles, club members squabbled over who was most senior. Some of these disputants had long since given up exercise. They surfaced occasionally only to assert status.

The tiresome involutions of martial-arts clubs measure how keen I was to study *gongfu*. I bit my tongue at the politics and didn't buy a water canteen. Fortunately, there were positive experiences to nurture my enthusiasm. I had moved to the UK as a university student. There my *gongfu* teachers included a White Crane practitioner who forbade me from learning the first sequence of movements until I could stand perfectly straight. He sent me to flatten my spine against the wall while the other students acquired the set. At times I lay on the floor while he pressed my knees in various directions to increase the flexibility of my lower back and hips. By then I had practised under the White Crane instructor for several months. I realized that he made extra efforts because he had decided I was worth teaching. My back improved. The first time a friend commented on my immaculate posture, I thought he was being sarcastic.

Undoubtedly I've displayed a touch of the Yang craziness. When I couldn't afford a car, *gongfu* commitments required me to make a half-hour bicycle trip to class, much of it uphill, while clutching an eyebrow-height staff. At least it was mostly downhill on the way back to Bristol, with me holding onto the staff again as though I'd invented long-distance jousting. When my call-centre employers allocated me too many shifts that interfered with training, I quit the job. For a time I got up early every second Sunday to travel across England by coach and local bus – three-and-a-half hours there, three-and-a-half hours back – to put in a couple of hours with an instructor, all because I believed that was the right art for me.

The fact that I wasn't ostensibly built for martial arts put me in surprisingly distinguished company. There are legends of child prodigies in *gongfu*, instant adepts. But there is also the story of an asthmatic and jaundiced boy named Huo Yuanjia, who would eventually found the Chin Woo Athletic Association, now an international *gongfu* organisation. The martial-arts journey of Wang Xiangzhai began when his parents, concerned at his feebleness, sent him to learn *Yiquan* – 'Intention Fist' – in which he became a renowned expert. And a long time ago, in an unremarkable Chinese village, a little boy's grandmother saw him tormented by local bullies, so she taught him *Taizuquan*, the Emperor's art, and this set him on the journey that would lead his life to intersect with mine. *Gongfu* holds the promise of remaking yourself. Some will progress to meditative practices that alter sensory perception. More immediately, a degree of physical transformation entails any regular physical effort. Those who begin with some bodily disadvantage, if they persist, get into the habit of hard work. This work never ends: with advancement, the bar is raised so that *gongfu* never seems easy.

When I had worked for some years, I wanted more than any available teacher could offer. More than that, I felt the way people went about martial arts was entirely wrong. The last club I attended pressured me to become a full-time instructor, but devoted most of its energies to leaflets, franchise management and new products, behind which the romantic figure of the warrior monk was hard to discern. And there was something amiss in the student's place in a group of twenty, miming what the instructor showed from the front of the hall. Surely this fudging wouldn't uncover the complexities of *gongfu*. The fantasy was to practice in close quarters with a great master, someone both knowledgeable and willing to share. Often my mind turned to the one true expert I had met, briefly, when I was a teenager. I wished that I could study directly with such a master. I was tantalized by the idea of where the art would lead if I made strong efforts with authoritative direction.

My break came about from another field of interest. Let this not be considered a betrayal of *gongfu*: it's traditional to study martial arts alongside calligraphy, philosophy, poetry, horse riding and music. By coincidence rather than knowledge of classical Chinese education, I was not only a *gongfu* enthusiast, but also a starving musician and a graduate student. In short, I spent most of my hours temping in low-paid office work. It was a bleak time. My band fell apart, and academic work was difficult to secure. But then a Singaporean university advertised two-year research positions. I applied to study portrayals of China in Western literature, and returned from honeymoon to a job offer. It was too good to be true. In a profession that rewarded publication above all else, I was to have very few teaching responsibilities, allowing me to write. The move would be gold for my professional profile.

From the moment I accepted the job offer in Singapore, I researched the local martial-arts scene in every way I could. I understood that many arts were excellent. The quest was to find the best teacher, to learn the most possible in the two years I had. Singapore had many groups, in a population of three-quarters Chinese ethnicity, and that number predominantly of ancestral origins in *gongfu*-rich Fujian province. *When the student is ready, the master appears*, goes a *gongfu* saying. The occurrence doesn't have to be as passive as that phrasing implies. It's not as though the only legitimate way to encounter a master is to bump into him in the street. Perhaps I was fated to apply my research skills to investigate the different teachers in Singapore, and fated by that method to find my master, my Sifu. And, despite Chen Changxing's lofty dismissal of Yang on their first encounter, masters need students too, or their arts will be lost.

A few years after he first heard the story of Chen and Yang, our teacher studied under Dong Ying Jie, a disciple of the Yang family whose technique was so good that many still refer to it as 'Dong style' in its own right. Yet it was another master whose arts would become the focus of our efforts.

A comet passes through our system to be witnessed by the experts who look for it, and by some chance watchers of the skies. Others will hear tell of it, but most will never know the phenomenon occurred. And so the trajectory of Chee Kim Thong. Those in his wake include devoted disciples and hangers-on; those who want to fight, those who only trade on his name, and those who see his arts as steps on the Buddhist Path to Liberation. High *gongfu* satisfies all of these mindsets – it is a discipline with a unique capacity to intrigue the brawler and the mystic alike – but we must disavow these inclinations and survey the entire picture if we are really to understand the pursuit. *Gongfu* is neither punching alone, nor meditation alone, but to conceive of it as crucially reliant on both of those activities simultaneously, however counterintuitive such a union appears, would be a significant step towards its essence. Therefore to tell of Chee Kim Thong's group I must introduce yogis and Tibetan lamas, but must equally treat of fighters with names like Sea Dragon and Iron Fist. Nor do these characters adhere to the roles we might instinctively ascribe them: there are renegade monks in temples, and there are transcendent saints living outwardly banal lives.

Furthermore, martial arts is a tale of mediocrity alongside mastery. Precious few practitioners are talented, or even dedicated. Journeymen are actually vital to the transmission of martial arts: they provide financial support and training spaces, administrate *gongfu* schools, and take sides in disputes. Each aspirant has a part to play in the future of the art. To know the art necessitates knowing its practitioners. The actions and motives of the supporting cast are as important as are those of the master in determining the practices that have reached us.

Behind these efforts loom the *gongfu* temples at Shaolin and Wudan. These are the considered the origins of, respectively, the Zen and Taoist martial-arts traditions. Their names persist as exemplars: negatively so, for their modern incarnations as tourist traps and purveyors of watered-down *gongfu*; positively, as the sources of ideals and legends that inspire practice. Many look to a master such as Chee Kim Thong to embody what is best of Shaolin culture. Notwithstanding their diverse purposes in learning *gongfu*, all of Master Chee's followers share a belief in him as a paradigm of the genuine master, in a world populous with disappointments and phonies.

For a time he lived in seclusion. Maybe the Old Man anticipated the problems that could arise if one developed the reputation of a Chen or a Yang. But Chee Kim Thong's quiet life was not to last. If it had done, I would never have heard of him, nor learned the real arts. Did mere coincidence lead me back to Chee Kim Thong's *gongfu* – of all the many martial-arts disciplines in Asia – or the machinations of mysterious forces, powerful enough to impel me across the world? The narrator at the start of this book would dismiss such enigmatic agency, but the narrator at the end is not so sure. Some practitioners are convinced that unseen powers exist that bring us all together. But it's the *gongfu* itself that draws us in to begin with. A little practise yields modest health benefits. A *lot* of practice brings us into strange realms of consciousness and bodily sensation. Those who attempt Chee Kim Thong's arts are forever changed.

THUNDER

1

EVERYONE KNOWS AH-THONG

Not yet two years old, a little girl named Semek wandered onto the Kuala Terengganu-Dungun Road one day in September 1956 and was hit by a bus. She died almost instantly. The bus conductor had some knowledge of medicine, but he was unable to save Semek. After two months and a local controversy, the coroner would return a verdict of death by misadventure. Semek suffered a terrible misfortune. To apportion blame would accomplish nothing.

The complication – which the bus conductor perceived immediately – was that Semek was Malay, while the driver was Chinese. Race was a volatile issue in Malaya. Here it would be difficult for the driver to argue that, unfortunately, accidents happen; that the blink-of-an-eye motor crash allows no reflection on ethnicity. In minutes, reports spread through the village: a Chinese man had run down a Malay child. A Chinese man *killed* a Malay child.

A mob of furious locals surrounded the bus, intent on vengeance and deaf to reason. Some brandished *parangs*. The conductor urged the driver to get back into the bus and shut the doors, and not to open them under any circumstances.

What happened next, Yap Cheng Hai explained four years later as his Austin A35 bounced down 382 miles of dusty roads and dirt tracks from Kuala Lumpur to Dungun, persuaded him that this bus conductor was a 'great man'. Cheng Hai recalled the newspaper's description of the conductor repelling armed fighters as though protected by a force field. Further details corroborated Cheng Hai's initial impression. It seems that once the melee subsided, the bus conductor tended to the wounds of his assailants. The next day the *penghulu*, the village headman, visited to wish the bus conductor well for his recovery, but found that he was completely uninjured.

Cheng Hai determined to visit the bus conductor whose name, he had learned, was Chee Kim Thong. Although it was essentially a village of fishermen, with an iron mine nearby, that offered limited opportunity to a hardware salesman, Cheng Hai concocted a business trip to Dungun. He was intrigued.

On the ferry across the Sungai Dungun, Cheng Hai conversed with a fellow passenger who had damaged his arm. The stranger intended to visit Chee Kim Thong for medical treatment.

'You know this Chee Kim Thong?' Cheng Hai asked.

'*Everyone* knows Ah-Thong.'

The ferry landed and the passenger entered a taxi, shutting the door with the instruction, 'Take me to Ah-Thong'.

Cheng Hai visited Chee Kim Thong on various occasions over the next few years. Now in his early thirties, Cheng Hai had seen enough *gongfu* to know he was on to a good thing. His accounts of the master's demonstrations impressed his young companion enough for him to endure the twelve-hour journey to Dungun. 18 April was a school holiday and, coincidentally, Chee Kim Thong's birthday, an auspicious occasion to visit a master. The boy enjoyed his opportunity to pass between worlds. English-speaking Tim Chan, student of a prestigious Catholic school in Kuala Lumpur, became Chan See-meng, an enthusiast for traditional *gongfu* who scoured the land in search of true experts. He grew up glued to the radio for stories of the legendary *wuxia*; with the bumbling Cheng Hai he set out to discover whether such 'martial heroes' existed in reality.

For two years See-meng studied under the great *Taijiquan* master Dong Ying Jie, but had struggled to find good instruction since Dong left for China. For the last year Cheng Hai had taught him the hard-style *Wuzuquan*, Five Ancestors Fist, he studied in Singapore. Hence See-meng was fascinated to hear that although Chee Kim Thong was also an *Wuzuquan* man, his art was different. Cheng Hai insisted that Ah-Thong's *gongfu* was more refined than any other he had encountered. The hitch was that Cheng Hai had not persuaded Chee Kim Thong to *teach* his arts. On every visit Cheng Hai pleaded with the master to accept him as a student. In 1959 Chee Kim Thong said to come back in one year's time, so here Cheng Hai was to try his luck again.

The Austin reached the perilous Sungai Dungun, which ranked just above bandits, cholera and tigers as the greatest regional hazard. The river's current was strong, and floods were frequent. Occasionally boats capsized. In 1958 a bus plunged off the edge of the ferry. It took a car with it and twenty-three people drowned. When the river reached its highest in 1959, Dungun lay under eight feet of water, stranding residents on their rooftops. The best of times meant dangerous river conditions. Cancellation of the ferry was a regular occurrence, although it was not a formidable vessel. In truth the 'ferry' was a rickety raft on a rope-and-pulley system operated by coolies. Fortunately it was functional when Cheng Hai and See-meng arrived. They crossed the Sungai Dungun for the final stretch to Ah-Thong's house. Cheng Hai and See-meng arrived at a shack with a corrugated-iron roof, where Chee Kim Thong sold groceries and scrap metal, and gave traditional medical-treatment to those who sought his help. He retained his stake in the bus company, but had shifted his focus to retail.

At first inspection the legendary Chee Kim Thong did not thrill See-meng. En route the boy prepared himself to meet a superman.

'But this guy,' he thought, 'looks like a Chinese farmer. The wide trousers, the baggy shirt with the sleeves rolled up, the suspenders; *aiyoh!*'

For what seemed an eternity, Ah-Thong fumbled in his pockets and produced immense bunches of keys, which he laid on the table with a series of clatters before sitting. See-meng winced. At least the master appeared happy to have visitors on his forty-second birthday. They drank tea while Chee Kim Thong conversed with Cheng Hai in the Hokkien dialect. See-meng didn't understand Hokkien; his family spoke Cantonese.

Occasionally Cheng Hai turned to give him the gist of the dialogue with Master Chee, but soon the boy became bored and his mind wandered.

'Hey!' Cheng Hai prompted. 'He's asking you to demonstrate.'

See-meng leapt up. He moved to the centre of the room and performed an *Wuzuquan* sequence. He imagined he unleashed ferocious power. The routine of strikes and parries took around two minutes. When See-meng finished, to his dismay, Ah-Thong laughed. He addressed See-meng in Cantonese.

'Your strength doesn't even come out. It's stuck in your chest.' The master rose to explain. 'The movements should all be circles. Yours are all straight lines. In this way you restrict yourself.'

He was in flow now. Chee Kim Thong opened up and, as he talked, alluded to every principle that the boy had taken two years to apprehend under Dong Ying Jie. Cheng Hai was right. See-meng could perceive that there was magic to the soft-spoken Ah-Thong.

Next, Chee Kim Thong himself demonstrated. It was, like Cheng Hai described, as though the wind came from Master Chee's hands. The visitors were entranced. They studied a version of *Wuzuquan* based on stiff, muscular strength. By contrast Ah-Thong's technique combined immense power with delicate skill. Unlike See-meng's direct hand-attacks, Chee Kim Thong used rotation of his waist to whip out his limbs like a slingshot. He manifested the elusive paradox of the highest Chinese *gongfu*, the union of hardness and softness. At one point Master Chee invited See-meng to attack him and flung the boy across the room effortlessly. See-meng picked himself up and beamed. It was worth the journey.

After some time Master Chee reached a decision.

'You will become my disciples,' he announced.

In accordance with custom, Cheng Hai and See-meng served tea to their new master. It was an occasion for great celebration, but also a serious commitment. Cheng Hai and See-meng would undergo ritual initiation as disciples. Because this was a formal arrangement of adoption See-meng, a minor, needed written permission from his guardian. Consequently he could not undergo initiation that night, but needed to wait until the master's next birthday. Nonetheless in 1960 Chee Kim Thong initiated Cheng Hai along with two locals who were keen to learn *Wuzuquan*. He asked them to swear obedience, and gave each disciple a special technique and a baptismal name. Afterwards Chee Kim Thong hosted a commemorative dinner, and invited his neighbours. Some questioned Master Chee's sudden decision to adopt disciples, while others bemoaned his choices.

'Shaolin has so many tenets. Why do you only have one oath?'

'If they can't give obedience,' Master Chee answered, 'why promise anything else?'

'This boy isn't even Hokkien,' exclaimed another. 'He's Cantonese! How can you accept him as a disciple?'

Chee Kim Thong trusted his own judgment ahead of old-fashioned tribalism. He had taken a shine to See-meng. Moreover, Cheng Hai had what he wanted at last. Afterwards the two visitors reflected on Master Chee's sudden change of heart to accept disciples, but this occupied them only momentarily. They were swept up in the excitement of tuition from a true master.

* * *

'Mr Chee,' Chan See-meng concludes, 'has a lot of treasures. If he trusts you, he'll tell you a lot of things. But if he doesn't like you, Old Man is like a clam.'

He turns his attention to his smartphone which, he has assured me, is the latest model. In the moment's silence I reflect on the two hours that have passed since we met at Chinatown MRT station. Ducking away from the pristine shop-fronts of Eu Tong Sen Street, Master Chan led me through a series of alleys whose labyrinthine twists emerged into an older Singapore, where the waiters speak no English and the menus are all in traditional Chinese characters rather than the simplified script of mainstream Chinatown. For me that transition was exhilarating, the hoped-for symbol of foray into the secretive depths of martial arts. There are rickety medicine shops to hand – so unlike the air-con-blasting chain outlets on the high street – and shadowy antique-stores of which it is impossible to tell whether they are now, or ever, open. It's as though I have found the priestess who can open the path to the underworld. Even 'Chinatown,' I have realized today, is an obsolete label from the British colonial past. The multi-lingual train announcements refer to Chinatown in Mandarin as *niuchi shui*, 'ox-cart water'. Modern Singapore has a sober exterior, but there always seems to be something beneath the surface, for those who look.

Master Chan ordered for us. As he converses, finished for now with the investment opportunity heralded by his smartphone, he has the contented air of a recently fed tiger. He revels in his own movements when he displays *gongfu* flourishes in his seat. Likewise he relishes telling anecdotes in which he enacts his teenage self, swinging his shoulders from side to side as he recalls carrying Master Chee's medicine case around Kuala Lumpur. In this cat-like enjoyment of his own being is an utter absence of affectation. He declares renowned *gongfu* practitioners to be 'crude' and 'rough' not for dramatic effect, but from total indifference to what people may think. Identifying the food for me, and speaking in a series of narratives of his past, he revels in the role of elder and host, which was prearranged. When I asked to meet, Master Chan offered to take me to lunch. From some inkling that it's customary, I brought a gift for the master, which I hand to him now over the table.

'How did you know I like single-malt whiskey?' he beams.

I had no idea whether he was a teetotaller or whiskey aficionado, but gravitated towards a representative of Irish culture; perhaps with some notion that Master Chan's acceptance of this offering might determine his treatment of me as prospective student.

My head spins from the amount of detail taken in over lunch. We have discussed the early days and how Chee Kim Thong's group became a national organisation; Chan See-meng's career as a banker; his victory in a *gongfu* tournament; a meditation group he hosted in 'KL' which, I realize, means Kuala Lumpur; my background in *gongfu*; what sort of family I come from; whether I can name the Eight Essences of *Wuzuquan*. I answer that I *think* I know about *four* of the Eight Essences, transmitted to Anglophone practitioners as the Four Principles.

'You must know all these things. Although we talk with our fists, you must understand the theory. Mr Chee may look like a villager, but he talks like a scientist. *Wuzuquan* is all circles and triangles. Did he mention these things in your seminar?'

'No.'

'Old Man just sat there drinking his tea, ah?'

'Pretty much.'

There are grounds for optimism in Master Chan's patience with what must occur to him as remarkable ignorance. In my novitiate toil with chopsticks I have even learned about table etiquette:

'The plate is only for bones and such. Mostly we use the bowl. Don't worry; even many Singaporeans do not know this.'

Now I know that it is acceptable to pierce a dumpling with chopsticks if it proves difficult to grab; about the tradition of annual performance for the deceased ancestors of the *gongfu* lineage; the *correct* name of Chee Kim Thong's primary art: Shaolin White Crane Five Ancestors Fist, or *Baihe Wuzuquan*.

'I can also teach the spiritual part, if you are interested,' Master Chan says, but he sees me balk at the word 'spiritual'. We change the subject. Finally we arrange to meet again.

'So you are coming one week from Tuesday?'

'Yeah.'

'*Hmmmmm?*'

'Uh, *yes Sifu.*'

'Good.'

We return to the MRT station and part on the platform to take trains in opposite directions. On my journey to Jurong I mull over the encounter. He exerted a strange presence over lunch. Already my memory plays tricks on me and recalls the last few hours like they were two separate events. We faced each other across a round table, yet I remember particular phases of discussion – such as when he demonstrated the various hand forms used in *Wuzuquan* – like he sat right beside me. Already too the setting of our lunch is a distant world. The train rattles past endless shopping-centres and apartment blocks. Now Jurong Lake stretches to my left, relief from the closeness of Chinatown.

There will be no sports hall, no uniforms, just a few students in a private group at Chan See-meng's home. I am apprehensive about the challenges of this new environment, but I hoped for this invitation. Of Singapore's rich *gongfu* heritage, Master Chan was the most fascinating prospect I encountered on my search for tuition. The private lessons will enable depths of practice beyond – I hope – the possibilities of the usual hobby groups and commercial classes with fixed syllabi. Yet uncertainties run through my mind. Why does such a distinguished expert live and teach in relative obscurity, rather than open a lucrative school? Is his critical manner insufferable, or are his lessons ruinously expensive?

Chan See-meng admitted he was lucky to meet some of the best *gongfu* masters. As the train slides into Pioneer Station, it excites me how few degrees of separation I would become, by training under Master Chan, from great names in martial arts: Dong, the Yang family and Wang Xiangzhai. Above all, Master Chan's proximity to Chee Kim Thong attracts me. I have invested time in *Wuzuquan*, and feel entitled to experience the real thing. In his account of their first year with Master Chee, See-meng and Cheng Hai 'were like a pair of chopsticks' who practiced, ate and travelled the long road to Dungun together. Chan See-meng described experiences that any martial-arts enthusiast would envy, and now I have the opportunity to benefit. But I can see too in what he told me that the seeds of discontent were sown in those early days.

* * *

'Be ready soon—'

For the first month, while we look for an apartment, Claire and I live in campus housing. The university is both beautiful and bewilderingly different from the Victorian villas of Bristol University, where we met. Our new campus occupies 200 acres of groomed jungle, populated by wild boar, snakes, pangolin and even – it is whispered – the endangered leopard-cat prowls amidst its 10,000 trees. Recently a group of children, who live with their parents in faculty apartments, confronted builders who were tormenting a one-armed monkey.

Cicadas shriek as I walk between buildings to complete umpteen administrative tasks related to my induction. Several times I become lost in the university's complexity and, with that, exasperated and drenched in sweat. The main blocks sparkle as though the public face of a Singapore that, as a colleague put it when he collected us from the airport, 'is like living in the future'. The streamlined, functional appearance of some structures appears defiant of the older European universities. Others are conspicuously forward-looking. They hint at Chinese characters, their facades ripple, they emerge unexpectedly from hillsides and have grassy roofs. But at the front of the campus is the Chinese Heritage Centre, a construction in classical Chinese architecture, and a garden dotted with octagonal pavilions. I gazed at this prospect online when I knew that I would soon leave my dire temping job and relocate to Asia.

One night the garden is covered with stalls, the trees adorned with lanterns, and a stage is erected to celebrate Mid-Autumn Festival. I don't see any of my colleagues from English literature – few of whom work on Asian writing – and all the students here are of Chinese ethnicity rather than Malay or Indian. Claire and I are served moon cakes in the Chinese Heritage Centre, and we amble around the stands, which are devoted to different aspects of Chinese culture. The sole discordant note in my head is concern that Claire will be unhappy so far from home. As an independent researcher I'm not bound to rigid office-hours, so I've taken it easy in the first couple of weeks to acclimatize. I am hopeful that novelty will distract Claire enough to settle in, both the vast catalogue of newness available to us in Singapore, and more immediately, the displays before us this evening. There are traditional games and laptops running programmes that simulate fortune-telling rituals. Under the lanterns, students distribute candles for visitors to carry along the avenues.

Today I obtained my Foreigner Identification Number, which enabled me to purchase a mobile phone. I decide to try out the camera by filming the lion dance that winds its way around the garden. Inexplicably, the footage appears distorted. Regardless, the occasion doesn't constitute a great moment in cinematic history. The participants aim to retrieve traditions that are in danger of becoming lost to them in the onward march of modern Singapore. The lion is awkward, inexperienced. There is no display of *gongfu*, but there is a troupe devoted to *wushu*, a *gongfu*-derived performance whose key predicates are that the Chinese Communist Party wanted rid of subversive Zen martial-arts, and that Chairman Mao's wife was fond of ballet. That there are far more *gongfu* groups around than in the West remains an observation of only relative significance. Few Singaporeans care about traditional martial-arts, a part of the nation's heritage that threatens to be swept aside by modernity.

At last, one Tuesday evening I take a bus from the campus, board the East-West MRT, negotiate the crowds to change line at Outram Park, and finally board a light rail service to Master Chan's building. The trains are packed, and the journey takes ninety minutes, but I arrive early. Master Chan – 'Sifu,' I should say – will not yet have arrived home from the class on breathing exercises he leads for elderly high-fliers in Orchard.

It's a starry night. Bluish-white Venus is brightest in the sky. I can discern little of the neighbourhood, just thousands of square lights that look out from the buildings around me. On a stone bench outside the apartment complex I think about the ways that people are brought together. Being in a room with Chee Kim Thong for one week becomes the pretext to contact his closest disciple, many years later, half a world away.

What will happen tonight? I imagine offending Master Chan on the grounds of arcane Shaolin etiquette. I'm convinced that his students will be advanced beings, who will resent how my low standard slows down their progress. Amidst these doubts, I decide not to tell Master Chan about my old spinal problems. For one thing, the deviation is barely detectable now. More importantly, I don't want to appear like damaged goods, and I don't want to cast my study of top martial-arts in Singapore as the sort of personal adversity-narrative that I find tiresome and narcissistic. Let Master Chan notice what he will.

Momentarily I inspect the new phone, and find that there's a protective film over the camera lens. No wonder my footage of the lion dance turned out blurry. I peel off the sticker and hope it's a good omen that life offers me such a metaphor for the possibility of altered perspective.

2

VOMITING BLOOD

'Chris, your technique is *beli-bad*. Do you know what is *beli-bad*? It's Singaporean; it means *very bad*. What you are showing me is not the correct *Tiaoqie*.'

Tiaoqie: qie is to 'cut,' and the *tiao* technique is named for a calligraphy stroke that flicks up and concludes in a sharp turn. These movements are the main focus of *Tiaoqie*, one of the sequences in which techniques are transmitted and performed. I infer that my routine lacks the finesse of fine brushwork.

'You can see,' Sifu continues, 'the front of my shirt is gone all red. Watch.'

Sifu demonstrates the motion that gives *Tiaoqie* its name. Deft rotation of the wrist deflects an incoming strike with the heel of the hand. The technique concludes with a Knife Hand to the opponent's ribs. Travis and I observe, then imitate.

Sifu watches me and shakes his head.

'I don't know why Old Man didn't teach.'

It dawns on me that the rear foot must push against the ground to drive the hips forward and give momentum to the hand. This is a matter of coordination. My real difficulty lies in the middle stroke. It's an upward block, but the way I generate momentum is incorrect.

'I *flip*,' Sifu emphasizes. '*Flip* up at the elbow. The arm is a rattan. It should sound like thunder when you cut through the air.'

Sifu shows us, with a whoosh when his hand cuts down and slices up. To produce the sound requires high velocity, but it will be silent if the muscles are stiff. I attempt to make the necessary change, and amend how I impel the motion rather than the outer form. An impulse from my waist whips my arm out like a bamboo switch.

'Ah, you're getting it,' Sifu encourages. '*Flip! Flip!* Now *turn* the wrist. No, the last one was better.'

The knowledge is not yet manifest in my practice.

'Now; you are leaning to the left, *juuuuust* a little bit,' he says, which infuriates me, as I had no idea I was doing so, and don't know how to fix it.

'Hip flexibility,' Sifu suggests. 'You are no longer a teenage boy, ah?'

I don't volunteer that as a consequence of my back problems, I have far more flexibility at thirty than I did at thirteen.

'Never mind. A little more Duck Walk can help this. If you go back to London you can show off a lot already,' Sifu says. 'But I want a higher standard; I demand perfection.'

Travis rubs imaginary silk between thumb and forefinger.

'Sifu's art is very fine. *Very* fine.'

'You're lucky I scold you,' Sifu declares. 'The Old Man will never tell you your mistake. One day I forgot my Thunder Fist and he sulked behind his newspaper. I pleaded with him to show me the next movement. "*Hmmmmph!*" He ignored me. I was so mad with myself! Finally after an hour I remembered. "I have it!" Old Man put down his newspaper and smiled. "Now that you have remembered, you will never forget it."'

'Sifu, I can think of the details, but I'm slow to integrate them,' I answer.

'Slowly, slowly. The Monkey King took three leaps to get to heaven. You think you can make it in one? Learn this well. Then we will talk of the Whipping Strength.'

Travis twitches, keen to comment.

'Sifu, can I say, he still not soft enough? Also, the waist, cannot.'

'Give him a chance, ah? If I pointed out all the faults, we would be here all day. You'd get frustrated and give up.'

'Sifu, I remember the corrections, but I can't—' Sifu interrupts me.

'*Can.*'

He gestures to Travis. 'Your turn.'

It's already a hot morning and I'm grateful for a break. Apartment blocks loom around us but conspire in their alignment to cast no shadow over the car park for now. It will take another hour for sufficient darkness to advance over the ground to offer me shade. At present, the only dark patches across the rooftop occur where my sweat has dripped onto the concrete. These blotches punctuate the progress of my recent *Tiaoqie*: three steps forwards, two back; a pivot 90° to the left, then 180° in the opposite direction; another 90° turn, two steps forward, two back; a stamp of the foot; a 180° turn; a kick, a jump, a turn; a block that flows into a crouched attack – 'like Elvis, combing the hair' – right hand then left, and the closing *Wuzuquan* salutation. Finally I drew my hands to my sides and lowered them to rest by my thighs.

'No, no, *no!* Don't you realize this is one of Mr Chee's favourite techniques?' Even this conclusive gesture requires total commitment. The concentration required to perform *gongfu* properly is exhausting. I require rest in alternation with bursts of effort. Watching a classmate demonstrate allows me to recover and to detect errors that might occur in my own routine.

As Travis begins I wince. His barrel-like stockiness and decades of martial-arts experience should assist his efforts, but he translates these assets to negative effect. Sifu reviewed *Tiaoqie* three weeks ago, but Travis has forgotten the corrections. The opening sequence doesn't look like our White Crane lineage at all, but appears to be *Taizu,* the Emperor's style of *Wuzuquan* that Travis learned years ago. Each variation of *Wuzuquan* accentuates a different one of its constituent Ancestors. The White Crane techniques are too subtle for Travis. He paints in broad strokes; he misses details and omits some movements entirely, and simplifies every part as the execution of muscular strength. It's a distant account of Sifu's demonstration, as though learned by hearsay. Unfortunately, Travis rejects all criticism. Recently he told me that Sifu's comments on his performance were intended as indirect feedback on mine.

'Travis,' Sifu calls from his pillar, 'why do you have to make me vomit so much blood? Don't tell me again you practice four or five hours a day; I don't believe it.'

Travis protests feebly.

'Actually, Sifu, not I no practice, I ever—'

'*Ever! Ever! Aiyoh*! You and your "ever". How many years you are coming now, and I'm still telling you? Eight years already. When my left foot is forward, I cut with my left hand. Right foot, *right* hand.' Briefly, Sifu diverts his admonishment to Cantonese, then back to English. 'Ah, so many pints of blood wasted. I tell you, you're like Long-Arm Lum.'

Long-Arm Lum, legendary idiot of the Chee Kim Thong Pugilistic and Health Society; he of the freakishly gangling limbs, a collector of every exercise he could get his inaccurate hands on and, as unauthorized instructor, the source of many debased *gongfu* practices that have reached the West, unworthy prizes of martial pilgrims to Kuala Lumpur. Forbidden to teach or be taught, nonetheless Lum exploited those vain enough to show off what they had learned. In turn, Lum was mentor to students greedy for new exercises and impatient of Master Chee's recommendations. Sifu implored the Master to castigate these deviations.

'But you've met the Old Man,' Sifu continues, 'you know he's like a kitten: *meow, meow*. One time I went back to KL and saw them doing all these silly things. So I asked the Old Man, "Why don't you correct them?" He answered me in this way: "I told them before. They never listen." "So why don't you tell them again?" He said, "They're adults." "But in *gongfu* they're babies!" Old Man just shook his head. This is a traditional Chinaman,' Sifu sighs.

On the first night Sifu warned me, 'I scold a lot'.

'You should scold,' I answered. 'It's the only way I'll get it right.'

I had come far enough in *gongfu* practice to realize I had little *gongfu* to speak of. Sashes and certificates wouldn't deceive me. In various martial arts groups I had improved my agility, muscular strength and flexibility. I had endured sparring classes whose participants clubbed each other for an hour and derived little other than burst lips and a bloody nose. None of these pursuits was the thing itself; true *gongfu*, I could see before me in Singapore, was a matter of refined skill and gradual comprehension. Sifu terms this 'realization,' seemingly a strip-tease of the physical world to reveal the essence of animated Nature, the great realization at which all arts converge when they are well-learned.

'All arts are the same,' Sifu tells us, 'it's just that people don't understand.'

This is not to say that the *techniques* of different arts are interchangeable – on the contrary, one should persist with a particular method – but that they should eventually result in the same relationship between practitioner and world.

On the night of their introduction, Chee Kim Thong guided Sifu to a first realization that would later be, in turn, my first lesson from Sifu. Against every impulse of masculine physicality, and the hard-style martial arts that Sifu had learned before, the Old Man exhorted him, '*Song-song! Qing-qing!*' Soft-soft, light-light.

Over the last few months, Sifu has showed me – repeatedly – that his soft-light skill could overcome any method of brute force I employed, 'Like the bull,' he said, 'and the matador'. I had heard other practitioners allude to soft strength, but few could apply it with conviction. At Sifu's insistence I aimed punches at him, shoved him, grabbed his arm and attempted to pull him over. Invariably Travis makes sycophantic comments at these demonstrations, but I disallow such hero-worship. Relegation of success to the realms of an enigmatically conceived Master would be counterproductive. I became fixated with knowing how I could replicate Sifu's techniques.

'Did I use any strength?' was his constant question.

'No, Sifu,' the eternal answer.

'*Think* of the rationale behind what I'm telling you. I can't match a young guy like you for physical strength. What did I use?'

'Technique.'

'Remember that when the four masters created this art at Shaolin, the nun watched them, and she bound them to a promise: "If my soft technique can overcome you, you must incorporate it into your art.'" Hence the Lady in the Purple Dress became the fifth and final contributor to *Wuzuquan*, Five Ancestors Fist.

'You must include these refinements. If you train only hard strength, you will end up with nothing. Your *Baihe*, White Crane, becomes *Daihe*, Nothing Crane. People will tease you: "Ah, I see you've learned Nothing."'

The nun's art is the most difficult component of *Wuzuquan*. Fortunately, Sifu allows no aspect of the art to be overlooked: 'I will keep on scolding you'.

Clearly Sifu's directness is a divisive quality. Distinguished martial-artists have left Sifu's company aghast at his appraisals. Chee Kim Thong said that the best etiquette was always to praise demonstrators – 'Very nice! Very good!' – but when pressed to comment further, Sifu complies with devastating honesty. I am lucky to have reached contentment with relentless criticism of my performance, and value Sifu's insistence on high standards. By now I have even learned to exploit his intolerance for imperfection, and time my practice so he arrives during the exercise I want help with.

'Hi!' he will greet me, and after we bow to each other: 'Your technique is wrong, ah?'

The unspoken condition is that I do not become discouraged by the constant threat of blood vomiting. The return is the possibility of constant improvement, incrementally in tiny realizations, newly apprehended subtleties. Each progression is a victory over a former self. 'You may think we're going fast, but to me, it's very slow. I want to teach you everything. My only fear is you cannot learn.'

Momentarily he appears an explorer surveying some magnificent prospect, urging the expedition to the summit so he can lead onward.

Today Sifu set the agenda.

'This morning I want to review your sets; your sets are *terri*ble.' In addition to performing the *Tiaoqie* routine we have concentrated on excerpts and 'practical applications,' meaning that Sifu aimed knees at our groins and back-fists at out temples to ensure that we could affect the principles of deflection. By the end of the lesson my *Tiaoqie* is an object of marginally less contempt.

'OK,' Sifu calls, and we return to his pillar. 'You can see the importance of specialized training, not five minutes of this, five minutes of that. A whole morning on one technique and still you can't get it! You see why I disagree when Tien-Hsiang says we should make up a rigid plan.'

It took me a while to infer that Tien-Hsiang is Sifu's son rather than the name of some *gongfu* principle. Currently prevented from practice by work commitments, Tien-Hsiang is established in my mind as an off-stage character, whose arguments with his father are reported to us regularly. In the latest dispute, Tien-Hsiang agitates Sifu to establish a public class, which would adhere to a fixed curriculum. Sifu tells us we'd better become good, as he doesn't want to teach the public group himself.

'Any questions?' Sifu asks, a sign that the session is near its end.

'Sifu, what is Whipping Strength? I don't think I've heard you mention it before,' I say.

'Coming Attraction,' he answers. 'I don't want to show it to you now, because I know you can't get it, and then you won't do the basic version right either. You'll muddle them up.'

'So it's the next stage of the same technique?'

'Yes. You must go through the stages, not jump ahead when you see some advanced art and want to do it, like these idiots in KL. Even my own son must go through the stages. If you can't understand *yin-yang*, there's no point in talking of the Four Words; without the Four Words, it's a waste of time to mention the Six Directions; if you don't know the Six Directions, how could you attempt the Five Elements? So, one thing at a time. For *Tiaoqie* you must also master the Heavy Hand, a related technique. Have you seen our Heavy Hand?'

'I've heard of the theory—'

'Forget theory. All bullshit.'

'Heavy Hand is this one,' Travis says, and demonstrates a few strokes: *cut, parry, retaliate.*

'OK, next lesson we will revise the foot technique.' Sifu nods towards me. 'It's time this young rascal learned the proper version. Any more questions? No? Please bow.'

I dry off with a towel and change into a clean T-shirt. While Travis fetches his car, Sifu shakes his head.

'This old goat has no connection between his body and his mind. It can't be helped. Forty-over years of practice, no *gongfu*.'

'At least you haven't given up on him,' I observe.

'When Alex is here, you can see I show him the correction and he practices over and over. Don't tell him I said something nice about him, ah? But *this* man … Once or twice then he gives up. Mr Chee would say, "Why didn't you do 1,000 times?"'

'I suppose it's hard to accept he's not very good by now.'

'I don't care! This is how I teach,' Sifu explains. 'I need to maintain my reputation. If you want to learn from Chan See-meng, you must have some *gongfu* when you leave. Recently Travis came to me and complained. He said, "Sifu, when you tell me off, you really whack me, you give me no chance." I said, "I apologize; it's just my style."'

Like Long-Arm Lum, Travis retrieves a sense of self-worth in *gongfu* by sharing what he has learned in his local park. He thinks Sifu doesn't know.

Travis pulls up in his Mitsubishi with the big spoiler. To make room for myself on the back seat I displace a stuffed animal and a feathered implement used in Taoist ritual. The pleather upholstery is searing to touch. *Shunk*: Travis activates the child-safety lock and starts to complain about his latest job. Sifu remonstrates with him for poor relations with his employers.

'Chris, make sure you never argue with the boss.'

'Yes, Sifu.'

We descend the storeys of the car park, spiralling down the roads and ramps, and emerge onto the Kallang-Paya Lebar Expressway.

'Travis, watch out for this guy creeping here!' Sifu taps the glass as a car attempts to overtake on the inside lane.

'Sifu, I see him already—'

'Saw him, ah? Hey, what you guys want for breakfast today?'

Debate ensues on the relative merits of *laksa* served in Punggol and *char kway teow* in Hougang. Travis clarifies that Punggol is 'Alex side'; near where our classmate Alex lives. I have still met Alex only once, on the first night we trained. He's been preoccupied recently, to Sifu's chagrin, with family matters.

Having decided on Hougang *char kway teow*, Sifu and Travis resume bickering over office politics. Silently, I enjoy the entertainment and look forward to the noodles. There will be no more talk of *Tiaoqie* today, unless Sifu sends an SMS later ('Still cannot do it! ! ! Use the circle – THIS is the way').

After lunch, Travis deposits me at Tampines MRT station. From there I make the long journey back across Singapore. Because it's Saturday I get a seat. Sleepily I think back over today's lesson, details to add to the journal I have started on my practice under Sifu. *Waist. Looseness. Flip wrist. Straighten damned spine.* While I am physically tired, the sheer amount of detail that Master Chan imparts also turns my brain to mush.

When I need to change lines at Jurong East, I remove the towel I have placed beneath me to absorb my sweat. I find that my sweat has soaked through onto the plastic seat. Has anyone noticed? I wipe the surface hurriedly and move onto the platform to await the last vehicle in a complex commute.

At the other end of the island, I emerge with leaden steps. We live in a condominium now, a forty-minute journey from the university by the erratic trajectory of public transport. There are several casual-looking guards, and I need to scan a resident's card to open the side gate. The condo contains eight towers standing around a swimming pool, and it offers a gym, barbecue pits and tennis courts. The actual reason we live here is that foreigners aren't allowed to rent the normal apartments administrated by the Housing Department Board. I like it well enough. The neighbours don't speak to us, but I'm not sure they speak to each other.

The muted-sweet scent of frangipani emanates as I amble to our tower. By the path sprout pandan plants, whose leaves are said to repel the commonplace intruder, the cockroach. I wait for the elevator in the lobby of our building which, like our apartment, gleams with marble surfaces. Seven hours after I left this morning I have arrived home, although it's still early afternoon. Claire greets me with commentary on my haggard appearance and vinegar-like odour.

Before an overdue shower, I experiment with the *Tiaoqie* once more. I attempt to replicate the contradiction of the technique, a deadweight relaxation coupled with an audible intensity that might cleave atoms. In this small room, with no noise to block out the sound, I can hear the rush of air. Although faint it is the thing itself, the thunder: distant but approaching.

3

THE OLD MAN

It's St Patrick's Day and Sifu has never tried draught Guinness before. He's only had the local variation, which is the stronger, thinner Foreign Extra mixed with lager. To rectify the situation, we have visited one of Singapore's Irish pubs for lunch. The International Irish Bar, not Ireland, is the experience on offer: suspended road signs to parts of Connacht, but never Dublin; photos of sheep; painted barrels in the corner; sprinkle of straw by the door; menu of Irish stews that nobody in Ireland eats. Yet the un-Irishness, akin to nothing of my upbringing, puts me in check. Who am I, and where am I going, given that my origins stand contradicted before me in this manner? It makes me wonder what other personal histories are dubious. I start to think about Chee Kim Thong's origins, and Sifu surmises that I have a question. He prompts me to speak up.

'Sifu, how can you call someone the "Old Man" who is only six years older than one of his disciples, and ten years *younger* than another disciple?'

'I cannot answer you,' he responds. 'Why don't you tell me?'

I groan and tell him that's a real *gongfu*-master kind of mysterious answer. He chuckles.

Was Chee Kim Thong ever young? In boyhood his life acquired the gravity that characterized *Laoren*, the Old Man. I've heard stories – some true, and many false – of Master Chee's adventures, which communicated a brave and compassionate man, yet when I met him I detected an ambiguity that I couldn't define. The *gongfu* beginner is attracted to the idea of a master with remarkable abilities, and wants to emulate those feats. Now it has become important to me to understand Master Chee himself. Why did he take up *gongfu*? What sacrifices were required by his dedication? As Sifu talks I begin to identify the elusive quality, the counterpart to Master Chee's gentleness and compassion, as a tremendous sadness about the Old Man. With this comprehension the mysterious smile playing about the right corner of his mouth becomes an expression of hard-won wisdom. When we juxtapose the different stages of Master Chee's life in our conversation, I become uncertain whether truer heroism lies in the drama of warfare or the *longue durée* of quiet altruism.

Palpably the child is father to the man. I attempt to imagine the boy Ah-Thong but can see only a Russian doll of Old Man, within whose exterior lie earlier Old Men. Poverty, servitude, separation, combat, war, imprisonment, torture, escape, flight, refuge: so definitively was Chee Kim Thong forged in youth by so intense a fire that while the various versions of Old Man occupy different positions on his chronology, they remain essentially indistinguishable.

'His family was very poor,' Sifu explains. 'His village was very poor.' Lowly origins in early twentieth-century Putian yielded few possibilities of social advancement. Young Ah-Thong had intelligence, but the only means for him to cultivate it was to leave his village. When he was nine years old he was offered employment as a pageboy across Fujian province in Xiamen. He would be a servant and companion for a merchant's son, in the course of which he would receive the same education. It was a stroke of good fortune but as Sifu describes the formal arrangement between Chee Kim Thong's family and the merchant, I imagine a solemn scene in which Ah-Thong watched his father sign the contract that would take him away.

The rich man's son was spoilt and idle. Often a Chinese man of means employed a pageboy in such circumstances to exert good influence. A wealthy parent might also enlist a prestigious *gongfu* master to instil discipline in wayward offspring. Hence Toh Yit Choon arrived in Xiamen. Toh was an expert in the Northern Shaolin art, and former bodyguard to the nationalist revolutionary Sun Yat-sen. But as he sat and sipped the tea Ah-Thong had brewed for him, waiting for his student to attend the lesson, Toh realized that his employer's son was uninterested in *gongfu*.

Of boredom, Toh told the pageboy to put away his broom and learn a few Shaolin strokes instead. Immediately, Toh saw that Ah-Thong was talented, and wanted to teach him. To formalize his relationship with Ah-Thong, Toh required the traditional *hongbao*, a red packet of payment. The merchant agreed to pay the fee, a kindness that I suspect may have been intended to motivate his son. For one year Ah-Thong studied Northern Shaolin under Toh.

Chee Kim Thong had good *gongfu* foundations in the *Taizuquan* art his grandmother taught him to fend off local bullies. The skills he advanced under Toh Yit Choon became crucial to ensure bearable working conditions. The merchant's son was a physical menace. He chased after Ah-Thong to torment him. The lowly pageboy couldn't retaliate without trouble. He could only elude the bully's grasp and evade his strikes.

Finally the boy tried to urinate on his servant. One day Ah-Thong stood beside the merchant's son at a rustic public-toilet, a bare plank over a pit. As he relieved himself the boy decided to turn and wet Ah-Thong. With remarkable agility the pageboy leapt to avoid the urine, without falling off the plank into the cesspool below. Among the spectators, impressed by Ah-Thong's *gongfu*, was the *Wuzuquan* master Lim Hian. He approached the page-boy and told him that if he visited a certain address he would learn something of interest.

'So a *gongfu* legend began with a stream of piss,' I suggest.

'If you like,' Sifu says.

By night Ah-Thong sought out the address Lim had given him. He waited outside for a while, with no sign of life inside the house. This was a standard test of an aspirant's dedication. Suddenly Ah-Thong was attacked, and he scrambled to defend himself. In the darkness he discerned that his assailant was a girl around his own age. The two fought until Lim emerged and halted the sparring. Unseen, Master Lim had watched the contest until satisfied that Chee Kim Thong had validated the impression he made at the public toilet. He introduced the girl as his granddaughter, Yit Leong, who was to be Ah-Thong's training partner in *Wuzuquan*.

Lim Hian was Carrying the Yellow Bundle, a Shaolin term for a *gongfu* graduate who travels China in search of great masters, worthy disciples and people in need of assistance. In his free time Ah-Thong learned techniques from the master and practiced with Yit Leong, who was similarly adept in her exchanges with childhood nuisances.

'Mr Chee saw a bully grab her by the pigtails,' Sifu tells me. 'She got him in an arm-lock and dragged him down the street behind her. The locals stood at the roadside and laughed.'

Under Lim, Ah-Thong studied *Wuzuquan* and traditional Chinese medicine. When it was time for the Lims to move on they instructed Ah-Thong to Carry the Yellow Bundle, with one stipulation: 'If you learn from another master, make sure he's a better one.' To add a repertoire of mediocre techniques to his skills would be useless. While Ah-Thong was encouraged to seek good masters, *Wuzuquan* would define him as a practitioner. As Lim's disciple he could study other arts, but not undergo ritual initiation with another *gongfu* master.

'How long did he spend with Lim?' I ask.

'Old Man only trained one-to-two years with each master,' Sifu replies, but Ah-Thong trained seriously and had brilliance for martial arts.

'You know,' Sifu reflects, 'I think the little girl, Miss Lim, is still alive in Beijing. There was one time years ago when the Old Man went to visit her. He asked if Cheng Hai and I could go with him. But then she said, "I don't want to meet them."'

'Why not? Weren't you disappointed?'

'Of course I was. But I suppose when you're at that level, you've seen so much, why do you care about meeting someone's disciples?'

When Lim Hian and his daughter moved on from Xiamen, Ah-Thong's grandmother suggested that he study with a friend of hers, Yong Yuek. The *Wuxingzhang*, Five Elements Palm, that Yong practiced had many commonalities with the *Wuzuquan* that Ah-Thong had learned from Lim. These arts complemented each other and deepened the boy's comprehension rather than simply expanding his repertoire. I'm curious to know more about Ah-Thong's experiences with his instructors, but few details are available.

'It's traditional for a master not to talk about his own teachers,' Sifu explains. '*I* like to talk about my masters, but it's not the tradition.'

Since *gongfu* was illegal for much of Chinese history, it makes sense that a practitioner would protect the identity of his master. Many *gongfu* origin-myths arose for this reason. Disciples under interrogation by imperial officials would claim to have devised new arts inspired by animals, dreams or deities rather than admit the existence of their teachers. We know little of Chee Kim Thong's masters other than his tantalizing allusions to their skills. Yong was reputed for his spider-like ability to climb sheer walls. Master Chee said that Lim could heat cups of cold water in his hand with intrinsic energy. With the details of their lives, those masters' arts have nearly been lost too.

'When Mr Chee went back to visit Putian years later, nobody had heard of Yong Yuek, or the Five Elements Palm.'

If the masters remain shadowy figures, it's clear that their student became an accomplished fighter. Champion of three provinces, Ah-Thong defeated China's best martial artists on the *leitai*, the elevated platform used for public matches. He was famous throughout Fujian. Masters sought out Chee Kim Thong, hoping that he would learn and preserve their arts. When Wu Jianquan – son of Wu-style *Taijiquan* patriarch Wu Quanyou – was due to visit Xiamen, Lim Hian advised him to look up his young disciple. Wu spent one week with Ah-Thong and taught him eight of his art's thirteen movements, although evidently Master Chee preferred to pursue the other disciplines he had studied rather than *Taijiquan*. At other times, renown created a need for Chee Kim Thong to conceal his identity.

On a visit to Singapore with the Old Man in the 1960s, Sifu recalls that local shopkeepers closed their stores and came into the street to see Chee Kim Thong. Cries of 'Ah-Thong is coming!' rang out among the Fujian community on Carpenter Street. We don't know whether Master Chee's reputation followed him from China with other refugees from the Japanese invasion, or arose in Singapore during his time there. In fact, Sifu's travels with the Old Man deepened the mystery of his master's past.

'Since one of our visits to Singapore,' Sifu continues, 'Cheng Hai and I are not 100 per cent sure Old Man's name really is Chee Kim Thong. A friend of the family was in Singapore. When I referred to the Old Man as "Chee Kim Thong," he laughed at me and said something like, "How can his name be ABC when his father's name is XYZ?"'

Therefore, I suppose that 'Chee' must be either a new name that the Old Man took in flight from China, or his family *was* called Chee, but one or all of them deviated temporarily to a pseudonym. If the Old Man felt compelled to create a new identity, it seems unlikely that he would abandon it in Japan-occupied Malaya. The question is whether he continued the greater part of his life under an alias, or reverted when the Japanese had left.

I surmise that two factors account for the Old Man's secrecy concerning his past; the first a disdain for violence, which I have come to perceive as the mark of a distinguished *gongfu* practitioner. The true expert stands above the need to prove himself. Recently I asked Kok Seng Pang, Sifu's fellow disciple, whether he had any good stories of Chee Kim Thong's duels, to which Seng Pang shook his head:

'Mr Chee doesn't talk about these things.'

The Old Man volunteered little, and few other than Sifu dared ask him outright. I suspect that there is a deeper, philosophical aspect to a master's avoidance of conflict than scpeticism over the worth of reputation, or anxiety over social disruption. The Japanese swordsman Yagyu Munenori wrote that his could blade only cut through evil. Therefore he considered his sword to be a life-giving instrument in matters of justice. Although Japanese arts tend to proceed from a more aggressive ethos than defensively-minded *gongfu*, Munenori was a Zen thinker. With Chee Kim Thong, and many top Chinese masters, I think he shared a belief that combat was to be looked upon as a chore, comparable to weeding.

The second reason for Master Chee's reticence, and the immediate cause for him to adopt a pseudonym, was that he left China a wanted man.

* * *

For centuries, Shaolin has fought. Long before the seventeenth-century Manchurian invasion, when the temple became a symbol for nationalist resistance, Shaolin fought. Strategically positioned and on fertile land, Shaolin needed to defend its estate.

In the seventh century, monks repelled an army of outlaws with designs on the temple's produce. Soon after, China fell into civil war as families contested the kingdom. One warlord, Wang, attempted to seize the Cypress Valley on the Shaolin estate. The monks took up arms and defeated Wang's men. Although they acted to preserve their lands, because the monks fought Wang's army, they were seen to have sided with the forces of Li Shimin, who would later be Tang Emperor. In gratitude, Li Shimin offered official posts to the thirteen monks that defeated Wang's army. One of these accepted the position of general, and trained the Tang army. The remaining twelve requested that they be allowed return to monastic life. This incident originates the legend that the Shaolin monks marched out to join the armies of Li Shimin, and enhanced Shaolin's reputation for participation in worldly affairs when injustice arose.

* * *

The War Against Japan broke out in 1937. China was such a vast and tribal place that atrocities elsewhere in the country might seem irrelevant, but a unified identity emerged in defiance of the Japanese invasion. The nation was particularly incensed by the Rape of Nanjing, a six-week period following the army's retreat from the capital in which massacre and sexual violation abounded at the hands of Japanese troops. The Chinese armies could not compete with the more numerous, highly trained and better-equipped Japanese forces in open warfare. Ah-Thong joined a guerrilla resistance faction, the Big Knife Army.

'Usually if there is only one male child in the family, they don't ask him to join,' Sifu says. 'But they needed Mr Chee's medical skill. Then they realized he had *gongfu*, and they asked him to teach.'

As the army's martial arts instructor, Ah-Thong trained batch after batch of men for eight weeks at a time. Because of the time constraint the troops specialized in four strokes of the Chinese broadsword, which they practised for hours on end.

The guerrilla fighters were wary of detection, but errors and traitors endangered them. Sifu says that one of Ah-Thong's students was a rickshaw puller assigned to a Japanese major. En route to the Japanese base one morning, the two encountered a street fight. The major insisted that they pause to watch the contest. The coolie scoffed at the poor show of *gongfu*, and the major challenged him to prove that he knew better. Proudly the rickshaw coolie revealed that while his own skill was comparatively modest, he studied under a great master. The major insisted that his servant take him to meet Ah-Thong.

I imagine a cinematic moment in which the student rushes in the door of Master Chee's house and apologizes desperately for bragging, which has brought the enemy to his teacher's home. In the coolie's wake come the assured steps of the Japanese major. Master Chee rises, intently concentrated. A Japanese officer always carries two swords, one long and one short. The major is not here to talk but to challenge. He draws the longer sword. The nearest weapon Chee Kim Thong has to hand is a *guandao*, a Chinese halberd. Ah-Thong seizes the *guandao* and the major advances.

'As the major attacks,' Sifu recalls from the Old Man's account, 'Master Chee slams the base of *guandao* against the floor. At the same time he deflects the major's strike. The sword flies out of the major's hand and he is knocked back.'

Undoubtedly the major would demand either death or tuition of the Chinese master who overcame him with ease. Ah-Thong required a new hideout.

Like the incident with the major, the few other verifiable accounts of Chee Kim Thong's duels are consistently brief. The gulf between expert and pretender was immediate, and insurmountable for Chee's aggressors. Mak Tian Meng, chairman of Master Chee's *gongfu* group, related a visit from Thai boxers who wanted Master Chee to stop teaching *Wuzuquan* in the border-town of Kota Bharu in the 1960s. One of the Thai boxers challenged Master Chee to fight. Chee Kim Thong settled the matter by a single, retaliatory strike to the knee. The high practitioner aims to cease conflict as quickly as possible.

'As Cromwell said,' Sifu glosses with a favourite quotation, '"In a moment of war, there is no time—"'

'Sifu, please don't quote Cromwell at me, today of all days,' I admonish, and offer a summary account of the Irish Campaign of 1649, and the rough course of Ireland's relations with Britain, broadly comparable to China's relationship with Japan. I know that the lesson is wasted; Sifu never absorbs the information that Ireland is not in fact part of Britain. On the other hand, I like the idea that we might have made an Irish rebel of Chee Kim Thong.

The Big Knife Army emerged from the trees to ambush Japanese soldiers. They employed their four strokes and retreated. Occasionally they dealt with traitors within the Fujian community. Probably it was one such informant who caused Ah-Thong's eventual capture and interrogation by the Japanese.

'They shoved bamboo under his finger nails,' Sifu says, 'and they used the water torture. He won't say any more than this, even to me. So when we discuss it between ourselves, Cheng Hai and I agree, it must have been bad.'

The soldiers would have executed Ah-Thong had he not escaped. He slipped out of his manacles and disappeared into the night.

'*How?*' I ask.

'*Luohan Ruyiquan*,' Sifu answers, the name of Master Chee's highest art. Yet even with such ability Chee Kim Thong could not go on indefinitely as a fugitive, relying on *gongfu* and his wits to survive. Life as an outlaw was a bleak prospect, and there were alternatives. Master Chee had contributed enough to the war effort.

'To the Chinese, migration is a fact of life,' Sifu says. It reminds me that Sifu, Master Chee and myself have all undergone versions of this upheaval. For a century Fujian migrants in search of a better life had braved the journey to Nanyang, the South Seas, much as Irish peasants sailed to America in the same period. The initial waves of immigration ensued the emergence of modern Singapore, popularly attributed to Stamford Raffles, who arrived in 1819. Under this East India Company employee, Singapore prospered as a port. For those who had nothing in China, Singapore offered a fresh start.

Equally desperate circumstances attended upon Chee Kim Thong's flight from Fujian many years later. By 1940 the war showed no promise of cessation. In the north and east, the major Chinese cities had fallen to the Japanese imperialists. There was little reason to believe that Fujian in the south would not follow, having been invaded for its importance as a port. The conflict would continue until the end of WWII in 1945, with some 80 million Chinese displaced and 14 million killed by the invaders.

The Japanese circulated Wanted posters with Ah-Thong's face. It was time to leave China. One of the Old Man's sons told me that Master Chee dropped his military uniform, medals and broadsword to the bottom of a well. Treasures that might identify him were a liability. In darkness he leapt from the banks of Fujian onto a sampan bound for Singapore and freedom: a *gongfu* genius, an exile and a war veteran, the Old Man at twenty-two years of age.

4

CAR-PARK CRANE

On top of the car park by your apartment block are tennis courts. Underneath, the highest floor has ping-pong at one end, but no-one ever goes to the level below *that*, the penultimate deck. It's not even needed for cars, which thin out as you advance the floors and are entirely absent before you reach deck 13.

As soon as the elevator doors ping open, you pitch yourself forward to take your weight on your hands, and navigate the perimeter of the floor in the Monkey Walk. Perhaps neighbours in the building opposite can see you through the bay along the side of the car park. You are too old to care what people think.

The Monkey Walk strains your hips and chest muscles. Blood rushes to your head. By the time you complete 189 steps to the faucet in the opposite corner, your palms are black with dirt. You wash your hands and move to the end of the car park. You crouch, hold your fists at eye level, and advance in the Duck Walk. In Sifu's version the leg movement is very small, so that the tension in the thighs is never released.

'Unless you go through hard training like this, you can never be top class.'

In 50 steps you reach the ramp that leads to the next deck down. For relief you walk down normally. At the bottom of the ramp you begin a variation – Duck Walk II – for another 50 steps. In this version, you move your hips through a tortuous stretch, which is, you admit reluctantly, more effective than static flexibility drills. At the end of the car park you remove your keys from your pocket and place them on a bollard by the space numbered 238.

On the first night Sifu showed you the *Bagua* exercise to loosen the joints.

'Imagine you're waving to people. *Welcome!*'

It is the wave of a fascist dictator in an open-top car. You acknowledge the hordes with a broad sweep from your centre line outward, and shift your hips in the same direction. At the extremity of the hand's diagonal trajectory you lean back and move your arm across, above your head to the other side. Now lean forward, and your hand glides across in front of your body and on in an arc beyond your spine. All the while your hips follow, shifting from side to side in unison with the lateral movement of your hand. Throughout the exercise the palm must face upward, as though supporting a ball that must not be dropped. The worst test is when the hand, reaching backwards, rotates around to move back towards the centre; it must turn at the wrist, without dropping the ball, then float back to the starting-point, repeating the cycle without interruption. Correct visualization is essential to improve circulation.

'Your arm is like a garden sprayer. *Pffffffffffffff!*'

As you rotate, imagine that a coloured energy blasts down your arms and out the fingertips, sprayed all over the walls of the car park. After ten cycles you practice with the other arm, and then both arms at once. The hands move opposite each other symmetrically: when the left hand moves in front of the left shoulder, the right hand circles back beyond the right hip. At first you thought you would never be able to co-ordinate the movement, but now the hands revolve concurrently, a sun and a moon.

'You must do both together to train the *yin-yang.*'

You cannot visualize *two* garden sprayers yet, cannot sustain concentration into two arms doing different things simultaneously. Your shoulders and hips ache.

In *gongfu* films the master practices in a graceful sequence, a trail of smoke in the wake of his fingertips. *Your* session is sweaty, panting and inglorious. Often the most effective drills are of little interest to a spectator. After the *Bagua* exercise, the real practice begins. You proceed to *Wuzuquan's zhangong*, 'still training,' which builds stamina through torment. Slowly you exhale and sink into a posture that emulates the *Luohan*, the Buddhist immortals. Your thighs are parallel to the ground. You push your knees forward and attempt to straighten your spine. Inhale over ten counts, hold for ten, exhale for ten and repeat. Your legs tremble. Your temperature rises. You do not feel like a fat, jolly immortal.

In for ten—

Unless you go through hard training like this—

Hold for ten—

You can never be top class—

Out for ten. Repeat.

'You should feel like there's a mist around you.'

(A mist? What mist?)

Repeat.

'Mr Chee doesn't teach this to every Tom, Dick and Harry, you know. This is *lineage* training; he keeps it back for the disciples. When I taught it to students in KL, Yap Cheng Hai scolded me. He told me it was secret.'

(Sweat dribbles down your forehead onto your lips. It concerns you that it has no taste, not even salt. You wonder whether you have perspired so much that there are no minerals left to expel.)

You finish with forced dignity, straightening your legs slowly, but then utter an exclamation that unites an expletive with a central figure from Christian theology.

Next the *tu*, 'patterns' of movement. Each routine uses the same opening sequence. The *qing* salutation gesture identifies the White Crane *Wuzuquan* lineage. The left palm moves forward from the navel with the right fist on top. All Shaolin arts identify themselves with a variation of the *qing*, yet it contains complexity beyond greeting. Sifu spent an entire lesson on the combat application of the *Wuzuquan qing*, and taught you to evaluate a practitioner's ability by performance of this movement.

The first pattern is *Sanzhan*, the 'Three Wars' of mind, body, breath and crucially, their union. Therefore the wars are against your own habits.

The movements are simple expressions of power that inform many of the more complex techniques of *Wuzuquan*.

'Master *Sanzhan* and you're the best in the village.'

In *Sanzhan* you advance three times and retreat three times. With each step your fingers spread like the crane's feathers, curve like a beak to attack the ribs and sink to waist height with the irresistible force of a waterfall.

'Train with a pure heart. Don't think of anything else when you practice.'

Sifu says not even to think of the details of the movements, simply to express them, like a dance. One should imagine an opponent not as an aggressor, but like a dance partner whose limbs you sweep into the correct position. Your concentration has improved. You can keep your mind on the performance, but find it difficult not to fixate upon particular details of the movements, or to think of a debate that might arise from some aspect of the exercise while your body has progressed to something else. To be in the movement is one of the art's elusive simplicities.

You continue into the Tail of *Sanzhan*, the epilogue traditionally withheld by the master until the student is deemed trustworthy. Sifu said that Lim Hian's students waylaid the master, and attempted to rob him. Lim used techniques from his hidden repertoire to retrieve his money.

Your performance accelerates naturally in the Tail. The crane is vicious now. You deflect an attack to the ribs, chop with the right hand and kick with the edge of the right foot simultaneously, then repeat the sequence on the left side. Finally your hands circle outward and return to the *qing* salutation.

After two repetitions of *Sanzhan*, you recover by walking to the opposite end of the car park. Windows, openings of a foot's diameter, covered with wire mesh, perforate the end wall. You grab one of the higher spaces and dangle by your arms for a minute. You see the local *Taijiquan* group practise under the MRT bridge. A music system – 'ghettoblaster' does not seem the right term for a sleepy, Singaporean suburb – voices sentiments about Energy and The Universe over traditional music. To most

45

practitioners *Taijiquan is* a dance, divorced from its *gongfu* origins. Yet when Sifu first met Dong Ying Jie at a demonstration in 1956, the master pushed a fellow practitioner with such force that he nearly went over the roof of Kuala Lumpur's Chin Woo gymnasium, saved from falling to his death only by the reflexes of a spectator.

Still gripping the wall overhead, you count the seconds. The building trembles momentarily as a train passes. The scent of incense reaches you. You wonder whether the *Taiji* group burns incense for relaxation, but you don't believe it could reach this height with such intensity. Maybe someone in the nearest tower arranges joss sticks so that the smoke drifts across as an offering to the strange ghost in the car park. You *are* a kind of ghost. When you were alone over Christmas the lights went out while you practised, as though no one was here at all. It seemed to befit your abnegation of personal commitments. You didn't want to travel at Christmas. If that substantiated a denial of your identity, it might justify switching off the lights, an act that cast doubt on your selfhood. Ridiculous to practise in that darkness, as though there was nowhere for you to go.

Remember that this is what you wanted. This is the bare minimum of practice to keep up with the onward rush of Sifu's lessons. You will train like this day in, day out. This is your duty in the pact between master and student.

58, 59, 60. You release the wall, drop down and return to space 238.

'Master *Ershiquan* and you're best in the province.'

The triple strikes of 'Twenty Punches Fist' use the waist to generate power. The correct technique requires continuous movement. Your stomach rotates back and forth like a wet dog drying itself as you deliver each triplet of punches. Constantly you step in different directions to fend off attackers from all sides.

After two rounds of *Ershiquan* you need to cup your hands over your face and inhale carbon dioxide. Possibly this is a good sign: Sifu warned that performance would become more strenuous as your deadweight strength developed. You complete the third cycle and walk up and down the car park again for relief.

'Master *Tiaoqie* and you're tri-state champion.'

Chee Kim Thong was tri-state champion.

After the patterns you progress to specialized training of individual strokes. Tonight you practice movements from the Mist component of the Five Elements. In one motion you block across your face with both arms and cut outwards, one hand at the neck, the other at the ribs. In the second movement your hand circles at the elbow in towards the body, then upwards, then strikes heavily outward and down with the back of the palm. Finally both palms strike the chest. You step forward to repeat the sequence on the other side, and continue to the end of the car park: *cut-backhand-palm strike*.

When it's time to go in, you grab your keys from the bollard. You swing your legs up to stretch at each step on you way to the elevator. Your T-shirt and shorts have been uniformly discoloured by sweat. Your partner makes an exclamation of horror as you enter the apartment. You may offer him or her your wet garment.

'Get away from me.'

Your last practice of the day, just before you take a shower, is a stretch that shifts from side to side in a low stance. The challenge is to press one palm to the floor and keep your spine upright. Sifu tells us the key is to 'think *inside* the Old Man' and manifest his movements. This is not an attempt to assume his identity, but to emulate Master Chee's higher facility to *discard* his identity and become the art. You remember a picture of Chee Kim Thong in this very position. He appears to be in his fifties. Impressively well preserved and with perfect posture, he smiles out at you like the custodian of some marvellous secret.

* * *

It's a Sunday evening. We decide to watch a DVD of *Jeeves and Wooster*. There is a Sundayish quality to *Jeeves and Wooster*. The series is an appropriate choice now, since Claire is English, and homesick, and the programme is not only Sundayish, but quintessentially English.

As we sit on the couch, and Bertie Wooster lands himself in a manner of Scrape, my right arm moves. It circles towards my torso and outward, an elliptical circuit that ends with my right hand dropping onto my thigh. Then it happens again. And again, so that my arm now moves continuously, the back of my right palm striking my thigh with a little thump. It is the second movement from my Mist technique.

Thump. Thump. Thump.

'Look at that,' I say.

Thump. Thump. Thump.

'What do you mean?' Claire asks. She's used to seeing me play around with *gongfu* outside my formal sessions.

Thump. Thump. Thump.

'I'm not controlling it,' I say. 'It's involuntary.'

Thump. Thump. Thump.

I can halt the motion by grabbing my right wrist with my left arm, but it resumes as soon as I let go. Likewise, I can stop it if I concentrate hard on *not* moving, but the moment I relax, or allow myself to notice Bertie Wooster's quandary, the circuit begins again.

Thump. Thump. Thump.

Claire considers the situation. Finally she says:

'You are a fool.'

5
BONE

'If it's a bone injury, Chee Kim Thong can fix it,' was the saying around Kuala Lumpur in the 1960s, 'and if Master Chee cannot fix your bones, nobody else can fix them.' To any patient who requested his help, Master Chee would answer, 'I will try'. But in truth he had learned extraordinary precision from his teacher, the *Wuzuquan* master Lim Hian. The Sultan of Terengganu awarded Chee Kim Thong the honorific title of *Dato* for his work as a healer rather than his feats as a *gongfu* practitioner. For a time it appeared that no injury was beyond the Old Man's skill.

While reclusive as a *gongfu* artist, Chee Kim Thong shared his medical expertise with anyone who needed assistance. It didn't matter if you had no money. 'I will try,' Master Chee would say nonetheless.

In Dungun, Kok Seng Pang first met Master Chee after he fell off his bicycle and damaged his hip. 'Everyone knew who Ah-Thong was,' Seng Pang said, so his family took the boy to Master Chee for attention. The treatment was successful. Seng Pang's mother had heard that the Old Man was due to take a fifth and final disciple, who would be initiated with Sifu. In appreciation of the care Master Chee showed her son, she suggested that Seng Pang dedicate himself to Chee Kim Thong's *gongfu*. The bicycle mishap occasioned a happy turn of events for the boy, who became Master Chee's youngest disciple in the ceremony of 1961.

Another thankful patient who could not afford payment insisted that Chee Kim Thong take her daughter as his second wife. The Old Man resisted at first, but became enticed by Yap Cheng Hai's idea that he could set up a new home in Kuala Lumpur. The city, Cheng Hai said, would offer ideal opportunities to disseminate *gongfu* and treat patients.

The Old Man's relocation would spare Cheng Hai the arduous trips to Dungun. More importantly, Cheng Hai wanted to start an enterprise with the master he had discovered. In a traditional Chinese martial-arts school, the master teaches the disciples, the disciples teach instructors, and the instructors offer public classes. Master Chee's presence in Kuala Lumpur might offer Cheng Hai and Sifu a new source of income at the top of a pyramid. Chee Kim Thong was always open to new business opportunities, particularly as his family grew. In time the Old Man would have thirteen children, and adopt two more. Most of Master Chee's children, Sifu says, acquired the '*kampong* mentality,' the unambitious attitude that permeates a sleepy Malaysian village. Hence the Old Man felt pressure to provide for his clan, even when his children were grown. Probably he assumed his disciples would run the *gongfu* club while he taught only them, treated patients and made profit as the master. Opportunities in Dungun were far more limited.

Shambolically unorganised and a poor planner, Master Chee made no announcement of his change of heart about Kuala Lumpur. Evidently the life Cheng Hai portrayed sank in. Master Chee took a bus from Dungun abruptly. His disciples learned of the Old Man's decision when news reached them that someone called Chee Kim Thong had arrived in the capital unexpected and was searching for Cheng Hai, whose house became the venue for the disciples' sessions while Master Chee established himself in Kuala Lumpur. For a few years he operated from a clinic on Pudu Road, and public *Wuzuquan* classes were offered at the Eng Hua Association, one of the social clubs for Hokkien locals. In time the Old Man settled in a purpose-built clubhouse off the old Klang Road that contained facilities for *gongfu* classes, and a clinic. The land was cheap because it had been the site of atrocities in 1942, during the Japanese occupation. Before construction of the clubhouse commenced, Master Chee and Cheng Hai performed rituals to exorcise spirits from the property.

In their early years together Sifu accompanied the Old Man on his rounds of Dungun. He carried Master Chee's equipment case on his shoulder, an unwieldy affair that housed assorted powders, liniments and other mysterious substances. Chee Kim Thong used herbal medicines and massage, but his speciality was bone setting, a technique reliant on the sensitivity and fine movements he had developed in *gongfu*. Sometimes Master Chee asked Sifu to crouch in an uncomfortable position for hours at a time and hold a patient in the correct position so the Old Man could align bone fragments, apply splints, or shove strips of bamboo into the marrow. Gradually he manipulated the parts of bone back to their original position.

Medicine and *gongfu* is a common pairing. Several great masters have studied both these disciplines. Like *gongfu* theory, Chinese medicine hypothesizes the *yin-yang* binarity, the network of energy meridians, the Mother and Child model of leader and follower, and the Five Elements in eternal cycles of creation and destruction. The traditional doctor examines complexion to determine illness; the *gongfu* teacher does so to evaluate progress. Cheng Hai wrote that in a tournament back in Fujian, young Ah-Thong was commended for his medical formulae in addition to his *gongfu* prowess. Master Chee hoped that Sifu would learn traditional medicine, but the disciple proceeded no further than the acupuncture points. Like consultation to determine the patient's symptoms, Sifu encourages me to describe the sensations of temperature, pain and tingling that I derive from practice. Ironically, Chinese medicine offers knowledge of the body that increases the effectiveness of martial techniques, while for a reclusive *gongfu* exponent the main appeal of the art is its benefit to one's own health rather than its potential to injure another. Ideally the martial-arts expert will learn both how to hurt and to heal, but never have cause to do either. Few masters ever knew such utopia.

The Old Man's skills were his legacy. As an *Wuzuquan* initiate he was duty-bound to impart his *gongfu*; as a father he wanted his sons to have means of livelihood. With his knowledge he could align the boys, set them in place like bones so their paths through life would be clear. Boon Teck learned massage. When Boon Seng, the sixth son, was due to move to Australia as a butcher, Master Chee made him work hard on his *Wuzuquan* so that a career as a *gongfu* instructor became possible overseas. In time Boon Seng could quit his job to concentrate on his *gongfu* school, in which he became known as

James Chee. But of all the Old Man's children it was clear that Boon Hock, the fifth son, had the most talent for martial arts, to his father's delight. Sifu never wanted to learn traditional medicine, and as the 1970s progressed he became ever more engrossed in his banking career. By 1975, the twenty-one-year-old Ah-Hock showed such promise that the Old Man began to hope that this son would inherit the *Wuzuquan* school. The club would need a director, and the boy was talented. It appeared that Ah-Hock's future was fixed.

Seng Pang implied that the accident was simply bad luck: Ah-Hock sped around a blind corner, without reflection that another vehicle might approach from the opposite direction. But club chairman Mak Tian Meng felt that the crash was easily avoidable. Tian Meng wondered why Ah-Hock hadn't veered away from the other driver. He suspected that something or someone prevented the boy from swerving; that the mishap was orchestrated by a higher intent that compelled Ah-Hock in his catastrophic trajectory.

'I don't know *how* he collided with the truck,' Tian Meng said. 'Maybe it was that he killed a white snake; you know that snakes are deities to the Indians. So maybe the snake was taking revenge. It is as if he was blocked off, and so he rammed into the lorry.'

When I asked Sifu to expand on Tian Meng's interpretation he shook his head and replied, 'These people'. Why mystify the incident? Road accidents were frequent in 1970s Malaysia. Ah-Hock's was a common tale.

The effects of the accident were indisputable, unambiguous, brutal. Ah-Hock's motorcycle collided head-on with a truck. News was sent to his father in Kota Bharu, a day's travel away: Ah-Hock was hurt and certain to die. Over the telephone the Old Man pleaded with his students to do what they could to keep Ah-Hock alive.

'Even if his bones are broken or fractured, I can fix him back. I will try.'

Master Chee rushed back from the Thai border.

'But when Master Chee came,' Tian Meng told me, 'he looked at Ah-Hock's body. The head was all shattered. There was nothing he could do, only cover the body with a sheet.' The Old Man would never be the same.

'It was the first time I ever saw him crying,' remembered one witness of that vigil beside Chee Kim Thong and the broken body of his son.

6

MASTER AND STUDENT

Through the stalls of incense sticks and effigies, decorous but flavourless cakes and traditional medicine, we make our way to the food court.

'Just one moment,' Sifu says, and bids me wait while he queues for a ticket in the pools. As I stand there, I wonder how to phrase a delicate question.

Recently a colleague at the university asked me to write for an academic journal that planned an issue on sport and other physical activities. I wrote an interview feature on *gongfu* with Sifu.

When I had drafted my dialogue with Sifu, Alex offered to read it and advise on the Chinese terminology. He corrected a few errors, which included the appropriate characters for 'Sifu'. It's commonplace pedantry that *gongfu* refers literally to 'work' and not to martial arts, yet this appears to be only the tip of the iceberg in the tortuous lexis of Chinese martial-arts. I was surprised to learn from Alex that there are two versions of 'Sifu' in Mandarin, and that even Chinese practitioners are often confused about which they should use. Alex told me that before I joined the group, he and Travis discussed which version of the term should prevail among Sifu's students.

The debate on terminology became heated because the variations define significantly different relationships between the practitioner and the teacher. 'Sifu' entered English as a loan-word from Cantonese *gongfu* movies, but in Mandarin there are two near-identical terms applicable to a master. *Shīfù* (师傅), 'Master-Teacher,' acknowledges a practitioner's authority in an art, be it *gongfu*, cookery or calligraphy. But *Shīfù* (师父),

'Father-Teacher,' refers to a special bond between master and disciple, and a 'disciple' is a more privileged order of life than a mere 'student'. The distinction pained Travis because he had not attained his desired status.

Officially the initiation ceremony distinguishes a disciple from a student. The master adopts the aspirant, who enters the formal lineage of the art. *Wuzuquan* allows only five disciples. Sifu is proud of his selection by Chee Kim Thong and is irked by pretenders who allege that they are 'Inner-Chamber Disciples' when they have merely purchased platinum club-memberships. A true disciple receives special attention from the master.

At the end of class today, in the time for questions before we set out for the food court, Travis declared his 'duty' to impart the muscular *Taizu*-style *Wuzuquan* that he learned years ago.

'How can it be your duty?' Sifu rebuffed. 'You are not an initiate of the *Taizu* lineage. You cannot say it is your duty. It is not your right.'

Other than Sifu, none of us is a disciple of *Wuzuquan*. Conversations on the matter arise sporadically, characterized by curiosity and neurosis. We wonder whether Sifu thinks we aren't good enough to become his disciples. Perhaps he awaits a prodigy. But he is 70. Master Chee took disciples at the age of forty-two. If not us and now, who and when?

In contemplations of status, a mysterious document that Sifu acquired on a visit to Mumbai in 1970 is a plentiful source of aggravation. While Sifu idled in his hotel lobby an Indian man, who introduced himself as an initiate of Kriya yoga, approached him.

'He had a long, white beard like a yogi,' Sifu recalled, 'but he was dressed like an English gentleman, in a suit and hat.'

Generally Sifu is happy to entertain different perspectives on life, and yoga is a cousin of *gongfu*. Bodhidharma, the founder of Zen, travelled from India to Shaolin Temple in China, hence the Shaolin arts are demonstrably indebted to yoga. When high practitioners of related disciplines meet, Sifu explained, they can sense their affinity although strangers. Sifu recalled that the Kriyaban made a beeline for him as soon as he entered the hotel.

The stranger told Sifu enough about Kriya to capture his interest, and left him with a curious inscription entitled 'A Pupil and a Master

Relationship'. This scroll hypothesises four tiers of students, which range from 'the Feeble Seeker' to 'the Supreme One'. The author – unknown, of course – surveys the traits of each classification in detail that includes appetite and personal hygiene. The text transpires to be excerpted from a centuries-old treatise on yoga. The distributor, disappointingly, did not disappear into thin air, but remained in contact with Sifu after their dramatic encounter in the hotel lobby.

A modified version of the Mumbai transmission recurs in Sifu's *gongfu* talk. He has derived his own model to determine a student's chances of success in martial arts. Two of the four categories are not worth teaching at all: 'With average and below, you shouldn't waste your time.' My rational mind knows that Sifu wouldn't waste his time on me if I was Average and Below. Yet another region of consciousness wonders whether he might realize his mistake and demote me, on the basis of some poorly executed stroke, to the unteachable realms of the Feeble Seeker. The heady concoction of students, disciples and pupils, Seekers, *Shīfūs* and *Shīfùs* has me in need of clarity.

The *kopitiam* is the best place to ask Sifu questions, where we eat and, as he puts it, 'cultivate the relationship'. After practice, in the food courts of north-east Singapore, Sifu tells stories of the old days, about Chee Kim Thong and other masters he has encountered. Much of his talk is practical advice: how to evaluate a practitioner on sight by particular body alignments, or tell whether a monk has *gongfu* from his bow. Other subjects of Sifu's conversation have little to do with *gongfu*, but he intends us to benefit from his greater reserves of – an important word to Sifu – Experience. To Sifu, good interaction between master and student is essential to impart the techniques correctly, not only because talk establishes trust, but as though a literal line of communication is constructed between us whose signal strengthens with usage.

'When you first came, it took you a while to open up,' he observed recently. 'You must cultivate! How did you win Claire? You had to chase after her.' Sifu grabbed my wrist. '"*Meh, meh, meh, I love you, I love you.*" Right? It's the same.'

In truth I had expected a *gongfu* master to be a tyrant, like the Hong Kong cinema portrayals. Many instructors model themselves on that stereotype, by turns irate and distant. Now I suspect that inferior practitioners adopt this facade to obscure their limited knowledge. Sifu had no answer when I asked him how the cliché of the ill-tempered master originated.

'My teachers were kind to me,' he explained. 'I must try to act the same way.'

Now Sifu returns, brandishing his ticket for the pools. We enter the food court. I wonder how to broach the subject of discipledom without seeming to agitate for a promotion, but Sifu anticipates me.

'Travis has been asking for initiation again,' Sifu says. 'Your bag?' He takes my rucksack and finds a table while I order drinks.

'Three *kopi si kosong*,' I request in the Singlish terminology of the food-court, a creole comprising Hokkien, English and Malay. The girl heats three cups with boiling water then empties them. From a pierced can she pours preserved milk, healthier than the condensed milk of standard *kopi*, which Sifu claims has made everyone in Malaysia diabetic. Finally she decants the coffee itself from a steel jug where it brews with a stocking for a filter. I take the tray and find Sifu – as Master Chee taught him for security – in a rear corner of the food court, sitting to face the entrance. As Travis has not yet arrived from parking his car, we continue our conversation.

'This relates to Travis telling us just now that he represents *Wuzu*,' Sifu says. 'I told him that without initiation, he does not speak for the lineage.'

'So Travis has asked you to make him a disciple before?'

'A couple of times he has asked me to give him initiation.'

'Why does he want it so badly?'

'He wants to show off, tell people he represents *Wuzuquan*. I will say it is also, in part, to open the chakras. With open chakras, the student can get it faster. I told him it's not necessary.'

'You can get it from practice?'

'Yes, in time, if you train correctly.'

'Did he have initiation in any of the other arts he learned?'

'I don't believe so. Who wants a disciple like that? Did you hear him in the car?'

On our way to the food court Travis mentioned a trip across the causeway to visit his old White Crane teacher in Johor Bahru, to whom he referred as 'My Sifu'. This was a solecism, as a student should follow only one master.

'This Sifu, that Sifu,' our teacher mocked him. 'You've got too many Sifus.'

Too Many Sifus, I thought to myself, *a musical waiting to be made.*

Travis arrives as Sifu recalls the details of his initiation ceremony in 1961: joss sticks, offerings on an altar, genuflection, special techniques, oaths and given names.

'The baptismal names follow a system,' Sifu explains. 'Don't reveal it! If you reveal the system, all these people will invent baptismal names for themselves. The internet will be full of people who say they had initiation.'

'Victor Chong go to China,' Travis says of a prominent local practitioner he knows. 'Study here, study there. Learn *Xingyi*, learn *Bagua*. All the masters ask him to be a disciple.'

I tell Travis that, from what I understand, important aspects of discipledom are already available to us. Sifu has taught us the secret arts imparted to initiates, while we can honour the promise of obedience without the need for a ceremony.

'Which would you rather have,' I ask, 'the ritual or the practice?'

'If the master won't initiate you, it means he don't trust you,' Travis sneers.

'Sometimes,' Sifu responds, 'it's true that the master doesn't trust or like the student. But just because the disciple has been initiated doesn't mean the master will teach. When I first started with the Old Man, Teoh Cheng Her bullied me in the Knock Hands. I was black and blue. I kept going because I didn't want to let him beat me. So I fought back the tears. Mr Chee saw, and taught me to overcome him. Teoh gave up around seven months after initiation. He asked, "How can this young boy improve so much in one month?" It was because the Old Man saw he was a bully. He only showed him sets, not the real *gongfu*.'

Another disciple, Tan Boon Pin, was 53 years old at the time of his initiation. Like Teoh, Tan learned some *gongfu* from Chee Kim Thong prior to acceptance as a disciple, but he quit in discouragement.

'Some people think that when they get initiation, they won't have to practice,' Sifu explains. 'Tan complained to me. He said, "I've been with the Old Man for some years. After a few years at university I can become a doctor or a lawyer."'

'You would still need to study and pass exams,' I observe.

Sifu smiles.

'We should be the disciples,' Travis insists. 'When Sifu die, we carry the coffin.'

Silently I consider the two men and don't fancy Travis's chances of outlasting Sifu, despite their age difference.

'Mr Chee has not told me to take disciples,' Sifu says.

'You need permission?' I ask.

'Mr Chee did not. Lim Hian was dead, so he could not ask. Old Man decided for himself. At first even I didn't realize how important it was, even though Mr Chee told me. He said, "You must act well, you have a duty to the lineage."'

Sifu pauses to drink some coffee.

'This is the best,' he exclaims. I notice that he didn't answer my question on the need for Master Chee's permission to take disciples.

The atmosphere is slightly tense. Amidst mixed thoughts on initiation, I sympathise with Travis. A couple no longer needs marriage to cohabit respectably in Western culture, but the average girl dreams of her wedding day nonetheless. Knowledge of traditional initiation is new to me, but it sounds like masters have left Travis at the altar over many years. For my part, I would rather be a disciple than not.

The fact remains that we are students, not disciples. Organised *Wuzuquan* has been torn apart by politics, and it seems to me that recognition of true status is one way our generation can ensure that we don't replicate the problems. One benefit of being a lowly student is *carte blanche* to be selfish, a chance to learn without the burden of responsibility. It's possible that Sifu thinks ritual initiation is an outdated tradition, in which case it wouldn't matter if we were the best *gongfu* students in history. Additionally it's clear from his club's power struggles that Master Chee's selection of disciples failed to prevent disputes of authority.

After a few moments, Sifu reaches a decision.

'Chris, I want you to try this carrot cake for breakfast.'

A delicious misnomer, Teochew carrot-cake is made from a white, Asian radish. As I queue at the Teochew stall to order, I continue to reflect on our conversation. Given the gradations of *gongfu* aspirants, I wonder what constitutes a master. I ask Sifu when I return with the carrot cake.

'No such thing,' Sifu answers.

'You mean …?'

'You must give up the idea that there's such a thing as mastery. The Chinese saying is that you keep learning, then die. There's no such thing as coming to mastery of the art. If you say you have mastered it, you're bold and arrogant.'

I'm staggered by this because it contradicts one of the basic and central popular conceptions of *gongfu*, which is that there is a master, who has *become* a master at a specific point, and that this means that his or her expertise has been verified and is now incontestable.

'So when do you start to describe yourself as a master?' I ask.

'When you feel confident to bluff people. Marketing and promotion. But you shouldn't exalt yourself in this way. Mr Chee says "the big tree catches too much wind." When *gongfu* men become famous it's for fighting. In KL we call them *sansheng*, the same word we use for gangsters. They have none of the wisdom we talk about in Shaolin.'

'What about "grandmasters?"'

'Same. No such thing.'

'And all these people we know calling themselves "grandmasters…"'

'Bullshitters.'

Like 'master,' *Shizu* – commonly translated as 'grandmaster' – only has authentic application when it describes a personal relationship. *Shizu* refers to an ancestor within the lineage.

'I don't care about being a master or a grandmaster,' Sifu says. 'People can call me they anything they want.' He frowns. 'Except "Timmy." "Timmy" is what you call a little boy.'

'But,' I persist, 'we still use some titles amongst ourselves.'

'Yes. When learning, in Shaolin tradition we never call our teacher by his first name, so we say "Sifu". All except Cheng Hai, who would only address Mr Chee by his first name, Ah-Thong.'

'Why was that?' I ask.

'I don't know.' Sifu sips his coffee. 'When I demonstrate,' he continues, 'people call me "Master Chan" because it's usual, but we don't give ourselves these honours. If you want to talk about someone great, in this sense I am not the master; I am only your classmate. Mr Chee is the master.'

Sifu pauses and, with a shake of the head, corrects himself.

'I mean to say, he *was*. I always forget he's gone.'

7

THE DEATH OF
CHEE KIM THONG

In 1990 the Old Man developed gastric pains. Doctors ran tests and told him he had cancer. Master Chee was due to undergo surgery on a tumour, but his heart stopped in the operating theatre. The physicians decided it would be pointless to perform the surgery. When he awoke from the anaesthetic, the doctors told Master Chee he had four months to live. The Old Man closed his clinic and cancelled *gongfu* classes at the club. Most days he rattled about the Chee Kim Thong Pugilistic and Health Society headquarters by himself. Once the classes ended, most of his students did not come. Perhaps they had abandoned him to learn from another expert, or were disappointed that a *gongfu* master appeared mortal. They did not visit the Old Man socially and they did not help with his medical expenses. Sifu suggested to the committee that members should help with the Old Man's financial hardship. The committee's response was not enthusiastic. Only a small group of club members kept a vigil by an altar in the clubhouse. They burned incense and prayed for Master Chee's recovery.

Sifu has just taken me for lunch at the Singapore Cricket Club, in the heart of the colonial district. The Cricket Club is a dazzling-white work of British neo-classicism that overlooks a knoll once known as Scandal Point, favoured for the exchange of gossip. The colonial district melds gradually into the financial area; a hint that one reason Singaporeans often look favourably on British imperialism is its contribution to the foundations of administrative efficiency. Near his old business haunts, Sifu likes to entertain visitors at the Cricket Club, or to relax there amongst the other members. Occasionally we meet at the Club when I wish to ask about particular aspects of *gongfu*.

We discuss Master Chee's illness as we amble back to the bus stop over the Singapore River. Our route exposes us to cruel sunlight, a searing brilliance in which nothing could be concealed. Accordingly at this point in the tale, Sifu suggests, the majority of Chee Kim Thong's students showed their true colours. On the Fullerton Bridge, Sifu stops in his tracks at the detail that most infuriates him.

'The seats were thick with dust.'

His eyes flash at the injustice.

Yet death did not come. As at the Japanese POW camp, the end seemed inevitable, but then normal life resumed. Four months elapsed and Master Chee's health improved. He began to treat patients again. After a year it was clear his cancer was in remission.

When *gongfu* classes recommenced at the Chee Kim Thong Pugilistic and Health Society it appeared that affairs were as they had been before the illness. Yet the Old Man had learned something about the prodigal sons returned. Evidently he decided that if practitioners were to view their relationship with him solely as a commercial transaction, so be it. For its number of high-flyers the Association had become known as 'the Mercedes-Benz Club' around Kuala Lumpur. Master Chee knew that many of the students cared more for status than the art or their teacher. He may as well profit from the situation. Connection with a great master became a commodity. Chee Kim Thong began to offer discipledom at a price of $5,000. Like it or not, his students helped with the medical bills.

'Batch initiations,' Sifu says contemptuously. 'Twenty or thirty students at a time. 168 disciples in total!'

Locals of Chinese ethnicity liked to be associated with a Chinese group. Visiting Westerners wanted a big name to back up their claims as *gongfu* experts. The new disciples did not undergo the same initiation ritual that Master Chee conducted with Sifu in 1961. The Old Man did not give them baptismal names or open the chakras. Instead of teaching a special technique to each student, he told them to tour the statues of the Eighteen *Luohan* in the clubhouse. Each student should stop under the immortal with which he or she felt particular affinity. Then the Old Man went around the groups and taught a technique collectively, based on the statue they selected.

'I filmed one group,' Sifu says. 'You can see the Old Man keeps having to simplify and simplify; they just can't get it. By the end of the videotape, the whole thing is lost.'

Privately I wonder whether this is the fault of the teacher, who introduces a complex lesson that requires individual tuition, or the aspirants, whose ability in *gongfu* does not merit the arts. Sifu tends to apportion most of the blame to the students themselves for 'seeking double-promotion,' for wishing to advance in status.

'We refer to these as *cai*, "adopted sons,"' Sifu continues. 'Not *tudi*, real disciples.'

The foster-sons had merely purchased certificates of their affiliation with Chee Kim Thong. Yet Sifu felt that the privileged relationship he enjoyed with Master Chee was degraded by this wholesale acceptance of nominal disciples. Strictly, once Chee Kim Thong had initiated five aspirants, *his* disciples should be the next to initiate new dedicates into the lineage. By tradition Cheng Hai, Sifu and Seng Pang could each take five disciples, but this didn't happen. People who studied under Cheng Hai went to Master Chee to purchase the higher association for $5,000 rather than asking Cheng Hai himself.

'I asked the Old Man, "Is it money? I can give you more money." But he told me, "It's because of our affinity." He said that he couldn't turn them away, because they must have some connection in a past life. *Which* I did not accept!'

Typically, the Old Man lapsed into silence when Sifu pressed for an answer.

This development caused chaos in martial-arts politics. While insiders knew that disciple-by-purchase was an inferior association with the master, the reality was that more than 160 people came to present themselves as disciples of Chee Kim Thong. Self-declared 'Inner-Chamber Disciples' boasted of close and exclusive relationships with Master Chee to attract their own students, who didn't know any better. It was especially difficult to regulate practitioners outside Asia.

The Old Man was aware that his acceptance of endless disciples would cause disputes about status and authority. He took steps to control the fate of his arts.

'But this Old Man,' Sifu tells me, 'isn't organised. He'll call me up asking if I can go to China at one week's notice.'

In 2001 Master Chee pestered Sifu to organise a seminar for *Wuzuquan* instructors with the goal of 'Standardization'. Too much inferior *gongfu* was taught in Chee Kim Thong's name, and he wanted Sifu to correct it.

'Some of this nonsense we didn't even recognise,' Sifu complains. 'I asked, "Where did this come from?" Old Man said, "*I* didn't teach."'

The clubhouse in Kuala Lumpur had become a wellspring of misinformation. Bill Moran, an Englishman who spent time in Malaysia, told me that the foster-son certificate was like a kiss of death. The club only provided formal classes for beginners. Whatever their standard, those who paid $5,000 for elite membership considered themselves too good for the lessons. People practised with their friends in various areas of the clubhouse, trading arts casually and even teaching *Taijiquan* and other *gongfu* they had learned elsewhere. Visitors from afar identified the opportunity to acquire new exercises, blind to the problem of reliance on dubious sources. Bill visited Kuala Lumpur hoping to advance his *Wuzuquan*, but to his surprise was asked to lead the beginners' class. Sometimes the Old Man emerged from his clinic and taught whatever group was assembled, but wouldn't remember which art he had showed them from one week to the next.

In view of the crisis over the quality of *gongfu* practised in the club, negotiations commenced in which the Old Man recommended as many days of Standardization seminar as possible, while Sifu pleaded for as few.

'Three days?' Sifu suggested hopefully. 'Old Man said, "See-meng, some of them are flying from Europe, and America! We need two weeks." So I said, "*Five* days?"'

Eventually they agreed that a ten-day seminar would take place in May. Additionally, the Old Man made Sifu promise to teach at the Quanzhou Shaolin Temple that year. The schools at Shaolin strove to retrieve traditional *gongfu* practices, lost to them when the turmoil of the twentieth century forced out the traditional masters. The Old Man encouraged Sifu with the saying, *What comes from Shaolin returns to Shaolin.* To restore true arts to Shaolin was a duty.

Most importantly, Master Chee made plans to name his lineage successor. This person would have authority over the dissemination of Chee Kim Thong's *gongfu* after the Old Man's death. He chose Sifu. The Old Man spread news that a formal succession would take place on 29 April. Mak Tian Meng booked a celebratory dinner in Kuala Lumpur.

Chee Kim Thong prepared two important documents. The first was a formal certificate that appointed Sifu his successor. The second was a personal statement about Sifu:

The bearer is my most precious disciple, Chan See-meng.

Master Chee wrote this by hand in mirrored script, so that the Chinese characters were reversed, and stamped it with his seal. He did not explain the purpose of this document, which could seem superfluous in light of the succession certificate. Additionally, Master Chee gave Sifu a Chinese fan stamped by the Abbot at Shaolin in Quanzhou to acknowledge that Sifu's name was recorded at the temple as the lineage holder. Master Chee gave Sifu the personal certificate and the fan immediately, but he locked the succession document in a bedside drawer alongside his personal *gongfu* notebook. From the drawer, the document could be retrieved for the celebration of the succession.

Sim Peng Choon, Deputy Chairman of the club, congratulated Sifu when he visited the headquarters that spring.

'I hear you're to be made successor. Well done!'

When all seemed to be in place, the plans began to fall apart.

'I didn't expect the Old Man to go so soon,' Sifu tells me. It never occurred to him that a personal motive urged Master Chee's sudden resolution to ensure standardization among instructors, the formal succession of the school, and *Wuzuquan* instruction at Shaolin Temple. The Old Man knew he was dying.

Depression had seized Master Chee. Stress induced his earliest gastric troubles, and those who were close to the Old Man became frightened that it would kill him this time. Students in Kuala Lumpur urged Sifu to fly over from Hong Kong more frequently to raise Chee Kim Thong's spirits.

We have reached the bus stop now. I reflect on the surprise that a living legend, a verified Zen master whose achievements centred on feats of bodily self-control, would be susceptible to ordinary anxiety. Surely, I say to Sifu, surely with his ability to do X, Y, Z, Master Chee could transcend everyday concerns. 83 years was not a very good haul for a *gongfu* master.

'When I was young,' Sifu responds, 'I went to a fortune teller, who looked at the lines on my palms. He said I would die at twenty-seven.' Sifu turns over his hands. 'This line was very short, no line here: big trouble. My father died at twenty-seven, and my grandfather died at twenty-seven. So my grandmother became scared. Desperately, she wanted to protect me, to keep me from getting hurt. But I didn't die at twenty-seven. Over time, the lines on my palms have changed.'

'I don't understand.'

'What I mean is that sometimes we make our own fate.'

'And Master Chee?'

'He wasn't happy.'

Whatever the Old Man's ability for transcendence, he lacked the will for it.

'What was so bad?' I ask.

'His second wife, and his second wife's son.'

Sifu tolerates all kinds of roguery but warns me never to take a second wife. When they were younger, Daphne accused him of keeping mistresses.

'I answered, "Darling, you give me enough of a headache. Why would I want a bigger one?"'

Sifu joked with Daphne but his principles were serious. He learned from the Old Man's experience. Chee Kim Thong supported in-laws and children by his second marriage. It was too much when he was required to give further financial assistance to one of his sons, who had taken a second wife of his own.

'Mr Chee's second wife was not good to him, she didn't take care of him,' Sifu elaborates. 'Some say he loved her, but I saw them and I don't think it was true. Then, second-wife's son wanted to take a second wife of his own. He looked at the Old Man and asked, "Why should he take another wife, but not me?" This guy gives Old Man a lot of stress; he's already supporting the boy's *first* family.'

I attempt to fathom how the domestic disputes of the Chee family amounted to fatal anxiety. I recall Sifu's account of an incident during his first year with Chee Kim Thong. The Old Man's parents were still alive then and lived with him in Dungun. One day Master Chee's parents scolded him. Sifu didn't understand their talk in Hokkien, but clearly filial piety was a serious matter to Master Chee. 'He knelt before them with tears streaming down his face,' Sifu remembered. Duty weighed on the Old Man. I imagine his angst at his family trouble, which his ancestors observed in horror from their tablets. This was compounded by the squabbles of his *gongfu* students, likewise seen from the clubhouse altar by the Shaolin patriarch Bodhidharma, and Bai Yu Feng, founder of *Wuzuquan*. Sifu explains that the doctrine of reincarnation troubled the Old Man too. While he suspected that he earned his hardships by the misdeeds of a former existence, he dreaded that failure to regulate his family would have consequences in his next life.

Stress, hypertension, thoracic aneurysm: a swollen aortic artery. When the artery ruptured, Master Chee died.

'I practiced with him on the Sunday morning,' Sifu says, beside me now on the bus to Dhoby Ghaut MRT. 'Then I went off to teach a class. That afternoon he was taken to hospital. On Thursday, Old Man was dead.'

Master Chee died on 12 April 2001, some two weeks before the scheduled announcement of lineage succession. Administrative chaos followed. Officially, only the five initiates were of consequence in the club's hierarchy. Of those, three had maintained their *gongfu* practice: Yap Cheng Hai, Sifu and Kok Seng Pang. But a horde of ersatz masters emerged from the woodwork to claim authority, clutching their foster-son certificates. The Old Man hadn't stressed the difference between these adoptees and true disciples. They themselves either didn't know or didn't care. Around the globe, website warriors boasted online of their claims to Master Chee's arts; 'Inner-Chamber Disciples' aplenty who dazzled the ignorant. The standardization seminar never took place, and the quality of taught *Wuzuquan* deteriorated, inversely proportionate to the increasing claims of pretenders to the throne.

'Why didn't you put a stop to it, as the named successor?' I ask.

'Because without evidence, I would only be making claims,' Sifu answers.

'*Without evidence?*' I repeat. 'How can that be?'

We reach Dhoby Ghaut – a place whose Indian name refers to an outdoor laundry – and continue our conversation on the figurative dirty linen of the Chee Kim Thong Pugilistic and Health Society. As we exit the bus, Sifu tells of escalating skulduggery on the club's committee.

Shortly after the funeral, when Sifu had returned to Hong Kong, the board met at the club headquarters. Mak Tian Meng raised the matter of succession. He addressed Sim Peng Choon because previously, to Tian Meng's recollection, the two had discussed the imminent celebration.

'Sim Peng Choon answered, "No, I don't know anything about that." Tian Meng struck the table in anger. But nobody did anything.'

'You're saying that someone *got to* Sim? Why?'

'People playing politics.'

That left the meticulously careful succession certificate that Chee Kim Thong intended to prevent the kind of argument that had erupted. Surely this unequivocal manuscript would settle the matter. Sifu accounts for this crucial evidence drily.

'I was told that when they opened it, the drawer by the Old Man's bed was empty.'

II

LIGHTNING

8

THE CRIPPLED IMMORTAL

It is said that the Zen master Baizhang was due to give a public lecture on the dharma. Finding that a crowd had gathered to hear him, Baizhang chased them away with his staff. As the people fled, Baizhang yelled, 'Hey! Hold on!' but when they turned around to look at him, Baizhang said, 'Yes? What is it you want?'

The sage Yaoshan was delighted when Baizhang's disciple related this incident. Yaoshan perceived the tactic Baizhang had used to enlighten the crowd, and was grateful for an anecdote that allowed him to observe the other master. Through such storytelling we can eradicate the distance between ourselves and the masters, know them, and so share their enlightenment.

* * *

Today we witness a long-promised demonstration. Although we will not leave the rooftop for a little while yet, Sifu insists that we bow for the end of class: our activity has ended. We may watch, but not imitate.

In a traditional *gongfu* school, the student might only see the master perform at rare celebrations. Usually the art is channelled through a hierarchy, as it was in the Chee Kim Thong Pugilistic and Health Society, in which Sifu taught only senior instructors, and in turn was one of only several people to learn primarily from the Old Man. Had the old days endured, I could have taken lessons in Kuala Lumpur and Sifu would not even know my name. In addition to the regular hands-on tuition from Sifu, this demonstration is one of the happy consequences, from my perspective, of dysfunctionality in Master Chee's club.

For some weeks Sifu has said he would perform *Luohan Ruyiquan*, of which I have heard legend, but devised little idea of what the practice entails. In the West it is known as The Art You Cannot Learn, for reasons that are unknown. You may not be good enough for the art, but what does that mean, specifically? Such prohibition has the effect of increasing one's respect for the practice.

I know that the *Luohan* are Buddhist immortals, and have a hazy notion that *Ruyi* relates to intention. How these concepts converge in *quan*, the fist, I cannot say. Sifu speaks of this *Ruyi* as the best art he has studied. I know too that *Ruyi* is the art Travis would most like to possess. When we drive to the MRT station later, he will agonise over what sum or favour might persuade Sifu to teach him *Luohan Ruyiquan*.

Now Sifu begins *Ruyi*, which resembles other arts I have seen only as points of departure. If *Taijiquan* strums a guitar chord, *Ruyi* picks intricate arpeggios. The actions are both fastidious and smooth; resolution of that apparent contradiction lies in the skill of the exponent. Sifu's expression is peaceful. The practitioner's mind should be that of a musician who plays a favourite piece.

Involuntarily I smirk in bemusement at the inhuman quality to Sifu's movements. He's not like a *gongfu*-movie actor, who performs a polished and more acrobatic version of what people attempt in the park. Sifu's performance is like seeing a new animal. The movement requires a different language rather than a set of comparisons. His *Ruyi* is difficult to characterize because of the protean flux between stances, hand forms, speeds and textures. It is a symphony of diverse sections rather than the simple verse and refrain in which *Wuzuquan* patterns communicate techniques.

After a few minutes Sifu stops, truncating the long exercise at an early stage. He beams.

'Already perspiring!' he says. Behind him the sun climbs towards midday.

With a moment's rest, Sifu begins *Ruyi* again. Now he narrates the motions.

'The Five Elements: Metal, Wood, Water, Fire, Earth, *Amitabha*;' with the greeting of 'boundless light' he joins his fingers in a prayer-like gesture. 'I play the ball... I *turn*... This is the wave... I *churn* the Vortex...'

Travis and I stand dazzled like children before their first magic show. Suddenly Sifu crouches low and pauses.

'This is not just *any* monkey,' he says. 'This is the Monkey King!'

He continues.

'The drunkard... This one, like lilies in the wind...'

Sifu stands finally with his feet together, but his weight almost entirely on the right, with his left leg bent at the knee so that the toes of that foot barely touch the ground.

'This is the Crippled Immortal,' he says, and ceases *Ruyi* again at this point.

'The Crippled Immortal is named Li Chuan,' Sifu says. 'He planned to meditate and told his friend, "While I am meditating, guard my body, don't let anything happen to me." During this meditation, Li Chuan attained immortality. But at the same period, after a long time passed, the friend became scared. "Hey, Li Chuan has been still a long time. No breath, no heartbeat. I think he's dead, you know." So he had a funeral and burned the body. A while later, Li Chuan's spirit returned. Of course, he could not re-enter his body, because it had been cremated. The only body he could find was a crippled, old beggar who had just died.

'Anyway,' he concludes, 'now you have seen.'

There's a pensive silence as we travel to breakfast in Travis's car. I know that Travis and I have both taken *Luohan Ruyiquan* – realistically or not – as the target of our own practice, and wonder how we can persuade Sifu to share it.

* * *

Seen from the amphitheatre, the upper section of One Raffles Place appears two-dimensional, upright over Maybank like a business card propped up on a table. Close to hand stand the two UOB buildings – like a father and son, one large and one small – with their multi-faceted, Sino-Gothic exteriors. Straits Trading is no less complex in its asymmetric roof, its byzantine projections and recesses. There are two void levels on this tower, in which I can see support pillars, but nothing else. These floors may be for trees or for smokers, but I can't discern. Other towers lurk in understated, black chic. Beneath the columns of the Fullerton Hotel, once a British administrative centre, the kitschy Merlion fountain spews water into the sea. Tourists have their photos taken next to the statue in its eternal act of vomit, facing the Marina Bay Sands across the bay. The three upright towers of the Sands, with an elongated building on top like a capstone, intimate a Chinese character. Next to that is the ArtScience Museum, modelled on the shape of a boat, or a lotus leaf, or Buddha's palm; I never remember which. We came to this place on our first visit to Singapore. We went to the top of the Marina Bay Sands and watched the laser show that is projected onto the water at night, and Claire said, 'We could live here,' and now we do.

Marina Bay exudes calm. As everywhere in Singapore, construction has followed the principles of *feng shui*. To Sifu, the ancient origins of *feng shui* are common-sense observations about Nature – 'You want a house that gets the sunlight, right?' – but the calculations of modern geomancy are intricate. The discipline descends to downright chicanery with consultants who suggest that people's lives can be transformed with the purchase of expensive paraphernalia, positioned in the home to quell an unfavourable current. Every mall has a high-end *feng shui* store, and every local market has a stall selling figurines of Buddha, the Three Kindly Ones and Guan Gung, the God of War. On the other hand, it's hard to dispute that a principle more elevated than a nice view is at work in Marina Bay, which captures, intensifies and reflects the ocean's serenity to us on land.

Claire and I dawdle towards the Fullerton Hotel to take afternoon tea for my birthday. There's an extra reason to celebrate, because I've made a breakthrough in *gongfu*. My movement feels different, and all morning I've played with techniques when I have thought no bystanders could see or not caring when they did. At last I have a sense – tangible if nascent – of how the energy system works in *gongfu*.

Mysterious flute-music sounds in Occidental documentaries that broach the subject of *qi* – 'energy' – in their surveys of Chinese culture, which inevitably glimpse at *gongfu*. Westerners, from travel-programme hosts to *gongfu* aspirants, tend to reify *qi*. We have heard, they will say, that *qi* is a vital aspect of *gongfu*. Presumably a master has a lot of *qi*, which we mortals lack. How do we obtain this *qi*? *Qi* is one of the dilatory devices of bad *gongfu* tuition; 'your performance is poor because you have insufficient *qi*'. But an appeal to quantities of *qi* for improvement is a sign that improvement will never come, for in one sense *qi* is important, but in another it barely means a thing.

In Chinese culture, *qi* is every bit as abstract a term as 'energy,' with limitless applications that include weather. Everything has – *is* – energy. Because of this broadness, the concept is virtually useless without specific application. Reification is incomprehension when we imagine that we can acquire and store *qi* as though it was coal. All that matters is what is *done* with energy. To make any use of *qi* in *gongfu*, it must be discussed in particular terms, comparable to the ways in which the energies of Nature have been channelled in the placid *feng shui* of Marina Bay.

Traditional *gongfu* theory refers to the *dantian*, the 'cinnabar field' where energy is stored. Sifu avoids this term, I think because the fertile potential of a field is too static. Instead he speaks of 'the Vortex,' and will make a spiral gesture up his abdomen as though a cyclone rises inside his torso. Concentration, movement and breath converge to churn this Vortex, and finally I can *feel* what Sifu means. Since last night, when I couldn't sleep and tried some of the movements in our living room, it's as though the various parts I have crafted with *gongfu* have suddenly slotted together and operate as a machine. Specifically, it is like a steam engine, which builds up pressure in my abdomen, then uses the breath to propel my limbs. *The breath follows the hand, the hand follows the breath.* Maybe it's small potatoes to comprehend an old *gongfu* saying. Sifu will find plenty to vomit blood over in my performance regardless of this change. Yet it is incontrovertible evidence to me of advancement, which for once can be felt in my body rather than relayed in another practitioner's observations.

I mention these sensations to Claire as we walk the bridge alongside Fullerton Road. She's curious, but I don't ask outright what she thinks, in case it's that I'm insane, or that I spend too much time on *gongfu*. Her official line on the more elusive concepts I report is an Agent Scully-type scepticism.

'You should come along to our practice some day,' I say, because Claire did attend White Crane classes with me when we lived in the UK.

'I get the impression he'll only want people who are very dedicated,' Claire says, and we have rehearsed both sides of a conversation that has occurred before.

Today I am oblivious to objection, because all the effort appears worthwhile. Absurdly incongruous as we enter the austere lobby of the Fullerton, I attempt the Swallow-Vomit one last time with my new skill; a wave rolling forward from my torso. The concierge guides us to our table in the cavernous lobby. Shortly afterwards, the waiter brings the drinks and cake stand that constitute the afternoon tea service. I fancy there is a metaphor for *gongfu* in our ascent from the sandwiches on the bottom level, to the more delicate arrangements of wafer-thin crackers, cheese, salmon and caviar in the middle layer, and finally to the desserts on the top tier of the stand, which include macaroons, opera cake and a subtle mousse. But when I finish the sandwiches, ready to advance, the waiter arrives to replenish them. I am on sandwiches again, and the symbolism loses its lustre just a little. Fortunately, I'm enjoying myself. I keep on eating.

9

CRUDE AND ROUGH

It was still night when I left home. The Calligraphy Uncle was out already, drawing immense Chinese characters on the paving stones with his mop as I made my way to the MRT station. A bloody sun ascended over my journey across the island. They say that Jupiter is visible at twilight during this phase, but I have not seen it yet.

A billow of incense when the elevator doors open. I turn left across the walkway and ascend to the rooftop. I am half an hour early for class.

Now the morning bursts with primary colours. The sun has assumed a corner in the blue. More traffic hums beneath. A few joggers and cyclists take advantage of the least cruel time of day. As the neighbourhood wakes I warm up with the *Bagua* exercise. In the tower block over my shoulder a man hacks up phlegm passionately. From the trees and railings opposite sound the cheep of a Eurasian tree-sparrow, the tweet of a yellow-vented Bulbul, the squeak of a Javan Myna and another bird I can never identify, whose song is the single note of a flute.

I settle into the Plank, a static strength-exercise that resembles a press-up position with weight rested on the elbows. My chest and abdominal muscles burn. With my eyes on the concrete beneath and my concentration on endurance, I don't notice Sifu steal up the ramp behind me. Until he speaks I am unaware of his presence.

'This is silly training.'

I scramble to my feet and we bow.

Sifu continues, 'Very crude and rough.'

Dark antithesis of Soft and Light, the bane of Sifu's existence is Crude and Rough practice. I stand to attention.

'You think I haven't tried all these silly things?' he says. 'When I was young I started body building and Mr Chee gave me hell. It makes you stiffen up, no good for our *gongfu*. Next I wanted to punch the sand bag until my knuckles bled, do one-finger push-ups, all this nonsense. Old Man laughed at me. He said, "You're not a labourer; you work in a bank. How will it look to your customers if you're covered in callouses and bruises? They'll think you're a gangster." He showed me this soft exercise to strengthen my wrist. No need for the rough stuff.'

Sifu demonstrates a simple flick of his wrist, the minute movement of a Renaissance artist contrasted with the broad shapes of a cave painter. Alex rushes up the ramp.

'Permission to join in, Sir?' Presumably this formality is a leftover from Alex's two years of mandatory National Service.

'Go ahead.'

Alex begins a warm-up routine. Meanwhile I am incredulous at the lesson.

'That's *it*? *That's* his alternative to one-finger press-ups?'

'That's it. Practice for 100 days continuously and your wrists will become round like mine, no more flat. You two were both skinny when you came. Alex, you had no chest. Chris, when I saw you I said in my heart, "*Aiya!* How can this guy have studied our *Wuzu*?" Now it's different. Veronica says she has to buy bigger shirts for Alex. But did I make you learn any of this crude training?'

He beams. We try the new movement, which reminds me of a priest sprinkling holy water.

'No, *lah*! Still too hard.'

'Sifu,' Alex asks, 'why did hard-style training become so dominant, when this other kind exists?'

'Not everyone can get the refinements,' Sifu answers. 'Many who went to Shaolin were uneducated, they wanted to fight people. Tell me, what do you do with a guy like this? He can't even write his own name. Do you think he's able to study the Buddhist sutras and scriptures? In Shaolin, people like this do all the manual labour. Their *gongfu* becomes like this too.'

Popular wisdom, perpetuated in *gongfu* movies, holds that the correct stance can only be developed by hours of sustained leg tension over a protracted period. To Sifu, this is another misconception.

'It means you're stupid,' he says. 'You can't get the technique of the stance so you practice it for months on end. But it shouldn't be necessary. You don't need a long time in these low, painful stances. I'll show you.'

Sifu holds out an arm across his body, several inches in front of his chest. He doesn't adopt a *gongfu* stance but stands upright.

'Push me.'

I push to no response, then lean forward to use the strength of my legs, without effect. No part of Sifu has changed position. Alex makes an attempt and does no better. Sifu is like a statue.

'It's the same technique,' Sifu explains. 'Once you have the method, it doesn't matter what stance you use. If you're an idiot, you'll never get it. Good thing you guys have some intelligence. With the Taoists, they're all very smart; their descriptions are poetic. If the guy can't understand, they won't teach him. But in Shaolin they don't want to turn people away. They find a way to make it easier for you, and this is where the rough kind of training comes in. You've heard of the Ten Tigers of Canton? The *worst* of them took refuge in Shaolin from the Manchurians. When he came out he made popular all of this basic, very crude interpretation of the art.

'People are impressed,' Sifu declares, 'by silly things. All this is nonsense. Breaking bricks is just physics. In KL the gangsters would come out hitting slabs of marble and pieces of wood. But there would always be a seam in the marble, and they'd make sure there were no knots in the wood. The Chinese saying is that if you train only hard strength, you end up with nothing. You just get old and deteriorate.'

'But Sifu,' I reply, 'some of our training is gruelling.'

'Different,' he answers. 'When Bodhidharma brought Buddhism to China he taught the Shaolin monks Stretching the Sinews and Changing the Bones. Not punching the rocks and breaking the hands. But remember we talk about balance, so you must have some strength. Look at pictures of the old *Taiji* masters. They all had strong shoulders. To be completely soft is useless, you wouldn't even be upright.'

This elicits memory of an illustration in my school science book; an artist's impression of a human body without a skeleton. It was a puddle of pink in what appeared to be a martini glass, with two eyes and a patch of hair floating at the top.

'Mr Chee spoke about different kinds of practice. In one, the guy barely moves, it doesn't look like much. This trains you internally. Two: it looks awkward, but builds power. Third is the very ornate stuff, completely useless. Alex, remind me what is the Chinese term for it?'

'We talk about the "Pretty Pattern."'

'Yes, this is the one. Just for demo, no application, learning sets for the sake of it. Frankly speaking, it's a waste of time. Just because something looks good doesn't mean it is good. Like a prostitute: she may look good, but don't put your dick in her or you're in big trouble.'

Leaving aside prostitutes and aesthetics, I suggest that even soft strength requires the structure to be sound in order to transmit force efficiently. Sifu insists on the flexible resilience of a willow tree, as opposed to the rigid oak:

'Which will survive a storm? The oak will fall over. This is why I always talk about the willow and the rattan. This is the correct kind of strength, not the rough stuff idiots are impressed by.'

'Often the rough and useless people end up as teachers,' I say. 'It sounds like the chance to find the right tuition is very small.'

'I know,' Sifu answers. 'When my *Taiji* teacher, Mr Dong, left KL, I tried all the schools and found nothing worthwhile. I even stood around Madras Lane hoping to meet masters. When I saw someone dressed like a traditional Chinaman I tugged at his sleeves and asked him to teach me. They all said, "Get lost kid, I don't know *gongfu*."'

Sifu is fatalistic about whether an aspirant will meet good masters, yet it is not enough to be a passenger of destiny. To me it is difficult logic.

He speaks of luck, but also intimates that a fate must be fulfilled by effort.

'You must continue the search,' Sifu says. 'This is where the Yellow Bundle comes in.'

The talk of refined practices leads Sifu to focus on the Swallow-Vomit technique that incorporates *Wuzuquan*'s most important breath control. He directs us to perform the technique with one step forward, so we repeat until we reach a ramp two-thirds of the way along the car-park, then return with backward steps. Between sets of repetitions, Sifu allows us to rest by strolling once up and down the car-park. Initially we were only allowed to walk as far as a van that had been left half way up. Gradually Alex and I have extended the recovery walks, hoping Sifu won't notice. One bold day we began to walk as far as the ramp. Now we venture all the way to the end of the car park, grab the rail momentarily, and look at the traffic and trees below before turning back to face the next bout of exercise and criticism. Finally the Singaporean sunshine approaches its worst and we have suffered enough for today.

'Chris, do you see my shirt?'

'Yes, Sifu.'

'What colour has it gone?'

'Red, Sifu.'

'You see how important it is to review? You can't just go ahead learning new things all the time. Any more questions? No? Let's go, baby.'

We cross the ramp. When the lift arrives there are people in it, so Sifu remains silent until we exit. Some time ago he rebuked Travis for discussing *gongfu* in the elevator.

'Never talk when there are more than three sets of ears present.'

Although we have made the short journey to the food court umpteen times, Sifu walks a few paces ahead as expedition leader. He holds his right arm out at shoulder height and beckons once in a brisk motion that uses all four fingers simultaneously.

'Come, come, come.'

Footsteps behind. Two small children overtake us and approach Sifu at speed.

'Master, Master will you teach us?'

'Yes,' he nods. Sifu turns back to us as the children run off laughing. 'But they never come.'

'How do they know?' I ask.

'Some see us practise from their apartments. I meet people who say, "Master, are you off to do your training?" I always say, "I'm just out walking."'

He pauses.

'Hey, let's see if my grandson is in the playground,' Sifu says. He inspects the slide and sandpit. 'No; they must not have taken him yet. I think this boy is gifted, you know. When I was getting ready to go out, he pointed to my shoes. He knows this kind of thing already.'

'Before he was born,' I say, 'you told me all Singaporeans think their children are gifted. Since Jun Jie was born the argument has changed.'

There is no answer.

We pass an old woman who gives me the Singapore Scowl: she glares, sticks out her lower lip and jerks her head up. Alex explains it's because I'm foreign. A few weeks ago someone in the lift asked Alex if *he* was foreign because she overheard him and his Mandarin sounded too correct to be local.

'People are racist here,' Alex says.

'Sometimes people will complain about foreigners,' Sifu says. 'I've had it in Singapore myself. Only a few weeks ago a guy in the street thought I was from Hong Kong. He told me to go home. I was getting ready to whack him! These are crude people.'

The area is changing and some locals blame immigrants. When I first came to Sifu's neighbourhood, there were a few dingy shops around the wet-market, but the space is in metamorphosis to become one of Singapore's ubiquitous shopping malls. It will be a clean and convenient loss of identity, a temple to monoculture distinguished by a few Asian eateries and traditional doctors. To the scowler, I presume, modernization is imported strangeness. The wet-market hangs on as a peculiar anachronism.

We negotiate the crowds, vegetable stalls and fishmongers to ascend the staircase.

The *kopitiam* is always thronged on Saturday. Sifu goes ahead to find a table while I queue for drinks and contemplate options for breakfast. There's a long queue at the Indian stall but they won't have biryani ready yet and I'm too hungry to make do with *prata* bread. We haven't been back to the Duck Rice stand since Sifu's portion was laden with tofu and unacceptably light on meat. I anticipate Sifu will want *mee pok*, his favourite in recent months: noodles, sliced fish, Chinese mushroom, fish balls, chilli and a deluge of balsamic vinegar.

It's my turn to order. I purchase two coffees and Milo for Alex, a hot-chocolate drink that he takes under protest because Sifu thinks it's good for us to have something warm after practice. Every time Alex struggles dutifully to the bottom of the cup. Tray in hand I set out to our table in unaccountable knowledge that, no matter how busy it is, Sifu always manages to find a table in the same spot. He sits becalmed while the blind hordes mill around with their trays. Here, as he puts it, the Yellow Bundle comes in. Here it is as though action belonged to the Hour of the Dragon. The Hour of the Snake was transitional, and the Hour of the Horse brings us into an entirely different phase, in which there is no exertion but to talk and listen.

10

CARRY THE
YELLOW BUNDLE

One morning our talk in the *kopitiam* turns to a current controversy.

'Did you read about this blog writer in the news?' Sifu asks. 'What was it he said?'

'He said something like, "In Singapore there are more dogs than men,"' Alex answers.

'He complained there were Uncles staring at him on the train, and such,' I say.

The Chinese exchange student in question has criticized Singapore in his blog, based on his day-to-day experiences here. His complaints have been reproduced in newspapers.

'I hope he doesn't lose his scholarship,' Sifu says. 'Such a shame for his parents! What do you think?'

'I'm surprised it's considered newsworthy,' I say. 'But I suppose you shouldn't bite the hand that feeds you.' Sifu nods.

'When I came back to live in Singapore in 1997, I complained, *Cannot do this, cannot do that.* Then my nephew said to me, "In Singapore you must like it or lump it." He was right.'

'Correct,' Alex says. 'Especially for a scholarship student. He's lucky to have the opportunity to come here from China.'

I'm uninterested in the blogger's petty complaints, but intrigued by the public outcry over his right to criticize. I decide to test the waters.

'Recently a colleague said it would be *good* if Singapore had a little more civil disobedience,' I venture.

'And what do you think?' Sifu asks.

'I think she meant the students should be a little more rebellious, the way we think of students in the West. But nonetheless, it's not the kind of comment you'd make if you'd just been robbed.'

'A lot of rules and regulations here,' Sifu says. 'Like I always say, it's free choice: if you want to come to Singapore, you have to play by the rules.'

'In the newspaper someone pointed out that Singaporeans are "free" to go jogging at midnight,' Alex says.

'In a way that wouldn't be possible in places that are supposed to be more liberal, but are also quite dangerous,' I answer. 'I see your point.'

'Once I went to visit LA,' Sifu begins. 'One day, I had some free time in the middle of the afternoon. I went walking. It was such a nice day, I kept on going. Then I heard a police car blast its siren at me. The police officer said, "*Sir*, what are you *doing* in this part of town?" I said, "I'm just taking a walk." The police officers thought I was mad. They said, "You'd better get in quick." They drove me to my hotel and told me not to return to that area. Coming back: what kind of society do you want to live in? It's your free choice.'

'The old freedom paradox,' I say.

For a few moments I concentrate on my *char kway teow* while Alex queues for a bowl of congee.

'Chris, I notice you are like a garbage truck; everything goes in.'

'I'm hungry, Sifu. It must be because I practise so hard, eh?'

'Don't worry,' Sifu says. 'It's a good thing.'

'Recently a Singaporean friend took me out to dinner. I think I really won her over by eating so much.'

'To the Chinese it means you give her face as host, you show she has provided for you,' Sifu says. 'You're not like this Long-Arm Lum. One day I was taking some guys to lunch at a restaurant. I met Lum at the clubhouse, so I invited him along, just to include him, you know? But at the restaurant, I noticed he won't eat anything, even though we've ordered a variety of dishes for sharing. I asked him what was the matter. He said, "*Meh*, I don't like any of this." He only wants a certain kind of tofu and particular veggies. So I said to him –' Sifu wags his finger – '"Now, Lum! I asked you what you eat, and you said to just order anything." This guy! And people like Lum are always the first to criticize. When younger students practice before him he'll interrupt at every stroke – "No, you're wrong; no, you're wrong" – not even give the guy a chance. Why are you laughing so much?'

'When an Irish student came back from a holiday in Malaysia he did exactly the same thing; "No, you're wrong." He must have got it from Long-Arm Lum.'

'So these friends of yours went to Malaysia?' Alex says as he sits with his congee. 'Why go so far?'

'The best *gongfu* was in Malaysia,' I answer. 'They were not as lucky as you, living down the road from the master.'

'It took you a while to realize,' Sifu says to Alex.

'I was an idiot!' Alex says. 'I met Sifu through Daphne at the International School. She mentioned her husband was interested in *Taijiquan*. Then she told me he studied with Dong Ying Jie! So I interviewed Sifu for *Tai Chi Magazine*.'

'But then how long before you came to learn my arts?' Sifu says. 'All those years you wasted! Chris, I kept telling this guy to come and learn *Wuzu*. He said my fees were too high. But I want you guys to feel the pinch!'

'Don't worry, I feel it,' I say.

'Eventually he came, but until last year he only wanted to learn *Taiji*.'

'But it's better late than never,' Alex says.

'For the Westerners, it's a lack of good instructors outside Asia,' Sifu says. 'On a visit to KL I watched them and I said to Old Man, "These guys are so bad! How can they teach?" Old Man just said, *"Aiya*. Let them train."'

'So they were tolerated rather than endorsed,' I say.

'That's right. Mr Chee wanted people in the West to have the chance to get *some*thing. But then, just because you go to Malaysia doesn't mean Old Man will teach you.'

'So you end up learning from Lum.'

Sifu waves to Travis across the *kopitiam*, and Travis walks over to our table, still talking on his phone, and hovers about without sitting.

'Hey, what took you so long?' Sifu says when Travis has ended the call.

'Downstairs full up already. I park upstairs is quieter.'

'OK, since you are on your feet, you may as well bring me another coffee. Better get your breakfast as well, ah?'

'Nothing for me,' says Alex, who is part of the way through his mandatory cup of Milo.

'Actually, the coffee is better in the place near me,' Sifu says.

'A lot of flies here,' I say.

'Notice that the flies don't settle on me. Observe for a while; then we will discuss further.'

Travis returns bearing a tray of drinks in one hand, and in the middle of another phone call. He follows the same routine of hovering and talking for a few minutes. When he sits, Travis explains that he plans to meet his friend at their durian plantation in Malaysia. He leans across the table and slaps my chest with the back of his hand.

'You want come?'

'I don't want him to go!' Sifu says. 'A Caucasian guy like this, all pale, in the Malaysian jungle? The heat would kill him! Chris, one of these days I'll take you to Chinatown for durian. Don't make that face. If you can eat blue cheese, you can learn to like durian.'

'Sifu, I bring you some back from Malaysia,' Travis says.

'Thank you,' Sifu replies, and inspects Travis's noodles. 'How is the *bee hoon* today?'

'OK only. Not like last-time.'

'I think the chef left,' Alex says, and we all glance towards the unfamiliar faces at the *bee hoon* stall. 'He's gone to a new place nearby. So somebody new has come in.'

'Actually, I wish we had our vinegar noodle today,' Sifu says, frowning at his empty bowl. 'This was too oily.'

Alex removes a weathered book from his rucksack.

'Travis, here's your book.'

'Did you read?'

'I read it; it was interesting, the differences and similarities in their training.'

'This *Yiquan* is related to our *Wuzu*,' Sifu says. 'Mr Han Xing Yuan taught me in Hong Kong. The inventor was Wang Xiangzhai. When the Beggar's Art players saw Mr Wang's push hands, they copied. They challenged the *Taiji* men and won. These are the ones who called themselves the Black Star of *Taiji*. Then, the *Yiquan* stance training became part of *Taiji*, all brought over by the Beggars.'

The Beggar's Art, associated with the Hakka tribe, cobbles together techniques taken from different arts. While many arts have absorbed practices from other *gongfu* styles, the Beggar's Art is unique in foregrounding its acquisition from diverse sources. For that reason the Beggars might be considered unusually honest in their account of their repertoire. The Beggar masters took what *gongfu* they could get, but when Sifu speaks of their art it sounds as though they were proud of their ability to penetrate the secrets of other schools. These are further stories of enthusiasts learning *gongfu* surreptitiously, in contrast with the outspoken blogger earlier in our conversation, doomed to an early university exit.

'Hey Alex, what time is your tuition?' Sifu asks. Alex starts and produces his phone from a pocket.

'Better rush,' Alex says. He leaps up, makes his goodbyes, and is gone to tutor for school literature exams. Sifu begins to talk of another clip he circulated.

'Did you see the video of the Cambodian magic pedlar? What did you think?'

'I can see he break the neck, the chicken not moving,' Travis says. 'Then he do the magic, the chicken alive again.'

'What about the levitating monk?' Sifu asks.

'For me they're both the same,' I say. 'The camera cuts away at the crucial moment. So there's time to go in and change something. You need a continuous shot.'

'*Yes*. All these are tricks. Look at that *Taiji* man in the Botanic Gardens. He says he has this-*qi* and that-*qi*, and it's all nonsense. The students believe, so they fall over when he waves his arms at them. Does this kind of technique really exist? For years the Chinese government has promised to make a millionaire of anyone who can demonstrate this *so-called* "Empty Force," so the military can turn it into a weapon. But the money has never been claimed. So, use your common sense. It's psychology and superstition. Crude people believe. That's why I sent you the video of the magician, Derren Brown. Did you see this?'

'Yes,' I say, and the footage of the magician tormenting the credulous with imaginary force really was like what Sifu says of the *Taiji* man in the park.

'It's good for you to see these things; it's all part of the search. Donn F. Draeger showed me the list of masters he met, with his observations. Most were bullshitters. But you need to be careful. Do you know how Donn died? They poisoned him in Indonesia. He got a bacterial infection, and was never well after. He was researching *Silat*.'

Sifu's friends Donn Draeger and Robert Smith were pioneers of western scholarship on Asian martial-arts. They travelled extensively to accumulate knowledge of different disciplines. During his investigation of the Malay art *Silat*, Draeger offended the wrong person.

'So be careful what you say about people's training,' Sifu continues. 'Mr Chee says you think of yourself as a rabbit before tigers. Be humble and cautious. Not showing off like this guy, ah?'

'Actually Sifu, not I show off, I ever—'

'*Aiya*,' he dismisses Travis with a wave. 'I travelled everywhere in search of these great masters, but they were all cons. I could find no-one like Mr Chee. If you ask me how much of his art I learned, I'd say there's no way it's more than thirty percent. But these tricksters have *nothing*. If you want to say I'm arrogant, then yes, I'm arrogant.'

I take a moment to resolve this equation of arrogance and humility by turns; modesty in approach to strangers who might know something worthwhile, but readiness to discard people and arts deemed inferior.

'But isn't part of it just depressing?' I ask. 'Isn't it a big disappointment when people boast and it turns out to be a sham? At least in the academic world we have a standard. I can look at students' records and know who we should let do a PhD. But these *gongfu* ranking systems don't tell you *anything.*'

'Now some Chinese arts use the Japanese grading system.' Sifu says. 'It's silly, it's too commercialized.'

'Sifu,' Travis says, 'I think we can only investigate the masters with good reputation, see for ourselves.'

'I think so. If you listen to what most people say, it's the blind leading the blind.'

'That's why I keep saying that it seems a student's chances of learning a real art are very low,' I say.

'You have to be lucky to find the right teachers,' Sifu continues. 'We talk about *affinity* with the art. I was lucky to meet great masters. *But,* effort was required. In the early days with Mr Chee, whenever we could, Cheng Hai and I went to Dungun. You must take the opportunity.'

By contrast, when Sifu travelled around Asia to investigate reputed witch-doctors and masters, he found that most were fakes, trying to sell medicines. Others disappeared when they heard Sifu intended to test their abilities.

'Let me share this with you,' he continues. 'In China I heard of a Mr Siew, who said that his arts could heal people. I went and stayed with him in Hebei for three days and four nights. The first day I practised what Siew showed me. Nothing happened. I stood there for half an hour thinking, "What the bloody hell is this?" Siew looked at me and said, "Mr Chan, your *qi* is very strong, you should begin moving soon." At this my arms began to sway. But back in my hotel room I realized it was autosuggestion.'

'So you only swayed because Siew gave you the idea?' I ask.

'Yes. After that, I didn't move because I didn't believe. This idiot! He warned me that he could bounce *qi* off the moon using his eyes to harm an attacker. Siew lost his job around that time. He worked in a hospital: a janitor or something, not a doctor. He told the patients to give up their medical treatment and practise his arts. They all came back to hospital a year later, seriously ill because they hadn't taken their medicine.'

'That's just stupid.'

Sifu checks his watch.

'Come, let's have one more drink. Ah-Chris, you go. Tea this time; *the si kau*.'

The queue for drinks is longer as noon approaches. I think of the different kinds of bundle-carrier we have discussed this morning, from the travellers in quest of the best masters, to those who come to us onscreen, to the travesty of the process in the exchange student whose insensitivity threatens to cut short his education. I order and a moment later the Tea Auntie slams the cups onto the counter with the unceremonious spirit of the food court. Strangely it is this gesture that causes me to reflect on my own journey, although we live on a tropical island, and have spent an hour discussing explorations around Asia.

As I return to the table Sifu laughs so loud that it drowns out Travis's attempts to contest some point. He chuckles still as he sips his tea.

'I was just saying that the *worst* adventure of all was with *this* man in Kota Bharu, four years ago. His brother was there too; they believe in all this nonsense. They caught me with my trousers down: we were already in Malaysia, and they said they wanted to go up this mountain. I was the only one who didn't want to investigate. So what could I do? I felt I had to go along. The people there believe in witchcraft. They said that invisible beings – the Jungle People – were coming in from another dimension to steal the local girls as wives.'

'Maybe they went to the city to find rich husbands,' I say.

'Maybe,' Sifu says. 'We climbed the mountain, me with my bad knee, and in leather shoes. Soon I was *soaked* with perspiration. We reached the top and this group assembled from the village.'

'So the top of the mountain is where these beings were meant to come through?'

'This is what we were told; that a meteorite had landed there, and it had special powers. These villagers started to chant and wave their arms.

They said they could feel particularly strong vibrations that night. *I* didn't notice a damned thing. After a couple of hours I thought we could go back down, but they told me we had to stay all night. We were sitting on cardboard boxes. It started to rain – *pssssssssh*, downpour! – and the boxes collapsed. I was furious! Saturated, a complete waste of time. Then on the way down, this idiot nearly got himself killed. He decided to *run* down the mountain. When he fell, a big gash on his face.'

'Sifu, maybe you see, you believe,' Travis says.

'There was nothing there!' Sifu says.

'When I go to park to practice last month, two black dogs approach,' Travis says. 'They bark at me, I think they want me to go with them. I shock. My neck, all the hair stand up.' He wriggles his fingers to suggest goose bumps.

'Doesn't mean there are ghosts, *lah*!' Sifu says. 'This is a very literal belief in the Chinese traditions.'

'Funny, the Irish are superstitious about black dogs too,' I say.

'I think this is in a lot of cultures,' Sifu says.

'I think something happen in the park, maybe someone die,' Travis says. He looks disconsolate that that our conversation has not led to mutual professions of belief in the supernatural.

'Sometimes, where something bad has happened like an accident, there are remains. This is energetic, psychological. It's nothing to be afraid of.'

'Like a fingerprint on a photograph,' I suggest.

'Something like that,' Sifu says. 'Not ghosts and spirits flying around, black dogs here and there. You should trust your intuition. If you get a funny feeling about a certain place, there is probably a reason.'

'Bad vibes,' I say.

'Yes.'

'Don't they call Singapore "Asia's most haunted city?"'

'This is because of events at Changi, the men who died there during the war,' Sifu says.

'A student from London told me Master Chee's clubhouse in KL was haunted,' I say. 'He said that the ghost of a monk appeared and told off one of the English guys for staying in bed while the others practised.'

'This is nonsense,' Sifu says.

'You mean I won't get to see a ghost there?'

'Why does London have so much superstition? Mr Chee was not like this.'

'Some people want *gongfu* to be magic,' I say. 'Possibly if it's magic they won't have to put in the hard work. Or it will transform their lives. They want to latch onto something. They should be opposite: on a search for the real thing.'

'Yes,' Sifu says, and with a grand sweep of the hand he adds, '*The Search for the Precious Gems*.'

'You make it sound like *Indiana Jones*,' I say.

'It *is* like *Indiana Jones*.'

11

DRAGON DANCE

Frenzied, the dragon flashes before us in pursuit of the pearl. It dips, soars and spirals through the smoke with eyes that glare and jaws that snap at the prize. Frantic cymbals rally the serpent, but unseen hands float the pearl from its reach. A second pair of eyes blazes from a corner. Now two dragons coil in opposite directions, one blue, one pink.

The Luminous Dragon Dance is the speciality of Seow Lim Teck Eng Tong, a traditional Shaolin group. The *gongfu* students perform the routine to raise funds for their club. To mark auspicious days, Chinese businesses often enlist dragon- or lion-dance troupes. A well-trained dance displays the firm stances and agility of skilled martial-arts. Many of the *gongfu* groups around Singapore practice the lion dance but the Luminous Dragon of Seow Lim Teck, Sifu explained when he invited me to this dinner, is 'something special'.

At an apartment complex in Bedok, under an immense marquee erected for the occasion, Seow Lim Teck celebrates its forty-fourth anniversary with a banquet and performances. Friendly with the former chief instructor, Sifu has sponsored a table at the event and invited his students. It's the first time Claire has met him.

'Hi!' Sifu began when he saw her. 'Chris is a good guy. He hates me when I mention Cromwell.'

Claire laughed and her anticipatory terror of Sifu appeared to dissipate. Now they chat freely, as the dragon dance ends and there is a break in the programme. Sifu looks smart in a low-key way, wearing a black, short-sleeved shirt and a Rolex. He asks how we met. Claire tells him it was at university, and he wonders about the factors that caused us both to choose the University of Bristol.

'Fate,' Sifu concludes, and points upwards. As a suckling pig is served Sifu comments, 'This is a good experience for you guys, like a traditional village feast.'

We are the only Caucasians in an assembly of hundreds. The speeches are all in Mandarin. Sifu introduces me to Eng Soon, who studies his soft arts, and Nikko, a young woman whom Sifu knows from some business venture.

As Eng Soon tells me about his background in martial arts, I reflect on the commonality between Sifu's students. Each of us has found Sifu after trawling through other arts: Alex in *Taijiquan*; Eng Soon in Karate as a youth; Travis in everything under the sun; myself in White Crane and a watered-down version of Chee Kim Thong's arts.

In a yellow, traditional Chinese suit Lionel Lee, who has recently taken over from his father as head of school, demonstrates *Liuhebafa*, 'Six Harmonies, Eight Methods'.

'I studied this art in Hong Kong,' Sifu says, and I can tell that the performance carries him far away and into the past.

* * *

In the late 1970s Sifu began to study under Chan Yik Yan and Han Xing Yuan, to whom he refers as 'the two Northern masters'. Han had learned *Yiquan* from the great Wang Xiangzhai, while Chan was the *Liuhebafa* expert. Sifu met these masters through Ian Fok, a business associate and fellow *gongfu* enthusiast.

Master Chee encouraged Sifu to explore other arts and deepen his comprehension. He wrote letters to Masters Chan and Han permitting his disciple to study their *gongfu*.

'Mr Chee was a very open-minded man,' Sifu explains. 'He told me that if you see only one art, you are a frog in a well.' Sifu enjoyed a good relationship with the Northern masters, although as Master Chee's initiate he could not become a formal disciple when invited. He addressed the Northern masters as *Laoshi* – 'teacher' – rather than 'Sifu'.

Chan described the practitioner's body as a dragon and likened the expression of force to a spring. Han placed great emphasis on *zhangong*, stance training. When Sifu complained that Han made him sit lower and longer than the other participants, the master would say, 'Those guys are my rice bowl'. The exploration of similar principles in different arts aided Sifu's *Wuzuquan*. At times he had struggled with Master Chee's terseness. When he told the Old Man about his new discoveries under Chan and Han, 'Mr Chee simply said, "Now you know."' I'm always grateful when Sifu acknowledges such difficulties under Chee Kim Thong: even Chan See-meng didn't always apprehend the principles immediately. The Northern masters were more patient in explaining the details to their students. 'But wherever I was, I always went back to my Old Man,' Sifu will say, 'because he had so many wonderful things to show me. The Northern masters were more famous than Mr Chee, but they were not as good.'

* * *

The demonstration continues onstage. Sifu must be evaluating this *gongfu* in relation to the versions he was taught. However, there is no question that Sifu would compare notes on *Liuhebafa* with the Seow Lim Teck practitioners, because he has never told them he studies *gongfu*. Sifu's friendship with the master's father, former chief Lee Seng Lye, arose in a very different context.

'One day I was walking in the Punggol Park,' Sifu told me. 'Two old guys were doing some exercise. I asked them if it was OK to sit on the bench and rest, in case it would interfere with them. So I sat and watched for a little while. When they finished, they asked me if I would join them for coffee. They were very friendly.

'We went to the food court in Mr Lee's van – he has a fruit and vegetable business – and we had our breakfast.'

Since then, Sifu has joined Master Lee's group three times a week to walk and exercise in the park.

'If I miss a session he'll worry. He calls up and asks me, "What happened?" This is a good friend, loyal and humble. The only problem is he'll never let me have a lie-in.'

Travis was appalled when he learned that Sifu hadn't discussed his background in *gongfu* with Master Lee.

'Have you told them who you are?' he demanded.

'I have never mentioned my history in *gongfu*,' Sifu answered. 'But Mr Lee knows. An old-time master like that? Of *course* he remembers the name of a champion from Singapore.'

Travis was disconsolate.

'Why you no tell them your past?'

'Because Mr Lee organised this group,' Sifu answered. 'He is the leader. What I have studied is irrelevant. One of the others is head of the *Taijiquan* association, but it's the same rule, he keeps quiet. Mr Lee is boss. This is a group of old guys who meet for health. We do the exercises Mr Lee shows us.'

These include a few basic martial-arts techniques from Master Lee's art. I infer that Sifu enjoys pretending he's an amateur, although Lee Seng Lye hints that he has not been deceived.

'Once I said, "Hey, why do you correct the other guys but not me?" Mr Lee answered, "*Aiya*. You already have it."'

* * *

Sifu has started to expresses hope that I will teach *Wuzuquan* sooner or later. I'm ambivalent about the prospect of *gongfu* instruction, for reasons that relate to my teaching duties at the university. I have a good rapport with the students, and enjoy helping those who are interested in the subject. But those who lack commitment exasperate me. When some colleagues gush that being a professor is a great honour, and that they *love* teaching students above all else, I suspect that it's cant for job interviews, or self-important distortion of their own significance. However, what if they really *do* enjoy teaching that much, and I don't?

A troupe of Seow Lim Teck's youngest students gives the next performance, some with staffs and broadswords. To sit here watching the Seow Lim Teck students perform makes the idea of instruction tangible. What place would I have in such a group? In *gongfu*, my merits as a potential teacher are idle speculation, unless some upheaval occurs in the *Wuzuquan* world. It appears that the time in which Chee Kim Thong's arts were widely propagated is past.

Mr Lee doesn't seem to sit down all evening, but monitors from the side of the marquee. Surely Seow Lim Teck has its own concerns with funds, *gongfu* standards and politics, I think, but tonight it appears the model of a martial-arts organisation that works. Maybe having a non-profit group obviates part of the common problems. My mind drifts to the book Travis showed us about the Malaysian *Yiquan* association. I was absorbed by the photos of the people who constitute a *gongfu* club, and imagined their stories. A suited man performed his routines with the seriousness of his professional work; a plump and cross-eyed boy whose parents hoped *gongfu* would set him aright; the group of women with their own decades of *gongfu* experience; the stern-faced master in traditional dress whose only identity in this setting, regardless of life outside practice, was that of the Sifu; the businessmen who appeared unfamiliar with exertion but edged into the group pictures to demonstrate their support of a Chinese organisation; a lean and sharp youth who might some day be the master. Each practitioner is a moment in the course of the art. The faces imparted this truth to me in the same way that Sifu's talk of the old days is populous with names of club members – Jerry Lee, Philip Tan, Tony Wong, Chooi Mun Sou, Yap Chin Tian, Mah Ping Kwong – and there is incantatory power in their number.

Onstage the Seow Lim Teck group creates a chapter of its own history, and celebrates its endurance in difficult times for martial arts. Inevitably I reflect by contrast on the Chee Kim Thong Pugilistic and Health Society, which once held celebrations of its own, biggest of all for Master Chee's eightieth birthday in 1998. Recently I have trawled through the records of these occasions to derive a sense of what the club was like at its peak.

Fortunately, a significant quantity of material evidence has survived from the club's heyday.

In 2000 Sifu bought a digital video-camera to capture as much footage as possible of Master Chee. He filmed their private time in the Old Man's clinic. They practised together and discussed important theory. In time Sifu hoped to record all of Chee Kim Thong's arts. He didn't foresee that only several months later he would film Master Chee's funeral.

Sifu urged me to purchase a hard-drive so he could share his footage of the Chee Kim Thong Pugilistic and Health Society, which dated back to the 1960s. In addition to the videos from Master Chee's final months, Sifu had paid to convert old film reels to digital files. Finally, after seven months, Sifu returned the hard drive, burdened with 330 gigabytes of video files. In the first clip I watched, Sifu is in the store in KL trying out the camera. As I opened the other files I realized there were untold hours of footage that demonstrated the breadth of activity in the Chee Kim Thong Pugilistic and Health Society. Even in the 1960s Master Chee's disciples thought to purchase a video camera to document their *gongfu*. The footage captures the vibrant lifetime of the organisation, with performances at public demonstrations, club dinners, lineage anniversaries and private functions that united the branches it had established throughout Malaysia and beyond.

No such occasion prompts my imminent trip to Kuala Lumpur, although Sifu has arranged for me to meet some old practitioners who will tell me about the club's history.

'I told them to look after my student,' Sifu reported. 'These are strong words to a Chinaman. They may ask you to demonstrate, but they don't have these refinements. They may criticize, but in their hearts they'll say, "Shit! I don't have this."'

To complete the juxtaposition of the clubs – with a gulf in character apparent between Sifu's reliable friend Mr Lee, and the current occupants of Master Chee's property – I remember Sifu's last warning to me about affairs in KL:

'If you do visit the clubhouse, beware of Sneaky Snake.'

12

A LEGACY IN RUINS

'So dusty!' Mak Tian Meng exclaims as we ascend the staircase. 'Nobody cleans the place. I don't know what's happened.'

A laden clotheshorse is the sole occupant of the concrete practice-area outside. This laundry foregrounded my first view of the club headquarters, whose parchment-coloured walls bear the emblem of a monk seated in meditation. Five concentric haloes surround his head, the innermost radiance of which expands to encompass the holy man's body. His soles are upturned in the lotus position; his robes are the orange of Shaolin. Under the monk's gaze laundry dries, weeds spring through the neglected concrete, and nobody practises *gongfu*. A few wooden benches on the perimeter glisten in wet decay. Floodlights testify to former affluence. I wonder when the lights were last needed.

Above the doorway a sign painted in golden Chinese characters and Malay text reads 'Chee Kim Thong Pugilistic and Health Society'. As we tour the premises I think, *Elvis has left the building,* but realize the comparison is inadequate. In Graceland I could at least revel in Presley's kitsch tastes and attempt a fried peanut-butter and banana sandwich. By contrast, Master Chee's old clubhouse is a shell. I have felt the Old Man's presence on Chan See-meng's rooftop when Sifu revives the early days, but I imagine his ghost shuns this museum. That we meet on a rooftop car-park underscores the separation of Master Chee's legacy into material inheritance and the transmission of his practice. The art is of every place and none. The sad reality is that the clubhouse needs Chan See-meng, but Sifu does not need it.

The clubhouse itself is an impressive facility. It has the air of a deserted mansion that longs to be occupied again, or a disappointed lover deluded by hopes of reunion. The building itself feels poised, expectant that the cobwebs will be blown off and the old times reinstated. Perhaps it's the *feng shui* of this building to stir the visitor with a sense of activity that is now sadly ironic.

When we entered, Tian Meng told me that two of Master Chee's sons were at home. One, Boon Teck, greeted me, although clearly without intention to endanger the fatted calf. Perhaps sixty years old, his features an insipid reproduction of Chee Kim Thong's, he smiled at first and invited us to sit opposite him at his desk in the main clinic. After he and Tian Meng exchanged a few words in Hokkien, Boon Teng's expression changed. He got up to busy himself about the room and didn't address us again.

'Because you are See-meng's student,' Tian Meng explained.

The nefarious Second-Wife's Son, Ah-Hwa, lurked in the other clinic but declined to admit me when Tian Meng announced our arrival.

'Because you are See-meng's student,' Tian Meng said.

The grand entrance-hall contains an arch decorated with the eight characteristics of a successful *Wuzuquan* exponent:

Honesty
Tolerance
Diligence
Humility
Courage
Wisdom
Intensity
Power

Repeated on the rear wall, the character 忍 for 'tolerance' stands out from a gold backdrop, immense in black paint.

On the windowsill Tian Meng indicates a wooden box full of pebbles. He explains that they are used to condition the hands, and demonstrates by stirring the pebbles with a gentle push-pull motion. That the pebbles are kept in a reception area is testament to a time when the clubhouse so teemed with students that every nook was used for *gongfu*.

'This is very good for building power,' Tian Meng tells me. 'When you strike someone, the strength is already in the hands.'

In nostalgic reverie, Meng circles his hands through the stones. Around us glows an eerie half-light that belies the sun's blaze outdoors, as though the brightness hesitates outside to accommodate the sense of ghostliness. In reality the windows need to be cleaned.

We leave the two clinics beneath us to look upstairs at the main facilities for *gongfu* practice. A tall man in his seventies, Tian Meng remains limber. He rolls around on the floor before the ceremonial altar to demonstrate a series of stretches, which he explains Master Chee taught him to loosen up. Tian Meng springs to his feet.

'This is the picture I want you to see,' he tells me in allusion to a portrait left of the altar. The Old Man is seated with palms rested on his thighs. 'Look at his hands. You can see how powerful they are.'

Tian Meng was right; the clubhouse is an enviable asset. It includes the two clinics, a dormitory for visitors and a room for ritual use. The practice area has a polished wooden floor. Statues of rugged Bodhidharma and compassionate Guan Yin look out alongside exotic Buddhas that appear to be from Thailand and Cambodia. There is a painting of the Eighteen Immortals above the altar in this room, a tea set for ceremonies and a large bell on a stand.

In one corner of the practice room an elderly man lights sticks of incense. Tall and lean, his antiquity, feline narrowness of face and his eyebrows – heavy and diagonal – fascinate me.

'Who is that?' I ask.

'That's a disciple,' Tian Meng answers. Agape, the stranger nods to us but doesn't speak. We leave him to his devotions and exit to the conference room.

'It's hot!' Tian Meng exclaims. 'How do I turn the damn thing on?'

When we pulled up outside, the thermometer in Tian Meng's Mercedes read 34°C, but this says nothing of the steam-bath humidity that clogs our skin and stifles us. He locates the controls for the air conditioner and invites me to sit. In accordance with the pervasive air of pessimism, the factory's plastic sheaths have been left on the swivel chairs, long enough by now for the wrapping to be discoloured.

We discuss the early days of the club. Master Chee's disciples worked hard to establish the group's reputation amidst a Chinese community dense with competitors. Some rival schools sent spies who posed as students, but many of these defected to become *bona fide* members of the Chee Kim Thong Pugilistic and Health Society. When challengers visited the school, Sifu opposed them. When Long-Arm Lum embarrassed the club in a push-hands contest, Sifu sought out and overcame Lum's adversary. While many of Kuala Lumpur's *gongfu* organisations were bedfellows with gangsters, they realized their violence would be ineffectual against the talents of Chee Kim Thong and Chan See-meng. The Old Man's art was simply in a different league.

'We were very good back then. But who wants to learn *gongfu* nowadays?' Tian Meng wonders. 'Nobody does. This is the modern man.'

As a boy, Tian Meng defied his father to learn *gongfu* secretly at one of the famous international schools, which had a branch in KL.

'If he knew I was going to Chin Woo he'd have killed me,' he says.

Tian Meng asks what interested me in *gongfu*. I said that I first studied in Ireland as a teenager. My instructor told us about an incredible man in Malaysia named Chee Kim Thong, and I attended the seminar when the Old Man visited Dublin. Since then I have searched for the real deal, true *gongfu*, but never encountered it again until I met Chan See-meng.

'This is your karma,' Tian Meng says.

The French can-can sounds again; Tian Meng's ringtone. His advisor calls intermittently to update him on trades. Legend has it that Tian Meng made a pact with the Diamond Monk, an ascetic at a local temple. In return for a blessing, Tian Meng agreed that if his business succeeded he would dedicate a portion to the temple of the Diamond Monk, so named for the reliability of his benefactions. Tian Meng brought an irresistible combination of know-how and arcane boon to his financial speculations. When he took me to lunch this afternoon, Tian Meng explained how

Wuzuquan's Four Basic Essences correspond to investment: 'When you breathe in, you hold on to your money. When you breathe out, you invest. Then, stock floats up in value, and sinks down.' Like my first encounter with Sifu in the restaurant, my conversation with Tian Meng has proceeded according to our predetermined roles. He, as the elder, has talked; I, the younger, have listened.

Tian Meng ends his call. Sifu has briefed him that I am here to learn about the old days, and now we resume our talk about the history of the club.

'I heard about Master Chee through the newspapers,' he says. 'They wrote that there's one Chinese man, and it's as though there's a magnetic field around him. No-one can penetrate. I heard there were thirty or forty Malays involved.'

'But I didn't practice here until 1969. Master Chee told me to come back at 6 am if I wanted to learn! He was very kind to me. The club was very good back then. Cheng Hai and See-meng were good disciples at that time. And Master Chee loved him; he really loved See-meng a lot. He said he was talented to learn martial arts. They said the same about him in Hong Kong.'

Eventually we address the current activity of the Chee Kim Thong Pugilistic and Health Society.

'Is it fair to say the club is dormant?' I ask.

'No, we meet once a week in here,' Tian Meng replies.

'What happens?'

'We talk about finance; repairs to the building. We talk about training, but nothing gets done.'

I reflect on the Dickensian prospect of a committee that assembles to raise funds, which facilitate only further meetings. I had an idea of this scenario from e-mails that Sifu has relayed to me in which he attempted to motivate Tian Meng to reform the club. Accusing the chairman of '*NO gongfu!!!*' Sifu blasted his thoughts in a maelstrom of block capitals, bold text and exclamation marks, with the cumulative impression that he is constantly shouting at the unfortunate Tian Meng. For me to volunteer knowledge of these tirades would entail a loss of face for Tian Meng, so I affect utter ignorance of the club's problems.

'What we lack,' Tian Meng continues, 'is teachers. See-meng would do very well here. Kok Seng Pang is good too. And *talk-talk-talk-talk,* but nothing happens. We need people who are motivated by love for the art, who want to bring forward the tradition. But nobody cares about *gongfu*. This is the modern man.'

I am surprised at the broadness of this claim against the Modern Man, since I have travelled all the way from Singapore to learn more about Master Chee's arts. Tian Meng continues to discuss the committee's disputes.

'I suggested we all contribute equally for repairs. Other members refused. They asked why I didn't just pay for it all myself. Some of us even wanted to sell the clubhouse and pocket the money. I don't know where they got the idea.

'So the club is fractured. It's like porcelain: you try to stick it back but the crack is there. If Master Chee had done the right thing, See-meng would probably have been very famous. This is the sad part of the story. When sons argue, the duty of the father is to resolve the conflict and solve the problem. But Master Chee didn't do it, and See-meng left.'

I examine a pile of blank certificates left on the table. They are headed with the club's emblem and await completion to award some distinction or other.

Tian Meng nods and repeats, 'This is the sad part of the story.'

He offers to show me more of the neighbourhood before he returns me to the hotel in Bukit Bintang. As we return downstairs it occurs to me that I should inquire whether there is any fried peanut-butter and banana sandwich of memento, if only because I find it unlikely that I will ever return here. I suggest the medical wine for sale in the clinic, which is rubbed on limbs after contact practice to prevent bruises.

'If it's his father's recipe,' I say, 'I may as well pick some up.'

I sit in a reception area by the rear door while Tian Meng inquires about the medicine. He returns and presently Boon Teck's son emerges. The two debate in Hokkien for a moment before the boy speaks in English.

'Fixed price, $70,' he says firmly.

I agree to the price and the boy returns with a small bottle of brown liquid. 'CHEE KIM THONG,' the label declares in large font and below, much smaller, adds 'CHEE BOON TECK'.

On our way down the driveway I notice that the clotheshorse has been removed in case, I like to think, I might choose this moment to photograph the building. But I saw it and committed the laundry to memory; part of the clubhouse as it now stands.

* * *

Who were the members of old? A diverse cast frequented the clubhouse in Kuala Lumpur, the epicentre of the Chee Kim Thong Pugilistic and Health Society, which had branches around Malaysia and some later in Europe.

Mr Ho, who made his millions as a durian farmer, had an epiphany that inspired him to set aside business. He spent his time at the headquarters upstairs beneath the statue of the Ear-Scratching Immortal. The exercise Mr Ho practised resembled running on the spot while rotating his wrists. He became a most contented man on learning this art.

Goh Thong Meng's son had no interest in *gongfu*, but came through the clubhouse on the occasions that a peculiar trance befell him. He appeared to be possessed by the Drunken Immortal, Zhongli Quan. At these times Goh Junior arrived hunched over and clutching a fan, like Zhongli. Any club members on the scene stood out of Goh Junior's way and allow him to proceed upstairs, where he performed incantations at the various altars.

Big shot Alan Ting called in regularly for short practice-sessions. Rotund and topless, he rehearsed his sets in a corner of the hall. His girlfriend crouched by his side, ready with a towel. After fifteen minutes Alan would reach out for his towel, and his session would be at an end.

Li-teng studied *Wuzuquan*, and for a time Daphne took lessons in the soft art of *Wujiquan*, 'Ultimate Void Fist'. Many women joined, but few remained in the club very long. I suspect it was masculine self-assertion in club politics that drove away the female members.

Alvin Yip was the only person known to have lost his mind since he joined the club. Already eccentric – he induced trances in which he acted as a medium for spirits – Alvin wanted to learn the Virgin Art. This *gongfu* was not suitable once the practitioner was middle-aged, married and a father. But Alvin insisted, and acquired the set, and was not quite right afterward, if ever he had been.

Yap Chin Tian and his brother Chin Khoo had a lumber business. True servants of the club, they studied diligently and became instructors in the Ipoh branch. Among the students there were the brothers KC Tan and KE.

These people and many more came to the Chee Kim Thong Pugilistic and Health Society by the old Klang Road.

* * *

When I meet Peter Seow and his wife Ling for dinner in Kuala Lumpur, I discern that word spreads fast between local practitioners.

'Hey,' Peter says when we stop at a traffic light. 'I hear Sneaky cheated you for the medicine. It's because you're Chan See-meng's student. Master Chee used to charge $4 a bottle.'

Mentally I estimate inflation since Master Chee's death and speculate a price of $8.

'I'm not surprised,' I answer.

'Too bad. And it's a pity Tian Meng didn't introduce you to Lum.'

Tian Meng presented me with some old yearbooks of the Chee Kim Thong Pugilistic and Health Society, which include progress reports from each branch, pictures to illustrate *gongfu* routines, and portraits of the committee. From the photos within I learned that the aged disciple at worship in the clubhouse was the prodigious Long-Arm Lum.

'You didn't invite him to dinner?' I ask. Peter and Ling giggle.

We met in the lobby of the Marriott on Jalan Bukit Bintang, five doors and several rungs of grandeur up from my hotel, which nobody has heard of and which lacks a car-park. For about fifteen minutes we drive across the city. The rush-hour traffic is heavy but not immobile.

'Master Chan likes to eat here,' Peter explains as we pull up at a steamboat restaurant set in a marquee.

A waitress assembles a hotpot apparatus – the steamboat – on our table, and lights the gas burner. We boil pieces of meat and vegetables, and eat them in turn. Finally, when the soup has acquired the flavour of the previous ingredients, we will boil noodles.

Ling tells me she practiced for a time. Nonetheless she explains she's bound Peter to an oath not to talk about *gongfu* all night. I say I'll do my best to help. We discuss the imminent election. Peter and Ling hope the Opposition will win for the first time.

'We Chinese pay most of the taxes, although we're the minority,' Peter says. The National Front reinforces racial division, and historically has retained power by appeal to the Malay majority. In this context I can see that a *gongfu* organisation would be an important environment in which Chinese identity could be celebrated. But for the first time Anwar Ibrahim's Opposition has encouraged a significant proportion of the electorate to overlook ethnic rivalry and support a progressive party.

Inevitably we veer back to martial arts. The fault is mostly mine because I'm so interested in reports I've heard of Peter's current teacher, the *Taijiquan* player Koh Ah Tee. Sifu began to mention Koh last year. He told a strange story in which Yap Cheng Hai coerced Koh into a contest with James Chee, the Old Man's son, who teaches *Wuzuquan* in Australia. Apparently, Koh had overcome Cheng Hai in a push hands challenge. Cheng Hai wanted James Chee to beat Koh and uphold the name of Master Chee's school. Sifu became intrigued by Koh's gentlemanly behaviour in this debacle, and they became friends.

For lack of an instructor Peter gave up *Wuzuquan* some years ago and started to learn *Taijiquan* from Koh.

'Mr Koh is very internal,' Peter tells me as we eat the noodles, the final stage of the hotpot dinner. 'Although the movements are simple, it's hard to see what's going on. He started under Cheng Man-ch'ing when he was twelve years old. Have you heard of Cheng Man-ch'ing?'

I've read a book about Cheng Man-ch'ing and seen videos of his *Taiji*.

Sifu met him in the 1950s after his studies under Dong Ying Jie. Later, Cheng migrated to New York and established a reputable *Taiji* school. Koh's depth of comprehension, Peter says, arose from prolonged, solitary reflection on the techniques Cheng taught him.

'He pressed me to the wall with soft strength,' Peter recalls. 'I couldn't even feel an impact. Does Master Chan demonstrate this kind of thing?'

'Sometimes,' I answer. 'Although he doesn't like to dazzle us. He prefers to demonstrate the next level, which should be within our grasp. When we reach it he shows us the next level again.'

'Now I practice everything softly,' Peter declares, and demonstrates *tun-tu*, the Swallow-Vomit technique of *Wuzuquan*.

'Do you prefer this training to *Wuzuquan*?'

Peter makes a face.

'I learn from the best teacher I can,' Peter says. 'In the '90s I went to Master Chee and asked him to teach me. He said, "My time is over." But I didn't want to learn from Sneaky. Kok Seng Pang had a training group, but it fell apart ten years ago. He got tired of the politics.'

Peter explains that Seng Pang didn't want to continue classes at the clubhouse once the Old Man died. It wasn't that he demanded payment for tuition, but that others stood to profit by any lessons held at the facility:

'The fees would all go to Master Chee's sons.'

* * *

Sze Yah Temple is overwhelmingly red and silver, lacquer and metal. Local legend holds that a spirit spoke through one of the migrant Chinese, promising prosperity if a temple was built on this site. The temple was built. The immigrants mined for tin and became famous. Modern Kuala Lumpur was born. Thereafter the Chinese community met here to debate community matters.

An old woman kneels before a statue of Guan Yin, the Goddess of Mercy. When she sees me, she rises and points to a wooden cylinder full of bamboo sticks.

'You shake the cylinder until only one stick comes out. One stick only.'

Before I know what I'm doing, I'm doing it. I rattle the canister and the bamboo sticks, of which there are perhaps a hundred, start to budge forward. One of them emerges from the container ahead of the others and falls onto the stones beneath. The woman the takes the stick from my hand and indicates two kidney-shaped wooden blocks resting on the altar.

She makes a clapping gesture.

'I bang them together?' I ask.

'Three times. Then you throw.'

She flicks out her fingers, flinging imaginary blocks to the ground.

A block in each hand, I clap three times and throw them to the floor. I see now that each block has one flat surface, while the other is rounded. One block has landed with the flat side facing up, the other with the rounded side.

'See the way they fall?' The crone points. 'It mean she is laughing at you. This no good. Start again.'

I start again. Shake the cylinder. Stop when a stick has fallen out. Clap the blocks together. Throw them down. My supervisor nods, satisfied with this arrangement. She consults a number carved onto the stick and wanders off momentarily. She returns with a slip of paper, which has a message written in Chinese characters:

> A treasure house of jade and gems awaits you.
> Why search in foreign lands for unknown gold?
> Like the man who holds the lamp and seeks for fire,
> Better pack your bags and set out for home.

With these words bubbling in my mind I am out on the street again. On my way back to the hotel, where I will shower and nap before my next appointment, I speculate on what the fortune-telling could mean. *Foreigners go home*, maybe? Thanks a lot, Malaysia. Or perhaps 'home' in my study of *gongfu* means Singapore. The visit to Kuala Lumpur brings me to the scene of important events and romantic anecdotes in the club's history, but these are all long passed. In a more metaphysical interpretation, 'home' could refer to inner knowledge and realization, rather than seeking answers externally. None of these is a particularly encouraging prophecy. While I have learned useful things about Master Chee and the club, part of me feels like a fool for being here.

* * *

Kok Seng Pang tells me to wait for his silver Mercedes outside Bukit Jalil station.

'What do you look like?' he asks over the phone.

'Like the only Caucasian I've seen for hours,' I reply.

The penultimate stop on the Sri Petaling line, Jalil is a suburb 20 kilometres from central KL. It does me good to be away from the clubhouse, the sense of adventure growing with each change of train line, with every increment of distance from the city. While I value my close training with Sifu, part of me wishes Kuala Lumpur was still abuzz with *Wuzuquan* practitioners. The clubhouse depressed me with a sense of my own belatedness. Irrationally, I can't help but interpret today's inert Chee Kim Thong Pugilistic and Health Society headquarters as a symbol that forbids my further progress in *gongfu*. It's difficult to contest such strong material-evidence that Chinese martial-arts are in decline.

The meeting with Seng Pang was difficult to arrange. We kept missing each other's calls. My day began with an ill-fated trip to Thean Hou Temple, some distance outside the city. When lost I became irritated. From divination of a vagary in my guidebook I took a wrong turn on foot from Tun Sambanthan and ended up drenched in sweat twenty minutes from my destination. I reached Thean Hou Temple in little mood for tourism, so I went directly to the food court by the souvenir stalls and had a drink to cool off. Then my phone received an SMS from Seng Pang: 'Pls call again.'

My Singaporean phone behaves erratically in Malaysia. To speak to Seng Pang I needed to use Skype via my laptop, which was in my hotel. I didn't mind. Thean Hou Temple hadn't captured my imagination. I'd been in Asia long enough to feel all templed-out. After a perfunctory survey of the six floors I went back to the Golden Triangle.

Sifu refers to Seng Pang as 'the little boy'. In a photo with Chee Kim Thong taken after their initiation in 1961, Seng Pang is twelve years old and Sifu eighteen.

'He was very naughty,' Sifu told me. 'In the first year, the Old Man's father died. During the wake, Seng Pang wanted to go off to play with the turtles in the pond. Old Man scolded him: "This is a time to be serious."'

On the journey back to the Golden Triangle I wondered whether Sifu's information would be of practical application when I encountered Seng Pang. At the hotel I called him to arrange a meeting then showered, put on fresh clothes, and returned to the streets. Kuala Lumpur was still new to me. I didn't mind re-crossing the city. Even the mysterious interrelation of monorails and trains fascinated me in the midst of this deep inconvenience. Busier trains have Ladies-Only Carriages. Signs in stations proclaim *No Indecent Behaviour* with a silhouette of a couple poised but doomed never to kiss.

KL is a place of poorly-signed changes and unnumbered platforms, where everything bustles along continuously but without direction, as though to slow down was a greater error than to take a wrong turn. So it was that I had to double back to change lines on the way to Bukit Jalil, which I accepted as symptomatic of life here. It is Singapore's amiable but wayward cousin, the college drop-out next to the investment banker. The traditional shop-houses here have not been meticulously restored. KL has grubby charm, a lovable, shabby authenticity, but I imagine too it's the kind of place where it's impossible to get hold of a plumber.

Seng Pang arrives and I see that he is not a small boy, but a tall, broad-shouldered man – 'the best physique for *gongfu* out of all the disciples, like Mr Chee,' according to Sifu – mirthful, blue eyes and a relaxed chuckle.

We drive to take lunch nearby. There's a little stretch of restaurants in this residential area, with food court-style plastic tables and yellow chairs. Seng Pang orders us a variety of roast meats with rice; entry-level Chinese food for the unknown foreigner. He asks about my meetings with Tian

Meng and Peter, although I sense that he has spoken to them. I tell him about Peter's reverence for Koh Ah Tee.

Chuckle.

'I told him to work on softness.'

'Can Koh's art be so remarkable?' I ask. 'Peter is very impressed by his softness.'

Chuckle.

'Softness is within the practitioner.'

Over lunch Seng Pang tells me that he once studied under Wong Kiew Kit, who has since made his name with a series of *gongfu* books, international seminars and a horde of instructors in his own martial-arts organisation.

'Was his *gongfu* any good?' I ask.

Chuckle.

'Not *gongfu*,' Seng Pang clarifies. 'He was my schoolteacher in Dungun. He studied *Wuzuquan* for a while with one of Master Chee's sons. But he didn't master it. Mostly he practices other arts. Master Chee could have done so much more than Wong, but he didn't have English. Have you seen Wong's *Wuzuquan*?'

'There are videos on his website.'

'He plays the sets differently,' Seng Pang observes.

We drive to Seng Pang's home north of the city. He points out the blue peaks of Banjaran Besar in the distance.

'I didn't know Malaysia had mountains like this.'

'Cooler up there.'

'See-meng has some land in Genting. Sometimes he talks about retiring up there.'

Chuckle.

We reach Seng Pang's house, which is stylish in a sparse way that creates a tranquil atmosphere. Seng Pang made his money in music and television. Currently he produces travel programmes for Muslim tourists. He tells me he has considered purchasing the apartment next door, to knock down the partition and extend his own property. He indicates a framed work of calligraphy on the wall, a single Chinese character.

'Master Chee drew it for me,' he explains as he serves tea. 'It has special meaning, just for me. Something about myself. I haven't figured it out yet.'

Like *gongfu*, calligraphy is a high art associated with Zen concentration. Sifu says that directing one's intention to the wrist in brushwork is similar to a fundamental skill of good martial-arts. Medicine, calligraphy, music and philosophy make a complementary skill-set for a *gongfu* master. The Old Man's favourite character to draw was 佛 (*fu*), the Chinese name for Buddha. Often he gave out graphs of this word as gifts.

Our lines of conversation tend to dry up quite quickly, although the lapses are not awkward. I think that Seng Pang is puzzled by the purpose of my visit, which Sifu described to him as a 'courtesy call'. When I tell him I'm gathering accounts of the early days under Chee Kim Thong, Seng Pang replies, 'Hasn't See-meng told you all this?' I explain that since I'm recording the club's history it's best to collect as many reliable accounts I can. Seng Pang is satisfied with this, but is wary in discussions of club politics. For my part I greatly enjoy the chance to meet another initiate. It's as though I've learned from the Wizard of the South and have now encountered the Wizard of the East.

Seng Pang has his own set of allegories for our practice, yet what he tells me is conceptually consistent with Sifu's version.

'You must make your body like a ball of dough,' he says. 'When you inhale, decide what you want to do with your lump of air.'

Like Sifu, Seng Pang talks about a small repertoire to be studied in profundity rather than a collection of novelties.

'I like to meditate and go through the sets in my mind,' he says.

'Have you ever thought about taking disciples?' I ask.

Seng Pang shakes his head.

'Too much trouble.'

Before I leave, Seng Pang tests my *Sanzhan*. He grabs my wrists and applies resistance at each phase of the pattern.

'Your stance is too rigid,' he explains as I struggle to move him. Eventually I pant to the end.

'Next I will rock you,' Seng Pang announces, and we repeat the exercise. True enough, his interference causes me to sway from side to side. I expect a gulf of standards between us so I am not badly demoralized.

'If you practised like we practised,' Seng Pang says of my years in *gongfu* before I met Sifu, 'you would be a master now.'

That *does* dishearten me a little.

Seng Pang leaves me at Gombak LRT station. I meander back to my hotel and on to the airport, where I receive an SMS from Seng Pang: 'Is everything in order?'

Now in the departure lounge, I confirm that all is well. I thank Seng Pang for his time and add, 'My teacher is right to say there is treasure in KL among those who learned the true art.'

Between spurious practices and sneaky sons, I wonder whether Master Chee's true heritage has been too thoroughly demolished to rebuild. It would require determination and unity among the three interested disciples. Hence it's a pity that I didn't meet Yap Cheng Hai too while I was in KL, but the suggestion drew a familiar refrain. Tian Meng said, 'I was thinking of taking you to meet Yap Cheng Hai. But I was afraid if he heard whose student you are, it would give him a heart attack.'

As I mull over this, Seng Pang replies: 'Some day the muddy waters will clear and you will see the truth'.

13

SWEAT

Early in our time together I brought a cloth bag to Sifu's classes. I got it free at a convention. I needed the bag to hold a towel, a spare T-shirt and a book to read on the MRT, along with items I didn't want in my pockets while I practised. When he noticed it, Sifu looked at the sack dubiously.

'You need a better bag than that,' he commented while I changed my T-shirt after class.

'My things are still in shipping from the UK,' I responded. 'My good bag is in there.'

'You must be a little bit vain,' Sifu told us. 'Always show the best face.'

The next time I saw Travis he had dyed his hair jet black.

Soon afterward our boxes arrived in Singapore. My respectable backpack was restored to me. The matter was complicated, however, by the state of my clothing. It wasn't simply that my sportswear became sodden from *gongfu*. It was *pungent* with a new and heinous variety of sweat. Long sessions under a teacher in the UK – founded upon interminable press-ups – left me drenched, but that excretion didn't reek like the sweat under Sifu's instruction, which he claimed carried more toxins than normal perspiration.

'Your urine too will smell terrible.'

I answered that I had already received incredulous complaints on this matter at home. The vinegar tang of my *gongfu* sweat posed another threat to domestic harmony.

Sweat prompted debate amongst Sifu's students. I knew some practitioners prided themselves on an utter lack of sweat during *gongfu* exercise, and believed this was a sign of correct technique.

'Bull*shit*,' Sifu laughed when I told him of the Sweatless Boxers, who could practice the *Sanzhan* routine 108 times without rest. 'Now your realization is coming, what do you think?'

'There are major differences in concentration and breath technique,' I say. 'Your way is much more difficult.'

'If you can do it 108 times, I will kowtow and call you my master,' he replied. 'How can you exert yourself without perspiration? No sweat means you have used no effort.'

Clearly, the sweat was here to stay. I couldn't expose my rucksack to my sweaty clothes or it would become irredeemably malodorous, so I brought a supermarket carrier inside to receive the contaminated T-shirt after every class. One day Sifu saw me remove the grocery bag from my rucksack.

'You need a better bag than that,' he announced once more. 'I'll bring you some of the Club's bags.'

While I explained that the grocery sacks were merely liners, Sifu insisted that he help out.

At our next session Sifu presented me with two flat, unused plastic bags. They bore the emblem of a yellow lion on its hind legs and the declaration, *Singapore Cricket Club. Established in 1852*. I accepted Sifu's donation with thanks, although it created a new problem: I never reused the grocery bags, because if I persisted with the same carriers they would become slimy and smelly.

The solution, I realized, was to continue with supermarket carriers but conceal them under the handsome veneer of the Singapore Cricket Club, and place *that* in the rucksack. So far I have had no complaints on this account. Perhaps I've deceived Sifu with the triple-bagging ruse, or maybe he tolerates the lapse of standards so long as it is kept from sight.

14

STEALING CHICKENS

Shaolin legend tells that in the fourteenth century, a young man of coarse appearance came to live at the temple. Stocky and silent, he went barefoot, wearing only trousers. No one knew his name or where he came from. The youth was sent to work in the kitchen. He conducted the menial tasks asked of him without complaint, practised devotions as was appropriate to attain merit, and revealed no interest in martial arts.

When the Red Turban Outlaws attacked the monastery, the youth took up a poker from the kitchen. Wielding this implement against the invaders, he displayed the famous Shaolin staff-technique. The young man appeared so ferocious that the Red Turban Outlaws fled in terror. The temple was safe once more.

When order was restored at Shaolin, the youth was nowhere to be found. The monks concluded that they had been in the presence of a Bodhisattva, an enlightened being who remained on earth to direct mortals on the Way. They celebrated this protector of Shaolin as an incarnation of Vajrapani, the guardian of Buddha, and erected a stele in his honour.

* * *

'Last-time,' Travis begins after Sifu exits the car, 'Sifu ever mention, four potion'.

This is a prompt, a test of my knowledge. 'Last-time' is Singlish to mean 'at some point in recorded history,' while 'ever mention' is a formulation unique to Travis that designates recurrence. He waits for me to name the exercise or principle he has in mind, which will doubtless precipitate an eccentric speech.

'Four *potions*?' I venture.

'Four potion, portion.'

'*Potions*? *Portions*? What are you talking about, Travis?'

This goes on a little while longer. After a painful excavation the 'potions' transpire to be 'postures,' but I don't recognise the practice Travis alludes to, and I say so.

'*Puh*,' he spits, glowering over the steering wheel. 'You don't listen to the Sifu.'

My failure established, the test ends and Travis assumes his usual gabble about *gongfu*, unrestrained by his terrible English. Travis was raised to speak Hokkien and has been disadvantaged as Singapore changed. He has found it increasingly difficult to win employment against competitors who are more fluently bilingual. He has drifted in and out of employment since I met him. Although he's evasive about his reasons for leaving jobs, Sifu suspects that Travis's communication skills play a part. Even when he attempts to offer advice kindly, he sounds abrasive. Meanwhile he gets into ridiculous situations because he is reluctant to admit that he doesn't understand what is said.

'I tell him to use this free time to improve his horrible English,' Sifu told me, shaking his head, 'but he's too proud.'

Gongfu offers Travis release from the drudgery of his existence. His dream of mastery flits between escapist fantasy from the present and expectation for his future, intensified, no doubt, by his employment problems. To be a wise old master – *harkened to* – would offer the greatest fulfilment of Travis's know-it-all-ism. He possesses an inexhaustible desire to impress people, and declares his expertise on any subject that arises. He even told me to eschew the medical cover provided by the university, and entrust my health to the traditional treatments his father taught him. Now in the car I feel compelled to humour his speeches on *gongfu*. I'm not sure he notices whether or not I listen.

Unfortunately, his talk tends to illustrate that he dooms himself in *gongfu*. Regularly Sifu warns us that *gongfu* must be learned for the sake of the art, with total immersion in the act. The progressive realizations that constitute improvement will be frustrated, according to Sifu, if the student is motivated by revenge or aspiration for status. Yet I think that the social benefit of attainment is the central reason for Travis's lifelong perseverance in *gongfu*. He wants to be a renowned master with a troupe of devotees and an air of invincibility. I think this ambition is dogged by another contradiction: I doubt that the mastery Travis craves could possibly coincide with displays of knowledge, which he intimates as the chief activity of the role. Mastery is a demonstrative state to Travis: fighting, talking big, acts of endurance. For Sifu's part, he gives Travis no grounds to believe that he is on the path to *gongfu* greatness.

On our car journeys Travis protests against the injustice of Sifu's criticisms, fantasises about the higher arts he wants to learn, and brags about his own abilities in defiance of imaginary aggressors. In Travis's anecdotes all manner of disputes – with *gongfu* practitioners, taxi drivers and business colleagues – escalate to physical challenges:

'I say to him, "Come. We try."'

He raises a fist. In other reports he invites people to test him by the gruelling Knock Hands routine or by punching his stomach. The stories tend to trail off at this point, without clarification of whether physical conflict actually occurred.

* * *

Before he met Sifu the object of Travis's attention was Lim Hai-Ling. To me, Travis always refers to this master by translating his name as 'Sea Dragon'.

'The Sea Dragon, not soft like Sifu, but still very good.'

In addition to the reflective glory a practitioner would derive from association with such a master, Travis believed that Lim would help to improve his art drastically. In fact, Travis exalts Lim's skills so highly that once I asked whether I could meet him.

'No, no,' Travis told me. 'He's dead.'

I heard two different accounts of why Lim wouldn't teach him. In Travis's version, he undertook a lot of personal favours for Lim – 'go here, go there' – but he couldn't afford the *hongbao*, the red packet of payment the master wanted. But Sifu knew Lim better than Travis did, and identified other reasons why his colleague rejected that aspirant.

Lim was a disciple of Sim Yong Der, the master who taught hard-style *Wuzuquan* to Cheng Hai in the 1950s. Occasionally in the 1960s, Lim took the overnight train up to Kuala Lumpur with Sifu. There Lim watched Master Chee's students practise, although he never participated himself. In turn, when Sifu visited Singapore from Malaysia, Lim would take the afternoon off work at the bank to have a lunch together and discuss *gongfu*.

'Then when I moved back to Singapore in 1997,' Sifu said, 'some friends came to visit. They told Lim to join them. But when the taxi pulled up in front of my house, he said he would not come in. He felt it was a loss of face because I didn't invite him personally. The only reason I did not call him was that I had just moved from Hong Kong, and I didn't have his contact details.'

The two never spoke again. Soon afterwards Lim died aged 62.

'He had a stroke,' Sifu said. 'You could see he was hunched over when he performed. How could he have done the correct breathing?'

When I mentioned Travis's anecdotes about Lim, Sifu laughed and told me that the reason he never learned from the master was because of his bad manners.

'One day, Lim Hai-Ling was taking lunch in a restaurant with some friends. Travis came in with some of his own students. They sat down at the master's table without permission. Already, this is very bad behaviour. Then Travis said to Mr Lim, "You will teach us." This means he is giving an order to the master. In short, he assumes equal status with Lim Hai-Ling. Can you imagine?'

Sadly I *can* imagine. In his disastrous encounters with masters, as with his succession of employers, Travis repeats the same errors again and again. Travis was allowed to attend public classes under Lim's instructors, but was never admitted to the inner circle taught by the master personally. It is unclear whether he was excluded from the private group because of his ill-advised approach to the master or his failure to distinguish himself in the classes available. I imagine that both factors contributed to Travis's frustration in Lim's group.

* * *

Travis first met Sifu around a decade ago at the house of Paul Ooi, a local master who likes to unite senior martial-artists socially. On this occasion, various bankers and *gongfu* players attended. Some of Lim's former students arrived, with Travis among them.

'His first comment to me,' Sifu recalled, 'was sarcastic: "*Hmmmph*. So you're the great Chan See-meng." Then he began to boast about how good is his Twenty Punches. Of all sets, he chose my speciality! He got up from the table and insisted on demonstrating *Ershiquan*.

'My lip quivered with rage. My friend was holding my thigh to restrain me. Eventually I couldn't take it any more. I got up and I gave him hell, pointing out all the faults. I really ran him down, you know. Then I demonstrated the triple-punch technique where I stood. Everyone had gone quiet. All you could hear was the cracking of the tendons as I punched. "*This* is how you do the Twenty Punches."'

The atmosphere was tense. Sifu explained that at this point, all present were required to perform as a matter of honour. Finally one of Travis's teachers defused the situation by inviting Sifu to dinner, a gesture to acknowledge Sifu's seniority, thank him for his explanation, and apologize for the student's bad manners.

Sifu was appalled by the encounter, but Travis was captivated by his critic. He began to court Sifu. Travis haunted Sifu's home and followed him on his walks around the Botanic Gardens, near where Sifu lived at the time. He pleaded to be taught. Travis brought gifts, wrote an impassioned letter and sent a friend to petition Sifu on his behalf.

'Why would I want to teach that asshole?' Sifu asked the messenger. For two years he refused to teach Travis.

In fact, while Sifu shared a few exercises with elderly students for health, he didn't impart his real treasures to anyone. For some time Tien-Hsiang wanted to learn *Wuzuquan* but couldn't persuade his father to share the art.

'He was too lazy,' Tien-Hsiang told me.

Travis became frustrated when Sifu told him he didn't want to teach *Wuzuquan* to anyone.

'If you won't teach your own son, who will you teach?' Travis demanded. 'It goes with you to the grave.'

'Then,' Sifu replied, 'it goes with me to the grave. I would rather it was lost than it went to someone undeserving.'

But Sifu changed his mind. He began to teach Tien-Hsiang. In accordance with the rules of *Wuzuquan* he couldn't only teach a family member; he had to take other students. One day, abruptly, he told Travis that he would teach him. When Tien-Hsiang hears criticism of Travis he says, 'I'll always be grateful to him'. Sifu hasn't confirmed it, but Tien-Hsiang is adamant that the unbearable pestering from Travis prompted the master's decision to teach, in which case I too am in Travis's debt.

* * *

Travis has practiced martial arts since he was a teenager, and is now in his mid-fifties.

'He told me,' Sifu reported, 'that his first teacher was Iron Fist, one of the gangsters who came out of Shuang Lin monastery.'

Shuang Lin is a Shaolin-affiliated monastery in Toa Payoh that once practised hard-style Shaolin. In addition to this illustrious association, Travis boasts that he has studied a range of styles: Karate, White Crane, *Taijiquan, Xingyiquan, Bagua* and *Taizu*. He has travelled to China and

Malaysia in search of teachers. Travis is a kind of stamp collector. He retains routines from many martial-arts styles and claims that he spends hours going through them each day.

'How long you practise every day?' he asks as we wait for the lights to change near Tampines.

'About an hour,' I reply.

'*Puh*. Not enough,' he answers, disgusted.

But his *gongfu* is terrible. He seems unable to integrate any correction to posture or technique. When Travis learns *Wuzuquan*, he produces a bizarre mixture of the arts he has learned, with the practical application of none of them.

'Travis, why are you mixing fish-head curry with salad?' Sifu demands, vomiting blood from his pillar. 'Your *Taiji* looks like Shaolin art; your Shaolin art looks like *Taiji*. Ten minutes of *real* practice is better than this nonsense.'

It may be that Travis suffers from an inferiority complex that manifests as its demonstrative opposite, an arrogant tendency to assume authority and criticize others. Yet my sympathy for Travis evaporates in partner-work, and the various other training contexts in which he attempts to establish his pre-eminence by disingenuous means, and at the expense of his classmates. He cheats wherever he can, and tells himself all the while that he is top dog. Many of *Wuzuquan*'s two-man exercises force the practitioners into positions of weakness. Deprived of ordinary strength, there is no choice but to use correct technique and build power in underdeveloped parts of the body. Pushing hands with straight arms promotes skill. It's painful, but the shoulders strengthen in time and the correct kind of force is acquired. *Anyone* could bend his arms to avail himself of abdominal core-muscles instead. This makes the exercise easier, but whoever does so will never develop the intended skill. While practice in pairs is intended to be mutually beneficial, Travis thinks only of victory over his partner. Whatever the required movement, he finds some way to cut corners and persuade himself he has triumphed.

'Travis, you are *touji*,' Sifu said one night. 'Stealing chickens. Alex, translate.'

'Stealing chickens means cheating, taking advantage,' Alex told me.

The consequence of stealing chickens is that Travis curtails his own progress. When he noticed that Alex and I were catching up fast on his four decades of martial-arts experience, he complained to Sifu.

'How come they improve, I don't improve?'

Sifu answered, 'Because you *touji*.'

It makes no difference telling Travis not to steal the chicken. He's too committed to the idea of success, and indifferent to the cooperative goals of the exercises. He believes that he is an attentive student and that the rest of us don't understand Sifu's lessons. Hence when Sifu gives instruction, Travis commentates. Occasionally he becomes aggressive, and forces his opinions onto the rest of us with raised voice and pointed finger. At other times he makes emotive speeches: he doesn't want to cheat or win, we all misunderstand him. He has stolen no chickens. He has turned over a new leaf. We never believe him.

When Travis does acquire new techniques from Sifu, he can't resist showing off to former classmates. Sifu recalled an occasion when Travis returned to his former Yongchun White Crane school in Malaysia and overcame one of the members using an *Wuzuquan* technique.

'But then,' Sifu recounted, 'He came back whining: "Sifu, it doesn't work." I asked him what had happened.'

On request, Travis had revealed the skill to the Yongchun practitioner. Subsequently the Yongchun man performed the technique better than Travis and was able to gain advantage over him. Hence Travis returned to Sifu, asking for another technique so that he could defeat his former classmate. In his account of this exchange was the only time I've heard Sifu say 'fuck off'. Sifu is angered by these incidents, but allows Travis to learn nonetheless.

'You can see,' he said, 'martial arts is so damn important to him. After all these years trying, we can't let him end up with nothing.'

When his arrogance falters and Travis realizes he is not doing what Sifu has taught, it can be heartbreaking to watch him struggle with a technique.

'You have to help him, you know,' Sifu told me one night, as we watched Travis convert a sliver of *Wuzuquan*'s finery to a coal-shovelling motion. Sifu tasks me to show compassion to this impossible man. But Travis doesn't want my advice, and I can't give him what he hopes for, which is reverence.

A further complication in our group dynamic is that Travis doesn't trust Sifu to teach him properly. With his resentment that Sifu now seems to disclose far more details on *gongfu*, I think Travis believes that Alex and I receive instructions that he does not. He suspects that Sifu withholds the real techniques that would elevate him. Sifu's opinion is that Travis doesn't listen.

'Some day,' Sifu told him recently, 'I'll be gone, and you'll say, "The Old Man wouldn't teach me." But I have tried. Thirty schoolboys receive the same lesson, then they all take the same exam; some become *A* students, others are *F*s. How do you explain it?'

At Tampines station I leave the car. I decide to take the bus from now on, although it will make for a longer journey by the clock. Travis drives away.

You'll say, 'The Old Man wouldn't teach me.'

I reflect on a dark sense that history repeats itself.

III

WIND

15

MOTHER AND CHILD

Alex pants, unable to move. Sifu holds him by the wrists and Alex is completely under his control. After a few seconds, satisfied that Alex is making his best effort, Sifu allows him to progress to the next technique of *Sanzhan*, in which Alex is soon impeded again.

'Sifu is *giving* us power,' Travis commentates. It doesn't look that way. It *looks* like Alex will drop lifeless onto the concrete within the next thirty seconds, which is what I felt like doing myself five minutes ago. There is a breeze up here tonight, but it's small comfort in this kind of practice.

Alex has completed the central technique of *Sanzhan* – *tun-tu*, the Swallow-Vomit – which is performed three times stepping forwards, then thrice retreating. The exercise speeds up. Sifu aims punches at Alex's stomach and solar plexus. Alex parries, then chops to Sifu's midriff. The master drops his arm heavily on the student's forearm and Alex is stuck again.

I don't know how literally I should interpret Travis's remark, 'giving us power'. It sounds like a metaphysical cop-out, a mysterious transmission of knowledge that would excuse him from the necessity of practice. Fundamentally *Mazai* – 'Mother and Child' – is a kind of resistance work. We perform the routine while Sifu applies contrary strength, although it is a more subtle kind of opposition than muscular force. His adjustments alert us to the nuances possible within each motion.

When Sifu arrived he was wearing his knee supports, which always indicates that he means business. Silently he pointed at me, then at the ground before him, to signal *Mazai* practice. I was knocked back when I tried to push out, and helpless when Sifu prevented me from lowering my arms. Sifu dropped his hand onto my wrist deadweight as I cut to his torso, and even when I combined the strength of my waist with the pressure of my legs against the ground, I thought I might be trapped for all eternity. *Mazai* is a test of concentration above all else; we must *will* the hands into the correct positions. Our intention fatigues easily and we resort to the primitive, muscular efforts of habit.

'I am the Mother and you are the Child,' Sifu declares when Alex has finished the set and mops away his sweat with a cloth. 'How does the child know what to do unless the mother shows him? How can he eat unless she feeds him?'

Now Sifu points from Travis to the same spot of concrete before him. Alex and I watch Travis labour through *Sanzhan*. Sifu only applies force that is adequate to test each student. As spectators we can evaluate the external precision of the movements, but we cannot tell whether anyone has performed particularly well or badly. Only Sifu knows this, based on touch. Inevitably I find *Mazai* humbling for the apparent ease with which Sifu restrains me, but I know too that the master will not perform this exercise at all unless he considers the students worthwhile.

The Mother and Child characterizes a key difference between Sifu's practice and any other martial-arts schools I have seen. With Sifu, every technique must be analysed and tested. All defensive and aggressive strokes are learned first as solitary exercises, and later rehearsed in pairs, in which one person attacks and the other defends. Even our static stance-practice is subject to examination by gentle prods and outright shoves. This recalls Sifu's early days with Cheng Hai, and the manner in which the two disciples did their homework between visits to Dungun. Sifu's approach to study leaves the aspirant with nowhere to hide, no possibility of pretence concerning inadequate technique.

'What are you thinking during the *Mazai*?' Sifu asks when he has completed the exercise with Travis, and sits on his favourite pillar.

"I'm thinking, "Shit, the teacher is testing me!"' I answer.

'Good! That means you can remember it, you're not having to think of the movements. You can concentrate on development of intention. Today, your strength is breaking up. It needs to stream like a river if you want to move against me. Flow, fluidity; this is why we call ourselves the Ocean School.'

I had no idea that we referred to ourselves as the Ocean School.

'When you improve, it becomes more difficult,' Sifu continues. 'Only once I succeeded in moving my Old Man off his stance. He said, "Good". But immediately he adjusted, so I could no longer move him. This is the way. The Mother uses just a little more power than the Child possesses. When you are at 50, I am at 60, but no more than that. If you couldn't perform the set at all, it would be pointless. The Mother must *lead* the Child up to the next step. Travis, why didn't I let you go?'

'Sifu, I say, not enough strength.' Travis shoves his arms forward into a position from the pattern.

'No,' Sifu says. 'It's because you were trying to use hard strength. This is the crude version. When you try the correct technique I will let you proceed. I don't want to stop you. Shouldn't the parent want the child to succeed to a higher level? In life, I want my sons to achieve better than I have. Of course, so far, they have not.' He shakes his head. 'Where was I?'

'You talked about using the correct kind of strength,' Alex answers.

'Good. You need to understand each of the Five Ancestors and how they contribute to the art. You must combine these attributes. The physical power comes from *Taizu*; the breath is the *Luohan* immortals; the White Crane gives us the speed and strength of the sinews; the Nun gives us the softness; the Monkey King is the agility.' Sifu nods to me. '*You* didn't know what they were when you got here.'

He dances around in a few postures.

'See how I come out: *this* is the crane.' Sifu relaxes his hands from feathers into paws. 'And the monkey. See, Chris? See the monkey?'

He resumes his seat.

'Also in *Mazai* I can tell if you understand our basic Four Essences. What are they?' His finger shoots out to point at Alex.

'*Tun, tu, phu, zhan*,' Alex replies.

'What does it mean?'

'Swallow, vomit, float, sink,' Alex lists the primary methods by which force is received and exerted, the conceptual building-blocks of skilful contact as opposed to blind struggle.

'*Yes*,' Sifu says. 'Forever you must never forget. You must understand these Four Essences! The Essences are like our alphabets. First we learn our A, B, C, D, in a certain order. But when we remember the sequence we can do what we like with the letters to make words. It's the same. I float up, then spit out, or whatever. Once you understand these principles you can change the sequence any way you want. Similarly, in our Five Elements we learn Thunder, Lightning, Wind, Rain and Mist. In application, which Elements? What order? It's up to you.'

'Sifu,' I ask, 'what's the relative importance of Mother and Child training, as opposed to solitary practice? Can you have one without the other?'

'No,' Sifu answers. 'You must have both. It doesn't matter if I'm the best teacher in the world.' He scratches a speck from the collar of his polo shirt. 'If you don't comprehend, and practice, a waste of my time.'

'What about practice without Mother and Child?'

'Also no good. You will never get the refinements. You need to learn by *feel*, how I apply the strength. This is why you can see how many are lying through their teeth when they say Old Man taught them. Have you seen how long *Luohan Ruyiquan* is? Do you think he could do Mother and Child with all these people who say they have studied? It would *kill* Old Man, even if there was the time. These people have only learned the shell from Long-Arm Lum or one of the idiots in KL. They haven't even *seen* Old Man do it.'

By contrast, I reflect, Sifu *does* take the time with us, although Mother and Child for *Sanzhan* takes nowhere near the amount of time as it does for *Luohan Ruyiquan*. Still the effort is there, with the attention to detail. The question of initiation has not arisen lately. I suppose that this is because Travis – who has been unusually quiet of late in consequence of regular and intense admonishment from Sifu – has given up pestering the master for now. No longer do I wonder whether Sifu waits for better aspirants to come along whom he might accept as disciples. Sifu will be 71 this year. I am fairly certain now that if we are not to be his disciples, he will take none. The question that remains, then, is whether our status as non-initiates reflects Sifu's evaluation of our quality as students or a separate and impersonal decision he has made on discipledom.

Tonight I remain uncertain of what constitutes worthwhile progress. I have become stronger and faster. I can improve the details of particular movements. Yet still I am plagued by a dread that I will remain unable to *get it*, one of those doubts that is magnified by the intangibility of its predicate. At worst, Sifu refers to a practitioner's *affinity* with the art: I don't know whether this is meant as reassurance, since we're learning from him in the first place, or as a hint that we may not reach the upper echelons. Effort may not be sufficient to achieve certain conceptual leaps such as softness and the tactile intelligence with which Sifu can detect, based on light contact, which way we intend to move. In this case my progress would level out. Any acquisition of new techniques would amount to alternate expressions of the same ability. I attempt to formulate this anxiety as a question.

'Don't think like this!' Sifu warns me against self-doubt. 'The you fall into the trap of Travis': limited by his own sense of limitation compared to the masters, outwardly arrogant in defiance of deep disappointment.

Sifu does want capable students, but seems fatalistic about whether or not he will get them, and ambiguous about the extent to which he might have them already. Surely the attributes of the Supreme Seeker are unworthy of realistic expectation. The wait for an ideal disciple could consume a lifetime and still end fruitless. Still I don't know how good is good enough, or whether Travis leads me astray entirely with the idea that Sifu might promote us to some platinum-level membership, or indeed if that would mean anything in relation to the standard of our *gongfu*. We may not be initiates, but what is discipledom in *gongfu* if not this kind of practice?

16

THE FUNERAL

'I am going to see my master for the last time.'

Dressed in black and white, Chee Kim Thong's family sits in vigil, cross-legged on the floor before the coffin. The casket is open. Master Chee's body rests under glass. In time all stand as club members assemble inside the Chee Kim Thong Pugilistic and Health Society headquarters. The mourners bow at each of three gong strikes. They intone the *aum* mantra, then sing a Buddhist dirge to Guan Yin, the Goddess of Mercy. Later in the evening, orange-robed monks chant as newly arrived visitors prostrate themselves before the master.

Outside the clubhouse, tables and chairs have been laid out beneath an awning, with food and drink for guests at the wake. Many attendants have brought flowers to Chee Kim Thong. In his narration of the film, Sifu introduces various visitors who are seated at the tables: 'young Peter Seow with his sexy moustache ... the famous Long-Arm Lum, in his late seventies now;' a Caucasian whose name Sifu forgets; two of Master Chee's sons from Dungun; Mak Tian Meng and Mrs Mak, whom Sifu notes has coordinated black and white throughout her attire, including purse and earrings; Tony Wong, who is heavily involved with a local temple to the Goddess of Mercy and assists with organisation of the funeral. The guests seem upbeat. They regret the loss of the master, but his death came to seem inevitable over the last few months. Since the Old Man nearly died in 1990, they are grateful he lasted into 2001. 85 is a good age, they say: Chee Kim Thong died before he reached 83, but the Chinese often add three years to a master's age to suggest longevity.

On Sunday morning a brass band marches around the clubhouse playing 'Auld Lang Syne' over and over to frighten away spirits. Sifu explains that the white lanterns outside celebrate that Master Chee had a long life, 'So it is supposed to be a very happy occasion'. Yet the First Wife sobs in a chair by the entrance, detached from the groups of attendants. She was betrothed to Chee Kim Thong by family arrangement during their childhood. She has known the Old Man her entire life. Her children attempt to console her. Didn't anyone tell her it was a celebration? Above the front door a black cloth has been draped over the sign that announces the Chee Kim Thong Pugilistic and Health Society: no *gongfu* today.

This morning the monks wear black. They lead a procession in which each attendant takes a joss stick and circles the coffin, which has been moved outside into the sunshine. Then the guests form neat rows and bow to the master again. All except the monks wear white shirts, the mourning colour. One teenage girl's white T-shirt is embossed with a Superman logo.

A monk sprinkles the closed casket with water. The brass band joins in as the monks chant *Amitabha*, for 'boundless light,' with clackers and bells. The coffin is loaded onto a trolley and transferred to the hearse, a white transit-van with the funeral-director's phone number on the back in blue letters. The photo of Master Chee in Malay ceremonial attire – from the occasion when the Sultan honoured him – has been taken from the altar and attached to the front grille of the van, with a wreath. The master leaves the clubhouse.

Footage resumes at the cemetery. Guests take refreshment indoors; Sifu monitors preparation of his teacher's resting-place. The funeral director wears a baseball cap and shades. A walkie-talkie crackles on his belt, expressive of his own, impatient energy. He gesticulates to his workers with white-gloved hands and leads them to the burial plot. His employees have sky-blue polo shirts with sweat patches on the backs. They chatter as they lower Chee Kim Thong into the earth.

Blue hills seen in the distance; it's a beautiful morning in Malaysia. Chee Kim Thong's portrait stands at the foot of the grave now, with fruit, incense sticks and two red candles for company. Inside the grave at each end burn three candles in little alcoves. The guests wait nearby under shade. When the coffin has been placed in the ground they will attend in turn with a last bow and joss stick for the master.

One of the funeral-director's team lowers a pole into the grave, which he uses to manipulate the position of the casket minutely for the most advantageous *feng shui* alignment. The adjustments are fastidious, in accordance with the voice that sounds from an elderly, bespectacled man of rather bumbling appearance. He is not a member of the funeral director's team, but conducts himself as a man of authority. *This way! Too much! That way!* Still he is not satisfied with the position of the coffin. The orders proceed from eldest disciple Yap Cheng Hai, who stands over his master's body with geomancy compass in hand, a spiteful enigma.

17

THE BIRD CANNOT FLY

He said that the hand should become so swift, so sensitive that a sparrow perched on the palm would be unable to propel itself upward. Whenever the bird attempted to take off, the master instantly would detect the pressure in its legs and manipulate the muscles in his palm so that there was no platform for the bird to push against. This technique is of the Wind. It occurs in *Yiquan*, but this version is from the *Wuzuquan* routine, *Cool Breeze*.

Has it anything to do with another technique we learned recently, whose execution Sifu likened to the Chinese character for 'Wind?' That night he traced the word 風, *feng*, in the air with his fingertip – *the hand must whip around like this character* – but I couldn't see. I needed Alex to write the character down for me.

No! You can say it's 'similar,' or 'related,' but it's not the same.

I learned this hand by trickery. Sifu announced a week in advance that he would be free earlier than usual. I knew the others would forget. When Sifu and I traded messages that day I concluded, innocently, *See you at 7:30*. He arrived at that time and said, 'This technique is called "The Bird Cannot Fly."'

The technique is one of my favourites. I practice daily in three sets of repetitions, each with the aid of a different visualization. For the first set I envision that the edge of my palm sharpens blades that face my body at an angle from shoulder to hip. *This will help you to get the correct movement.* In the second instalment I deflect unseen punches. 'The Bird Cannot Fly' deflects strikes with minimal effort by speed and precision.

In the third segment of my practice I imagine that I strike Sifu back and forth across the shoulder, because that is how he taught me. He stood before me side-on and invited me to apply the technique, to smack one side of his shoulder as my hand turned outward, the other with my inward motion. Now I smack imaginary Sifu, my joints aching in the final stage of the practice. There are peculiar pains from this movement, as though my bones twist inside my forearms.

Other techniques too have their memories and stories. The Tail of Twenty Punches will forever evoke a night of unaccountable difficulty with the snap punches, which none of us could snatch back on impact *just so*. On a Saturday morning Alex and I advanced to the next level of breath control; a long-anticipated occasion that came upon us unexpectedly in the end, as Sifu assumed we were already doing it. There was the time Sifu showed us a technique to bounce away an opponent who pushes against our stance; no matter how forceful the attack, he said, 'Nothing is insurmountable' by skill. Travis echoed, 'Nothing is unbounceable.'

And one evening Sifu told us of the foolhardy students who wished to see the legendary Tiger's Back Kick so badly that they tricked the master into execution. In secret they drew lots to decide who would test the master. The unlucky one of the group set upon the master with a broadsword and pursued him through the forest. Reluctant to harm his student, the master coils around trees but realizes he cannot outrun the younger man, cannot evade him forever. The student closes the distance and at last the master leans forward to execute the Tiger's Back Kick, fatally for the student and to the benefit of none, for the others have kept their eyes screwed shut in terror all the while.

Sifu smiled to himself as he stood there to let me practice The Bird Cannot Fly. Student hits master; the situation might raise a momentary smirk, but wouldn't account for Sifu's self-satisfied and benign expression. That, with his gaze into the middle distance as the sun set, was to me the outward sign of a memory rekindled. At times when he teaches in great earnest, Sifu has the air of a man who strives to keep a promise. I concluded that the technique must be taught that way because it was so decades ago in Malaysia, when a teenage boy slapped the shoulders of Chee Kim Thong.

18

YAP CHENG HAI

It was Cheng Hai who complained at the time of Master Chee's death.

'The night of the funeral we had a dinner,' Sifu recalls. 'Cheng Hai grumbled, "The Old Man didn't teach me. He would only teach people who lived far away." After, I was told that this was a reference to me. Cheng Hai was jealous that the Old Man went to see me in Hong Kong and that we practised privately when I visited KL. That night I answered him in this way: "Old Man *did* teach you; he showed you a lot of different things that I haven't learned."

'The last time I saw him was at a South Shaolin Association dinner in 2005. He seemed surprised but acted happy to see me. All those years I didn't know how much he was stabbing me in the back.'

Some say he changed. One student – attuned to the tonal possibilities of the past tense – looked back on the 1960s and said, 'Yap Cheng Hai was an open-minded and benevolent man then.' When he wishes to be diplomatic, Sifu says, 'I will always be grateful for our early years together.' It was Cheng Hai who introduced Sifu to Chee Kim Thong, Cheng Hai who persuaded the reclusive master to teach publicly, and Cheng Hai who suggested that they form the martial arts association that obtained international reach.

Now the eldest disciple, in his late eighties, is in a Kuala Lumpur hospital after a debacle over a minor car-accident. At breakfast we pore over the details. Cheng Hai took a taxi that collided with another on Petaling Street. The drivers sprang out of their cabs to assign blame for the mishap. As the debate became heated, the passengers emerged from the cars too and argued with each other.

'The other passenger snatched at his spectacles,' Sifu says over breakfast. 'Cheng Hai tripped on the kerb and fell backwards. He hit his head and had a brain haemorrhage! Doesn't matter if he's old. What *gongfu*, letting someone snatch at his spectacles like this? He always wanted new things but he never practised! He also lost his gift for *feng shui* some years ago. You see, if you do bad things, later on you suffer. I think this kind of retribution exists.'

'Do you mean karma?' I ask.

'I will not say *karma*,' he answers, 'because karma is from past lives, and people use it to make excuses for their behaviour. A guy I know is always late everywhere. He comes along and says' – Sifu affects an Indian accent and waggles his head – '"I cannot help it, Sir, it's just my karma." This kind of excuses I will not allow. We should take responsibility for our actions.'

'Sifu,' Travis says, 'you should go see Cheng Hai in hospital.'

'*Aiya*. If this was a *movie* I'd go to see him,' Sifu answers. 'I'd sit at his bedside, and *grab his hand*, and we would both have the tears coming down our cheeks. A big, happy reunion. But this is not a movie. I would be a hypocrite.'

Various accounts I have heard intimate that a poison took hold of Cheng Hai after years of quiet resentment. While much of his malignity centres on Sifu, Cheng Hai was angry with Chee Kim Thong too. In part it was the bond between the two that he resented. Evidently, in addition to envy of Sifu's personal closeness to the master in itself, Cheng Hai suspected that favouritism was at fault for his limited progress in *gongfu*. However, to fathom the first disciple is a wasted effort to some club members.

'Don't expect Cheng Hai to be forgiving and kind to you,' Mak Tian Meng wrote to Sifu last year. 'The hatred for you is deep-seated. But he is what he is and there is no point even trying to understand him at all.'

Their relationship started badly. Around 1959, a mutual acquaintance introduced the *gongfu*-crazed young Chan See-meng to Cheng Hai, who then studied the *Taizu* lineage of *Wuzuquan* with the Singaporean master Sim Yong Der. Cheng Hai invited the boy to attack him. The precocious See-meng complied. Seated at the table, Sifu demonstrates the Praying

Mantis combination he used on Cheng Hai; two parries to lower the opponent's guard followed by a high strike.

'*Pap-pap-pap!* I left three finger marks on his temple. Then I saw his complexion darken with anger. Quickly I said, "Mr Yap! Please teach me your *Wuzuquan*."'

It seems that Cheng Hai didn't *really* want Sifu to throw a punch at him, but expected the boy to hold out his arm in a representative fashion; an arrangement that every worthwhile *gongfu* teacher I have met considers useless.

'This is why I have no respect for people who say they know Chinese *gongfu*,' Sifu declares. 'Too many are like this, all theory but don't fight. To me this is NATO: No Action, Talk Only.'

The augurs were unfavourable. To me, there was little prospect of a harmonious association between Sifu and Cheng Hai. Furthermore, for Sifu to study under Cheng Hai at all sounds impractical.

'Why would you want to study with him in the first place?' I ask.

Sifu was at a loose end in martial arts. His teachers had come and gone. When Dong Ying Jie left Kuala Lumpur, his son taught *Taijiquan* for a short time, but then followed his father to Hong Kong. Next Lim Pak Yen, Sifu's Praying Mantis instructor, resigned his *gongfu* tuition, annoyed that his former students had surpassed him under Dong's guidance. Pressed to recommend another teacher, Lim introduced Sifu to Cheng Hai. The salesman Cheng Hai offered See-meng the chance to learn something new. More importantly, he might introduce the boy to good masters. Cheng Hai had studied many arts, and could prove useful as a connection, if limited as a teacher.

Conversely it surprises me, on first reflection, that Cheng Hai would want a to teach an ill-mannered boy who had shown up his own poor *gongfu*. However, Sifu had already gained a reputation as a *gongfu* talent. He was known as The Tiger of *Taiji* around Kuala Lumpur. Cheng Hai could boast that Dong Ying Jie's prodigy was now his student.

For one year Sifu studied *Taizu Wuzuquan* under Cheng Hai. In that period Cheng Hai spoke more and more of the 'great man' in the far reaches of Terengganu, which kept Sifu interested. Finally they set out to visit this master.

'Cheng Hai must know he was having initiation,' Sifu says, 'because Old Man would have to obtain all the supplies for the ceremony; the fruits and the dried offerings. Then Old Man has to set up the altar.'

The surprise for Cheng Hai was that Master Chee would ask young See-meng to become a disciple too. Nominally Cheng Hai was ranked first of the five disciples, but initiation placed his former student at an uncomfortably close level. I suspect that he hated Sifu from this time, if not on some level from their first encounter. Arcane mastery brought Chee Kim Thong, Yap Cheng Hai and Chan See-meng together. Their undoing lay in the commonplace frailties of human relationships.

At first, it was simply that circumstances favoured the development of Sifu's bond with Chee Kim Thong. Cheng Hai was not excluded intentionally. An adult with a wife and children, he was in a very different situation to the teenager.

Sifu was an orphan. As World War II spread across Asia, Sifu's father made provision for the likelihood of his death by asking his best friend to ensure the well-being of the infant. Sifu's first guardian was Scottish, and in 1942 he took the baby See-meng to live in Glasgow. By this time, Sifu's father had disappeared, presumably to a Japanese labour-camp. When Sifu was nine years old, his grandmother requested that he return to Asia, for fear that she would never see him again. Robert, Sifu's older brother, was raised in Singapore. Sifu's mother was still alive, but had remarried.

'This was unheard of,' Sifu says. 'My grandmother told me, "Your mother has denied you." Years later I met my mother and couldn't look her in the eye. It was like talking to a stranger.'

The family decided that his paternal aunt in Kuala Lumpur should raise Sifu. The Chan family was successful in business, to the extent that the Istana Negara – presently the palace of the Malaysian King – was formerly owned by Sifu's uncle, Chan Wing. They could provide the boy with the best education. So it was that Sifu returned to a family of strangers who spoke Cantonese amongst themselves, of which he was then entirely ignorant. Worse, Sifu's aunt was hostile to him because of superstition.

'My auntie called me the Devil Child. She said that I killed my father, because I was in my mother's belly when he died. This belief is the old Chinese way. Because I came at the same time she thought it was connected.' He shakes his head.

The pattern of Sifu's childhood was alienation within a well-to-do household, extravagance interlaced with abuse. In the canteen at school, one of the Chans' domestic servants arrived daily with food for Sifu, laid out a tablecloth before him and served his lunch. At home he had lower status.

'My auntie would burst into my room at night with no warning and beat me. Although we had four servants, I had to do chores like clean the chicken coop. *Her* son never did any chores, and he could bully me all he wanted. This was before I learned *gongfu*. After that he didn't dare try to bully me.'

Sifu's solution to his domestic problems was to assert his independence as soon as possible. He enrolled in the military academy for its decent salary and to further his education. In the guise of house sitter, he moved into a nearby cottage owned by the family. His recollections waver between the tale of the self-made man and the privileges of a well-to-do family, depending on the desired emphasis. Sifu's residence in the cottage – a bid for liberation, on a platform provided by family wealth – shows that the contradictory origin-myths can mingle.

Sifu lacked a father figure; Chee Kim Thong sought a talented aspirant. The Old Man treated Sifu to meals and bought a Volkswagen Beetle for Sifu to travel to the *Wuzuquan* classes he taught on Master Chee's behalf, usually housed by Hokkien clan associations. Years later, to celebrate Sifu's wedding, Master Chee hosted a dinner and served wine to the guests, the role the groom's father plays in Chinese tradition. Aside from the question of which disciple was more capable, Cheng Hai's business took him all around the Malayan peninsula. As a teenager Sifu had more free time than Cheng Hai did, so he grew closer to the Old Man.

Gradually, the situation worsened. Cheng Hai was officially Master Chee's first disciple, but it became clear that Sifu was the Old Man's favourite and, as the one who faced challengers, *de facto* premier. It's equally valid to suggest that Chee Kim Thong replaced Cheng Hai in Cheng Hai's relationship with Sifu. Now that Sifu received direct tuition from the master, Cheng Hai was not needed as a mentor. He and See-meng were classmates instead. With one stroke Cheng Hai had been usurped in two interpersonal dynamics. When I put these ideas to Sifu he hardens, dismissing their importance by citation of realism: that the Old Man preferred Chan See-meng, and that was that. Yet it would take a remarkably circumspect mind for Cheng Hai to accept such logic as events unfolded. The Old Man should have anticipated that tension would arise between his initiates.

Master Chee devoted himself to his disciples and began to split his time evenly between Kuala Lumpur and Dungun. During his studies at the military college – and later, his employment at the bank – Sifu's day began at 5 am when Master Chee arrived for practice.

'Then after work, training from 10 pm to 2 am. I asked the Old Man why we must practise so late. He said, "It's good for the energy meridian." I answered, "Can't we use another meridian?" For two weeks every month I could go out and party like a regular guy. But the other two weeks it's full time with the Old Man: Old Man, Old Man, Old Man.'

On weekends and holidays, Sifu helped Master Chee with his medical treatment, and his other business around KL.

'When we met in the morning, I wouldn't even know what we were going to do that day,' Sifu recalls. 'All that mattered was I was with the Old Man.

'One morning we went to Montfort Boys' Home in KL. I said, "What are we doing here?" Old Man said, "You'll teach the boys some of our art." So I had to show these 200 orphans how to punch. No warning!' In video footage from that day, Sifu and Chee Kim Thong perform the Mother and Child on a stage, before an immense group of shirtless boys.

At times I need to remind myself that there were not only two initiates, but five. While Teoh Cheng Her gave up *gongfu* entirely rather soon, Tan Boon Ping served on the committee when the club was officially registered in 1968. This leaves Kok Seng Pang, twelve years old on initiation. At first,

Seng Pang underwent a similar regime to Sifu's. The two weeks Master Chee spent in Kuala Lumpur each month meant that he spent the rest of his time in Dungun. There Seng Pang endured the same early starts and rigorous practice that Sifu did in KL, but it didn't last; either because, as a young boy, he didn't commit entirely to *gongfu*, or because Master Chee spent ever more time in Kuala Lumpur. Eventually Seng Pang relocated to Kuala Lumpur too, and returned to train intensely. By then, the central dynamic of the club had taken shape: a triangle of Chee Kim Thong, Yap Cheng Hai and my Sifu, Chan See-meng.

Masters have favourites. Yet it was not as though Cheng Hai stood by neglected while Master Chee devoted his attention solely to Sifu. Group practice for the initiates took place at Cheng Hai's house in the early years, at which time the only formal disciples based in KL were Cheng Hai and Sifu. But Cheng Hai did much to lower himself in Chee Kim Thong's estimation. Sifu recalls that Cheng Hai would say, 'Don't teach this to See-meng' at the end of his lessons with the Old Man, and would ask that the younger disciple be excluded from social excursions: 'But Mr Chee would always say, "No, See-meng must come with us."'

In later years, friction arose as Cheng Hai put pressure on Master Chee to go into business with him. One instance was investment in a pyramid scheme that soon collapsed. Fortunately by the time this happened, the Old Man had withdrawn his funds, on Sifu's advice and to Cheng Hai's irritation. Another of Cheng Hai's schemes was *Yan Shou Gong*, a simplified martial-art drawn from the vast body of exercises Master Chee had studied.

'In any case,' Sifu says, 'Cheng Hai never gave Old Man a cent for this art. And he never gave Mr Chee credit for teaching him *feng shui*. In an interview he said he got this gift from some monk in China, so it's all mysterious. I tell you, Chris, when he received initiation from Mr Chee, Cheng Hai was already a disciple of various other masters. This – so to speak – is not done. You can only have one father. *You*,' Sifu points at Travis. 'Why do you think I always scold you when you say you *got* this *Sifu, got* that *Sifu, got too many Sifus*? Chris, how would your father like it if you changed your name to Chris Chan?'

'I don't think he'd be too happy.'

'Exactly.'

'Did it happen often that people would become disciples of more than one master?'

'Sometimes there are people like this,' Sifu says. 'They would take multiple initiations out of greed for different arts. Sometimes they were spies sent from different organisations. During the oath they would write the word "no" on the ground with their foot to mean that they weren't swearing sincerely.'

Sifu traces the character 不 for 'no' on the table.

'Like crossing your fingers?'

'Yes. Like I always say, you must learn with a pure heart. In Cheng Hai's case, he learned a lot from the Old Man, but he wasn't sincere.

'The day he died I went to see my Old Man in hospital. He cried at the disappointments in his life, especially family trouble. Certain names in the club were also mentioned. But Mr Chee said the *biggest* disappointment of his life was Yap Cheng Hai.'

The Old Man devoted considerable time to Cheng Hai. This is obvious from the enormous *gongfu* repertoire, from every art Master Chee had encountered, which Cheng Hai in turn disseminated to club members. Yet Cheng Hai emerged opposite to Sifu; with a breadth of exercises, but no depth, an endless assortment of techniques that he was unable to apply in combat. I suspect also that Chee Kim Thong's genius for *gongfu* worked against him as Cheng Hai's instructor. Master Chee intuited the principles of *gongfu* in his own, tactile language, but he was not expert in communicating this to others in words. Chee Kim Thong had no patience to repeat himself to people who could not apprehend the subtleties of the art. Giving up on Cheng Hai's capacity for comprehension, Master Chee satisfied the disciple's wish for a skin-deep repertoire of *gongfu* instead. However, it was not solely Cheng Hai's attainment in *gongfu* that dismayed Master Chee, but his treatment of his fellow disciples. Eight years before the Chee Kim Thong Pugilistic and Health Society was officially registered, its foundations were already weak.

It would be easy, from Sifu's accounts, to blame Cheng Hai exclusively for the problems in Master Chee's group, but that would ignore other, important questions. For instance, how did Cheng Hai *expect* to be treated once a member of Chee Kim Thong's lineage? And what was Chan See-meng like in his late teens and early twenties, the formative period of his relationship with the lineage members? Those specific issues relate to wider, cultural forces at work in Asia.

One day Claire and I went to the cinema to watch *The Monk*, an adaptation of a novel that I taught at the university. We arrived late and soon suspected we had entered the wrong auditorium. Instead of the debauched antics of a fallen cleric, we saw a Singaporean in his National Service garb, anguished by the bed of a dying relative. The sequence ended after a few minutes. We realized that the cinema had preceded Matthew Lewis's supernatural sex-a-thon with a short film that exhorted viewers to venerate the elderly.

Respect for the aged is a striking difference from Western society. The code of conduct in Chinese culture dictates that any older person is automatically entitled to a certain esteem. Accordingly, older strangers are addressed as 'Auntie' or 'Uncle'. Yesterday a Taxi Uncle drove me to class. A *Kopi* Auntie served my breakfast. I refer to someone who indulges his curiosity at the urinal as a Penis Uncle. The big picture is that people are raised to respect their elders. It would follow for Cheng Hai to expect young Chan See-meng to behave towards him with deference. However, in the context of a *gongfu* club, social rules could complicate matters.

Bill, the Englishman who spent considerable time at the clubhouse in KL, lamented that protocol undercut correct practice. Saving face was a particular hindrance. When pushing hands with Long-Arm Lum, for instance, it wasn't acceptable to make him lose face by overcoming him. Furthermore, in the labyrinthine intricacies of Chinese etiquette, if I cause *you* to lose face, *I* lose face. Bill was in a situation that tacitly forbade practitioners from testing each other. This is a reality check for anyone who assumes that the best *gongfu* environment is a traditional, Chinese community: aspects of the social code effectively impede the necessary effort. A version of this absurdity is common in Western groups, centring on Seniority instead of age. Those who have been club members for longer command a certain amount of respect; literally, in the form of ordering 'Juniors' around. This does not reflect anyone's martial-arts ability. Some people remain in martial-arts groups simply to tyrannize others as Senior members, in compensation for their own inadequacies. Sifu likes to cite a Chinese saying that *he who enters first is senior, but he who masters the art becomes the sage.* Strangely, this maxim is rarely circulated in the martial-arts world, while the Senior-Junior hierarchy is a keystone and too often *raison d'être.* Such codes were not always inherent in martial arts; they may reflect changes that occurred with the Ming policy of syncretism in the seventeenth century, which promoted the conflation of Buddhist, Taoist and Confucian philosophies. But now these philosophies are widely considered part and parcel of one unified and ancient Chinese culture. Hence, martial artists are burdened with protocols that are potentially detrimental, and which were not influential when the arts were actually devised in Zen or Taoist contexts.

Gongfu practitioners in Kuala Lumpur adhered to the spirit of Senior-Junior hierarchy *and* the expectation that older people are entitled to deference. In the midst of this complex etiquette, Sifu threw a punch when the older man expected him to hold out an arm and submit to his technique. Sifu explains his attitude by reference to his 'Western education'. While Sifu is not sceptical of all Chinese culture, he feels entitled to pick and choose whichever aspects of Western and Chinese values suit him. From Sifu's perspective, saving face might be an important concept in business relations, but he wouldn't allow it to encroach on his *gongfu*. He likes to declare, 'I give you no face' when we commence a new exercise. I am sympathetic with that position, but I can see too that it contradicts what was expected of Sifu as a young member of a traditional martial-arts group in the 1960s.

Success is another factor that may not have endeared Sifu to his associates. Sifu tells me that as a schoolboy, and subsequently as a cadet in the military college, he swam in galas, ran races and rode horses, and did all of these things very well. It sounds like he was a born athlete, but also insufferable. Yet Sifu has also told me that, 'When I was a boy, I suffered fits: F-I-T-S, *fits*,' which he attributed to malnutrition during infancy. From that anecdote Sifu emerges as a version of the sickly aspirant strengthened by *gongfu*, which is a charming, underdog heroism. The revelations concerning his early family troubles and ill health as a baby are new to Alex and me, as trusted students. I wonder whether compromising the ever-victorious persona more frequently in his everyday dealings might have made Sifu a more humane figure to his peers.

Evidently Cheng Hai's envy has fermented, as Tian Meng put it, to 'deep-seated hatred'. Perhaps he would say that this brat pulled the wool over the Old Man's eyes. Yet Chee Kim Thong was one among several great masters who saw something in Chan See-meng, and I feel content to be allied with that camp. Mindful that Cheng-Hai and Sifu was each vitally necessary to the group in his way, and both were unquestionably at fault, Tian Meng is right to say that the Old Man should have done more to marshal the difficulties between the two initiates.

In a debate on the club's future, Tian Meng urged Sifu to forget Cheng Hai and move on:

'My advice to you is to immerse yourself in what you like to do in life and in Chinese martial-arts. Always be humble and kind, and above all, live a life which causes no harm to others.'

When I visited KL even club members who attempted to be diplomatic to both parties – Sifu and Cheng Hai – corroborated the main facts of Sifu's account. After Master Chee's death it was Cheng Hai who proposed selling the clubhouse to divide the money. Decades before that, when he could tolerate the young disciple no more, it was Cheng Hai who brought about Sifu's expulsion from the Chee Kim Thong Pugilistic and Health Society. Rather than the consequence of a dispute, the incident was the epilogue of a great celebration for Master Chee and his organisation.

19

THE TOURNAMENT

'Why do you want to fight?' the Thai boxers asked Sifu when he came to Kota Bharu.

'*We* fight because we are desperate. We have no food and we have no work. We start to train when we are eight years old, and to compete for money when we are teenagers. By 27 we are finished, and we retire from the arena to train the next generation. But *you* have a career and a wife. We don't understand why someone like you would want to fight.'

Sifu explained that he was preparing for a martial-arts tournament.

'Why come here? Why don't you fight with people in Kuala Lumpur?'

Sifu answered that there was no-one left to fight in KL. After he challenged the other martial artists, he fought the gangsters, paying them for their time. But he found that these thugs possessed little skill. Sifu wanted more practice to ensure he was ready for the competition. Who knew what kind of contestants would travel to the tournament from overseas?

The Thai boxers complied because Sifu offered good money. They warned him about the risk of injury, but unnecessarily. Chee Kim Thong had exhorted him repeatedly to be cautious.

'You must think of your opponent as a tiger and yourself as a rabbit,' the Old Man said. 'Never underestimate young guys, or the elderly, or women.'

Fortunately too, Sifu could take care of himself.

* * *

In May 1969, 200 fighters and thousands of spectators converged in Singapore for the First South-East Asia Pugilistic Invitation Championship. Some contenders were *bona fide* martial artists; the majority were bruisers from Chinese gangs. The Singapore Shaolin group led by the notorious *sansheng* Iron Fist contributed many contestants. The participants from Hong Kong and Taiwan were often policemen, their teams composed substantially of *judoka*. Sifu led a team of Master Chee's students to compete at the Gay World Arena, an old site of cabaret, gambling and sports events that was becoming outdated like its name, and would pass out of existence within the next decade.

The tournament was one of the motives for Master Chee to formalize his group. His students demonstrated in Singapore by invitation in 1965 and 1967. The organiser, Alex Chan of the People's Association of Singapore, announced his intention to arrange a martial-arts competition in 1969 rather than a display. He was keen for Master Chee's students to participate, but they could only do so if they represented a registered club, in accordance with regulations on public assembly. Hence the creation of the Chee Kim Thong Pugilistic and Health Society in 1968. While Master Chee's student, the lawyer Chooi Mun Sou, helped the unorganised Old Man to make his group official, the disciples selected five students to complete the team, with Sifu as captain. His teammates were Chin Yoon Kong, Goh Thong Meng, Charles Chang, Yap Siew Tat and Chan Ming Chai.

Sifu's preparation for the event was meticulous. In addition to an exerting *gongfu* programme, Master Chee instructed Sifu to abstain from ejaculation for 100 days prior to the competition. 'Is there something in it?' Sifu says. 'I know that some athletes masturbate before competing, to relax. But I do what my teacher asks.' Amid protests, Master Chee put the entire team on a diet.

Sifu specialized in the Twenty Punches and Thunder Fist routines, the source of his favourite fighting techniques. Thunder Fist provided one of his favourite strikes, a back-fist whose deadweight drop he likens to chopping wood. The back-fist is injurious even to an opponent who attempts to parry, and jars against the intercepting limb to deter further attacks. Similarly, the Twenty Punches set subdues an attempted kick using a punch to the thigh.

Expertise in the triple-strike would give Sifu his nickname, Whip Punch. The torso whips the arms out to attack with the upward trajectory of a flicked towel. Recently I became able to generate the correct strength for the whip punch. The effect was like a fairground ride whose motor jerks the body from underneath, so that the head follows a split second later. I wasn't prepared for the power, and realized the importance of a rooted stance, and precise bodily alignment. The triple punch turns the stomach back and forth to produce a barrage that one alarmed spectator of Sifu's technique described as 'like a tank'. Master Chee, of course, tested these techniques repeatedly: 'Old Man performed the Mother and Child with me over and over again. This is the *real* training, only for his disciples.'

The Mother and Child counterpart for the Twenty Punches routine is more like conventional combat than the first pattern, *Sanzhan*. Master Chee would deflect Sifu's strikes and retaliate in accordance with the sequence. As during my own *Mazai* experience, Sifu hints at a mystical process of transmission in those sessions with Master Chee. Hence Sifu said that he found the Mother and Child practice more beneficial than free sparring. When challengers came to the club, Sifu fought them, and he sparred in other *gongfu* groups before he met the Old Man. Most decisively, he competed under the free-fighting conditions of the 1969 tournament. However, Chee Kim Thong insisted that free sparring practice was unnecessary as preparation. Anxiety impelled Sifu to seek out people who would fight him, against the Old Man's advice, but he found that Master Chee was right. He was already equipped to overcome opponents.

* * *

Free sparring means that, with a few restrictions for safety, martial artists engage in combat. To be told that experience of free sparring is unnecessary to apply *gongfu* in a contest was a revelation that astonished me. Intuitively, one would presume that there are obvious benefits to an exercise which most closely simulates the conditions of fighting. And yet.

My main experiences of sparring have followed two methods. One group encouraged participants to stop their strikes just short of the target, in the belief that this developed self-control. No protective equipment was needed. Other groups adopted gum shields, groin guards and boxing gloves, and a semi-contact approach that flared into full-contact as we became aggravated. Free sparring was weekly in these groups, but my sparring skills improved quite modestly in several years of regular bouts. For one thing, the clumsy boxing gloves precluded any *gongfu* finery. Secondly, the practice of free sparring is inherently flawed. All except advanced practitioners will quickly descend into scrappiness. One clean punch is thrown at the start of the round, and all that follows is flailing limbs. Too little *gongfu* occurs in a conventional, two-minute round. The result of this group's efforts was that the former body-builder tended to prevail, as he had since the first session. The true winner was the instructor who – charging by the hour – spent the sparring sessions seated with a newspaper.

Why did I persist? The most persuasive factor was that masochism has its own, insistent logic. That mentality considers pain as gain and, once adopted, it's difficult to think otherwise. However, it's not as though I didn't enjoy the sessions. I felt that I could struggle against my longstanding sense of my own frailty, and my tolerance of discomfort improved. These were benefits. But – refrain of my martial-arts past – I reached a point where I realized I hadn't advanced significantly.

None of these concerns had particular relation to combat, which I perceive as having only tenuous relevance to my study of martial arts. As a Humanities academic, seldom do I have recourse to physical conflict. *Gongfu* served different needs in Chinese history, but now the art is primarily its own pursuit.

* * *

Sifu spent the final few weeks prior to the tournament in Singapore, where he attended meetings with the other team captains. As part of his preparation, Sifu ran up Mount Faber every day accompanied by his team-mate Goh Thong Meng, now an eminent *judoka* in Kuala Lumpur.

'There was no cable car back then. By the time we reached the summit my friend was half dead. But I performed *Ershiquan*, my Twenty Punches set, fifty times at the top of Mount Faber.'

'*Fifty times?*'

'Hey, this is not for fun, you know? To be a champion, you must do extra. To prepare for a 100-metre gold-medal swim, you should do 200 metres. This Whip Punch is my favourite technique, so I concentrated on it.'

According to organiser Alex Chan, Sifu was the sole competitor with an office job amidst the labourers, policemen and gangsters who came to fight. The endless disclaimers signed by the combatants – in which the organisers abnegated any responsibility for injuries – were elaborated by participants in *gongfu* talk. Sifu recalls that these documents, and the safety regulations, were the official subject of meetings between the captains. In fact the gatherings were dominated by imaginative assertions of the harm that certain contestants envisioned inflicting on others. Commonly, the participants used the meetings as platforms to talk up their own chances and badmouth other arts. In accordance with a cosmic law of *gongfu*, however, those who made the boldest threats beforehand tended to fare badly when the actual tournament commenced.

'Wear face-guards if you wish,' one fighter sneered at the safety precautions, 'but they are no match for our finger-jab.' Inglorious, first-round defeat followed for all six members of his team.

'Once you have signed the disclaimer, I cannot show mercy,' another contestant declared. He lost an eye in combat, and withdrew from the tournament.

The many fighters to proclaim that 'our [*insert as applicable*] Fist is invincible!' tended to exit with weak excuses for their poor performances.

A man versed in the accomplishments of his antagonists declared, 'Chan See-meng is famous for his Twenty Punches. But I don't care if he throws 1,000 punches!' He was defeated in fewer than twenty punches.

A kind of ingenious metanarrative seems to have proceeded from an individual whose arrogant self-assertion hinged on identifying that others' threats were merely arrogant self-assertion. 'You *talk* big, *lah*' he observed. 'No *gongfu*, *loh*.' Nonetheless, in the ring he clawed at his opponent scrappily, displaying little evidence of any particular technique.

'It will take me only one strike' was the pronouncement of a fighter who, in the course of time, incurred a knock-out blow during a lapse in concentration.

Master Chee arrived for the start of the tournament. He remained ringside to treat the participants' injuries, while Sifu's brother Robert acted as his water boy. Sifu incurred no serious strikes and won the Middleweight category. Even Cheng Hai, in an article on the history of Master Chee's Society, conceded that the competition offered few serious challengers to Sifu's ability.

'My toughest opponent was Teo Choon Teck in the first round. He was then champion of Singapore. I knocked him down and he kept getting up again! He gave me one whack here, a *biiiiig* bruise on my shoulder.'

Teo's *Taizu Wuzuquan* was hard, but hardness is brittle. Sifu maintained his favourite techniques, and struck his opponent's shoulders until Teo could no longer lift his arms. As it happened, the opponent's group would profit from Sifu's success. Sifu's victory increased public attention to all forms of *Wuzuquan*, the art that contributed the greatest fight of the tournament. Eventually Teo's club – 'thinking this Chan See-meng must be dead,' Sifu laughs – began to claim that their master had won the 1969 Middleweight Championship. Although Lim Hai-Ling's school did not participate, an Indonesian group from their lineage did take part, so Sea Dragon advertised his club on banners around the arena. Sifu claims also that *Sanzhan* practices and the various White Crane arts became more prominent internationally following his clash with Teo and the eventual victory for a White Crane *Wuzuquan* fighter. For this reason, jubilation over Sifu's triumph was widespread among the *gongfu* community.

'But when I had won,' Sifu recalls, 'Old Man wouldn't even let me leave the hall until everyone else had left, because of the race problems between Malays and Chinese.'

The Malaysian government had declared a state of emergency because of race riots on 13 May. Violence between Malays and Chinese resulted in nearly 200 deaths. It was possible that the violence might be replicated in Singapore, where there was similar sectarianism in an inverted ratio: the Singaporean population was predominantly of Chinese ethnicity. Master Chee recognised that it might be provocative for Sifu to parade himself as a hero.

'The Malays might want to kill this Chinese champion,' Sifu says. 'The way out of the arena was very narrow; someone could come in with a knife and I might not see him. So Mr Chee made me sit and wait. I wanted to go out and celebrate! Only when the arena was completely empty he let me leave at last.'

Sea Dragon shared Master Chee's concern.

'Lim Hai-Ling was so worried that he hired eight bodyguards with pistols to protect me while I was in Singapore. So what if I won a *gongfu* contest? If a guy shoots you with a gun – what *gongfu* then, *lah*?'

* * *

In time the celebration of Sifu's victory was overshadowed by its protracted epilogue. The tournament dissolved into the argument between Sifu and Cheng Hai. Although the culmination of that tension followed several years later, it appears inseparable from the competition. That Teo's students now claim that *he* won the 1969 tournament indicate how quickly spectators forget the details. By contrast, such trouble arose in the aftermath of Sifu's triumph that I wonder whether Master Chee would have foregone the competition for the sake of better relations between his disciples. The tournament occasioned the Chee Kim Thong Pugilistic and Health Society, but the outcome threatened the club's future. The success that followed for the organisation came despite disharmony between its senior figures. Registered officially, the Society could recruit members without risk of infringement on public-assembly regulations. The group expanded into many parts of Malaysia and continued to attract students throughout the

1970s, including international visitors. Yet the Society could have achieved even greater success, as Mak Tian Meng told me in the ghostly clubhouse, if more durable foundations had been laid amongst the initiates.

If Master Chee had done the right thing, See-meng would probably have been very famous. When sons argue, the duty of the father is to resolve the conflict and solve the problem. Maybe See-meng got a bit arrogant.

Sifu concedes that Master Chee mismanaged aspects of the club.

'When students came in, they were given a choice of which instructor they wanted to train under. I mean, come on; wouldn't *you* want to learn from the competition winner? Old Man should have told us to divide them up: "You go here, you go there."'

Cheng Hai looked on as the hordes arrived to study with Chan See-meng, the champion. As they did so, uncomfortable questions arose for the elder disciple.

'People kept asking him,' Sifu says, '"Are you as good as See-meng?" He didn't know how to answer them. Actually, it's very sad to be like this. Cheng Hai was a good person, but as he grew older he became petty.'

'Why didn't you compete in the 1971 tournament?' I ask.

'It was my intention to be champion three times,' Sifu replies, 'but Cheng Hai was causing a lot of politics. Instead, Teo Choon Teck and I gave a demonstration to open the 1971 championship.'

The South-East Asia Pugilistic Invitation Championship was discontinued after the third tournament. It became incurably infested with gangs that supplied poor fighters and threatened other competitors with assassination. *Black Belt* magazine described the final event as 'a blood bath'.

Sifu sips his coffee. Travis has left to do his grocery shopping in Malaysia. The hawker centre teems with customers on a Saturday morning. For a few minutes we watch the crowd fluctuate. There are families, couples, friends and solitaries at the great Singaporean social exchange, the food court. We enjoy the silence until the context reminds me that one dispute between Sifu and Cheng Hai was over who bought dinner more often for whom in the early 1960s. Meals together, probably enjoyed without question at the time, became another point of contention decades later.

'Chris, in life, you might as well be happy.'

Sifu repeats the phrase with a caesura every second word, like a little poem:

> *You might*
> *As well*
> *Be happy.*

'Look at me,' Sifu continues. 'I enjoy my coffee, my food. *You* have learned to take your time. I'm teaching you to be an Oriental. Only the good parts; not the bad parts, ah?'

'Yes, Sifu. I won't take a second wife.'

'My life has been good. I had no parents, but then Mr Chee was both a father and a mother to me. The bank treated me well and I rose like a comet. In *gongfu* I met top masters. If I could choose my next life, I would be Chan See-meng all over again! So you can see, there's no reason for me to care what Yap Cheng Hai thinks.'

As a student I'm loyal to Sifu. Yet, while I'm inclined to condemn Cheng Hai, I can't certify that I'd behave better in similar circumstances. What happened was a terrible shame, that's all. The schism worked out in everybody's worst interest. I've heard Sifu declare he doesn't care what Cheng Hai thinks too many times to accept it at face value.

The tension between Sifu and Cheng Hai reached crisis after Sifu opened a new class in Petaling Jaya. Cheng Hai was incensed when he learned of the tuition fees that Sifu charged, and complained to Chee Kim Thong. Petaling Jaya was also Cheng Hai's neighbourhood in Kuala Lumpur, which can't have helped matters.

'People asked, "How can you charge $100 a month, when Old Man only asks for $30?"' Sifu says. 'I told them, "When people hear Chan See-meng is teaching, they will pay!"'

This was the excuse Cheng Hai wanted to move against the younger man. As far as he was concerned, the class in Petaling Jaya was unauthorized by the club. Cheng Hai took action.

'How can Old Man be asked to sign anything in English?' Sifu says. 'It's not fair. He didn't know what it was. Cheng Hai told him it was just some admin that needed a signature.'

So it was that Sifu received the administrative item: a letter that informed him of his expulsion from the Chee Kim Thong Pugilistic and Health Society, signed by his beloved Old Man.

20

GELEK RIMPOCHE'S MAP

Black clouds sweep across the sky. To escape the oncoming storm we have moved down one level from the roof of the car-park to the uppermost deck. There is space to practice here but it's even warmer and, with Sifu's flow interrupted, I doubt we will resume exercise. As we hurry away from the storm, Sifu tells me how he learned the Tibetan-lama arts.

'Did you watch the documentary I sent you?'

'Yes Sifu,' I answer. 'I was surprised how similar some of their techniques are to ours; the way they use the shoulders and the index fingers.'

'When I saw this, it shocked the hell out of me. It's supposed to be something very secretive, but people got it into the YouTube. So you see, people cannot be trusted; they simply put it up without permission.'

'Why did they let the cameraman into their lamasery to begin with?' I ask.

'The lama, after much persuasion, agreed to let him into the school, because the guy was so interested. The lama said, "The condition: it's for yourself, not to show people. If you practise this wrongly, it's going to be harmful to yourself." Which is true.'

'And you learned these arts?' I ask.

'Yes. Shaolin, yoga, the lama arts: all different, but they all have the same purpose, to prepare the body for meditation by energization. That's why I say, "meditation" itself is a very deep word. Many people misunderstood. They thought that "just sit down and close your eyes means you're in meditation." That's not true, you're wasting your time. We must always energize our bodies, like us when we train our *qi*. That's why at the end I make you do the *zhangong*,' the 'still training'.

'To boil the water?' I answer, beginning to comprehend why 'meditation' seems a dirty word to Sifu, and why what I practice at present doesn't constitute meditation in his definition, but a precursor which he terms 'contemplation'.

'Yes; boil the water before you make tea. 90 per cent do not know this in the world. They say you sit down and try to be empty and it's all bloody nonsense. If a guy comes along and says he just started meditating one day – with no preparation – I'll humour him just to be polite, but in my heart I say, "no way."'

'The fixation with "emptiness" sounds like hippy stuff,' I say.

There are ways in which my encounters with meditation and associated ideas in Asia are diametrically opposite my experience of the concepts in the West. Many practitioners attempt meditation by the method Sifu has just attacked; they 'sit down and try to be empty,' perhaps lighting a little incense. The benefits of this method depend on one's susceptibility to being told that 'you are feeling very relaxed'. These efforts aim to deepen relaxation towards enigmatic meditative-states communicated by esoteric terms such as 'mindfulness,' 'emptiness,' and 'no-mind'. Meditation too can cast progress as an event infinitely deferred, with former instructors telling me that to attempt is to fail, and that one should simply arrive at the elusive state, with intimations that further explanation would be futile.

'If you think you can just make yourself empty, bull*shit*,' Sifu says. 'Emptiness is fullness; think about it.'

How does 'emptiness' equate to 'fullness'? I reason that if I tip the contents out of a vessel, a scientist or a pedant will say that it is not 'empty' but full of air. Comparably, it's impossible to think of nothing, but with practice it is feasible to sustain concentration on a single object. This fills the mind like an 'empty' vessel, banishing the clutter of other thoughts. Yet there is no reason to privilege the notion of emptiness, and likewise the esoteric status afforded to 'mindfulness' and 'no-mind' can be negated by attention to one's concentration.

Sifu's theory of meditation is simpler than that professed by other practitioners, but the attempt itself is difficult. First, as Sifu has just reminded me, we 'energize' our bodies in preparation for meditation. It occurs to me now that the bedevilled idea of 'Shaolin martial-arts' might be explained as the physical routines of ascetics whose goals were spiritual, but whose mundane concerns often related to the safety of their temple. For that reason, the energisation techniques of Shaolin acquired combative aspects that are absent from their origins in older Buddhist, Taoist and Hindu practices. Asia had many fighters and many meditators, but circumstances at Shaolin caused the two to be combined. Contemplation, like the energisation of *gongfu*, requires skilled breath-control. Visualization of energy flows is also important in contemplation, to which any distraction is the enemy. Sustained concentration for the duration of a *gongfu* technique that meets physical resistance, with which I struggled in recent Mother and Child practice, is preparatory for mental exertion in contemplation, although the body remains still.

As I advance in *gongfu* and contemplation, I am reunited with an old enemy. Like a cosmic joke at my expense, I have learned that the spine is of central importance in *gongfu* and meditation, known to the Chinese as the Celestial Pillar. Maybe it's not a celestial prank but a stroke of good fortune that I've had to focus obsessively on a detail that transpires to be key. The spine is the central energy-channel of a *gongfu* practitioner's body. A year ago the lama arts might not have looked anything like Shaolin *gongfu* to me. Now the similarities appear indicative of their most important aspects, and I want to know more.

'Emptiness is fullness,' Sifu repeats. 'The guy who helped me realize that is the same who taught me the lama arts.'

'Who was that?'

In 1984 a Tibetan lama fell into a fever on a visit to Kuala Lumpur. As he slept, Sifu tells me, the lama dreamt that there was a cure nearby. Still asleep, he took pen and paper in hand and began to draw. The lama woke and realized that he had drawn a map.

'So obviously he had a map of KL,' I say, 'and wrote on it?'

'No; he just drew it on a blank sheet of paper, in his dream.'

The next day, as he explored Kuala Lumpur, the lama remembered certain landmarks from his dream, such as a petrol station and a Buddhist temple. He used these recollections to help navigate the unfamiliar city using the map. The lama's name was Gelek Rimpoche. His driver, Tony Wong, founded a local temple to the Goddess of Mercy and had invited the lama to speak in KL.

'"You go here, you go there,"' Sifu paraphrases the lama directing Tony Wong in the car. '*The federal highway, turn right, and where-where-where.* "This is what you will see, that's where the house will be."'

Finally the lama concluded, 'This is the place, let's look around,' and the two exited the car. Tony Wong said,

'This is Chee Kim Thong's house.'

I blink.

'Tony came in the door with this lama,' Sifu continues, 'and said to him in front of me, "Ah, if you'd told me you were coming to my master's house, then I would have brought you directly here!" But this lama didn't know where he was going or who was Mr Chee. When they were driving, Tony Wong only knows that these were the directions Gelek Rimpoche gave.

'So anyway, this is how I met him. One morning I came back from Hong Kong, I was training in Mr Chee's home. The lama came into our hall, he saw me, he walked over to where I practised. He knocked his forehead against my forehead three times and rubbed his nose against mine three times. I was just in my short pants, training bared-bodied because I was just so sweaty like hell. He embraced me, knocked the forehead, rubbed the nose again, and he asked me, "Don't you recognise me?"

'Of course I can't recognise him; I mean, who the *hell* is he? He said, "If you do a little bit more meditation, you will remember that we were colleagues together a long time ago." Of course, at this time I didn't know what that was all about.'

'Was he wearing the lama's robes?' I ask, attempting to visualize the scene of a Tibetan holy man embracing my sweaty *gongfu* teacher.

'Normally Gelek Rimpoche does not wear the robes, just dresses in an ordinary way. Anyway, he came to see Mr Chee, who said this lama was having a kidney problem. Mr Chee tested his pulse and all that, and asked him every day to eat twenty ginkgo nuts. "So you brew it, break it up, and you just chew. That will help you to clear your kidney problem."

'That's how I met Gelek Rimpoche, a cousin of the Dalai Lama. He belongs to the Yellow Order of the Dalai Lama. Then Gelek at the same time told me, "I am coming to Hong Kong on such-and-such a date. Will you entertain me?" I said, "Sure." So he came and stayed with me for four days. And every morning he would do a *puja* with me, with his chanting and bells, *ding, ding*. I said, "You can't do that so early in the morning!" I was quite scared that we would upset the neighbours, but surprisingly, nobody complained. And during the four days, he taught me the lama arts, which later came out on YouTube, many years later.'

'But the story of the map – that's incredible.'

'These are some of the uncanny things that can happen,' Sifu answers. 'If I've not experienced it, I wouldn't believe it. In my life I live among the coincidences. To we Asians, these occurrences are part of life. Believe or don't believe; it happens.'

If you believe, you believe; don't believe, you don't believe. One of the subtexts of the story with Gelek Rimpoche is that Sifu thinks the machinations of fate have similarly united me with him. I've never give much thought to the concept of reincarnation, tending to dismiss it as a consolatory belief for mediocre people who tell themselves they were once Napoleon. To learn his arts, Sifu doesn't ask me to make any leaps of faith. But I realize that I will never comprehend the decisions of Chee Kim Thong and his disciples unless I come to terms with their perspective.

21

THE FALL OF SINGAPORE

In February 1942 the Japanese army swept through the Malayan peninsula to Singapore, a strategic base for control of the South China Sea. Immigrants who had fled the carnage in China saw those scenes re-enacted in their new home. The stench of death filled the streets from bodies left where they fell: British soldiers, native resistance, whoever got in the way. The Japanese raised the Nippon flag over Singapore. Some local shopkeepers did likewise, hopeful that by demonstrative compliance they might be spared looting, rape and murder, the working-day atrocities of warfare.

But the Japanese newcomers did not trust the Singaporean community, significantly composed of Chinese immigrants. Hence followed the Purge, *Suqing*. Men of Chinese ethnicity were ordered to report to screening centres, where they were assessed as potential allies of the Chinese army. At the centres – concentration camps of squalor wrapped in barbed wire – the men waited for days to be evaluated. The soldiers examined their prisoners for Triad tattoos and interrogated them, or reached their conclusions based on the claims of informants. Those who satisfied the Japanese interviewers that they did not support the Chinese army were released. The rest were ushered onto crowded trucks. Waiting to depart, they whispered speculation on their fate. Most presumed that they would be transported to labour camps that assisted the Japanese war effort with weapons manufacture. Had they known the truth, they might have posed greater resistance: they were taken to the beach and machine-gunned.

In a feature published by a Malaysian newspaper in 1998, I was amazed to read that Chee Kim Thong had survived a firing squad on Changi Beach;

that he collapsed to the ground and played dead until the Japanese soldiers fled indoors from a storm. As I researched *Suqing*, I became absorbed by the accounts of witnesses. It was extraordinarily fortunate to survive the executioners, but it was not unknown. Some prisoners were struck by Japanese bullets, but not fatally. They crawled out of mass graves when the coast was clear and walked home, or swam out to sea, navigated the island and returned ashore elsewhere. Others, indeed, simply pretended to have been hit. Often the Japanese soldiers did not have the appetite for mass murder, and did not concentrate on their task. They shot carelessly and neglected to inspect their victims afterward. They assigned sympathetic locals the task of digging and filling the burial pits, or left their victims on the sand for the tide to claim the dead.

I imagine the stages of Ah-Thong's assessment. The wait to be interviewed would have been terrible. Even if these soldiers did not know that Master Chee was wanted by the Japanese for his role in the Big Knife Army, his Fujian accent was likely to condemn him. The Carpenter Street crowds that shouted his name in the 1960s might have contained an informant to betray it in 1942. What did he think while he lay among the dead, wondering whether he could maintain the deceit, or if a soldier would find him alive and settle the matter at point-blank range?

'It's not true,' Sifu tells me over fish-ball noodles.

'*What?*'

'Old Man was not in Singapore in 1942. He's gone to Dungun a couple of years already.'

'This is printed in a newspaper!'

'Yes. Mr Chee was very upset when this thing came out, but you know what Old Man is like. He keeps it in his heart, doesn't say anything.' Sifu adds, as a consolatory gesture, 'He did escape from the Japanese POW camp in China; this part is true.'

I shake my head dismissively. I've heard that one already. What I want really is for Sifu to say that the story of 1942 *is* true, that this is one more thing we know about the reticent Master Chee. The article is based on an interview with Chee Kim Thong. The prose lapses mysteriously out of quotation from the master in the account of the *Suqing* episode. I attempted to contact the journalist through the Malaysian press association, but she seems to have vanished.

'Disappeared,' I put it to Sifu and Alex, 'off the face of the earth.'

I allow a pause, in case our mercurial teacher chooses to reveal that he is playing a trick on me. Silence prevails.

'Where would she get this nonsense?' I ask after a time. 'A journalist could get into serious trouble if she made something up whole cloth.' Then add: 'She could get into serious trouble *somewhere that wasn't Malaysia*.'

'This woman needed an interpreter to interview Old Man,' Sifu says. 'Who translated for her?'

'Cheng Hai.'

'*Aiyoh*.'

I have hit a brick wall. I expected that with research the Old Man would emerge into daylight, but detecting falsehoods appears instead to have thickened the smoke. While I can discount the biographical accuracy of certain stories, they have added to my confusion, not simplified my pursuit of Master Chee. *Suqing* looms large in the identity of modern Singapore. To place Master Chee there untruthfully is like a corny historical fiction whose protagonist happens to meet every significant person of the era and ticks off every famous incident on his trajectory. You may as well say he shot Kennedy or walked on the moon. The real Ah-Thong recedes as the dramatic stereotype comes into focus. Today's revelation over *Suqing* prompts me to investigate other dimensions of the Chee Kim Thong legend.

'When he was named National Living Treasure of China,' I say, 'people made a big deal of the title in the West. I assumed it was because the government realized the mistake of eradicating real martial-arts in China, and hoped Master Chee would come back.'

Sifu laughs.

'Nothing to do with *gongfu*,' he says. '*I'm* a National Living Treasure of China.' Sifu tells me he was awarded the honour on a visit to China with the tycoon Ian Fok. 'The father did so much for this place, Nansha, that they call it *Fok-Seng*, "Fok City." The officials gave me a certificate to say

I'm National Living Treasure, all because I was there with the son.' By the end of the anecdote I suspect that the Chinese government makes National Living Treasures of people when it wants something from them: 'It was because Old Man sent money back to his village, to build a school. The Chinese government wanted him to keep giving money, so they came up with this award.'

Another aspect of the Chee Kim Thong legend which proves problematic is the incident that brought Master Chee to Cheng Hai's attention in the news. Mak Tian Meng and others said that the fight broke out with Malays over the death of a Malay child, an accident for which I have found evidence in the press, but Sifu disagrees.

'A Chinese bus-driver talked his way into trouble with the Malays,' is Sifu's minimalist account. 'It seems this guy was a real A-H.'

'Where did this version come from?' I ask.

'Cheng Hai translated for me,' Sifu answers.

'*Cheng Hai*,' I repeat, 'elsewhere considered such a *reliable* source of information. How could this guy talk his way into trouble with *so many* Malays at the same time?'

Sifu glowers and we abandon the conversation. Now we have reached another impasse.

'Then the Old Man is unwritable,' I declare at last.

* * *

It's 2:40 on a Monday afternoon and I'm sitting in the Spinelli Coffee Company, where I try to bribe myself into progress on the Chee Kim Thong narrative. I stare at my notes. There is nothing to do other than add the *Suqing* incident to my collection of Ah-Thong Apocrypha alongside fictitious duels, unsubstantiated feats and dubiously attributed quotations, often inaccurate aphorisms about *gongfu* on the lines of 'Always X!' and 'Never Y!'

The inventions communicate more about the students than their master. Some club members knew little about Chee Kim Thong. They used fictions to plug the gaps in their knowledge and complete a picture. Perhaps the resultant paradigm inspired them to practise. Still I don't see the need to concoct these additional Chee Kim Thong stories. It's possible that certain students felt that an exaggerated Master Chee would enhance their own reflective glory. Instead their deceit implicitly insults his achievements as inadequate. No wonder the Old Man was disappointed with his students. The reluctance to work with the biographical materials to hand parallels many students' refusal to focus on the *gongfu* practice the Old Man emphasized, when complicated routines seemed more glamorous. Tales of Master Chee arose for various reasons, serving different functions: how the Old Man's temperament became so; how he settled in Malaysia; how he was a gifted being in some manner that casts into more favourable relief his mortal students' failure to achieve. *Everyone knows Ah-Thong*, indeed.

'Just stories,' Sifu says. 'They're just stories.'

Sifu's own reliability as witness varies with the context. Other members of Chee Kim Thong's circle told the same stories as Sifu does concerning his disputes with Cheng Hai. In this conflict it appears that Sifu recognises adherence to the bare facts as the best tactic. Generally Sifu's memory is accurate, aside from occasional errors over names and places of a kind typical to people excessively confident that their memories are accurate. When it comes to the Old Man, Sifu describes his master's skill by reference to what he discerned in physical contact rather than by tall tales. Despite what he says, though, Sifu does reveal a sense of ownership over Chee Kim Thong, which is evident in his tendency to downplay the extent to which Master Chee taught people such as Kok Seng Pang. Consequently, Sifu is motivated by a wish for his version of a story to be the correct one, regardless of his source; that his account of the incident between the bus driver and the mob relies on what he recalls Cheng Hai translating fifty years ago is a pertinent example.

It would be fair to query the extent to which it *matters* whether certain stories of Chee Kim Thong are true or not. Furthermore, it's possible that some tales of the Old Man, while not factually accurate, could be said to contain 'truth' in the sense of illustrating an essential quality that nobody could dispute he possessed. Yet too many of the legends are misleading, not only because they put Master Chee in the wrong time and place, but because they distort his personality by illustrating traits he *didn't* have. For example, attendants of Master Chee's seminar in Dublin years ago were terrorized with a threat that if the palms were not held flat in the Swallow-Vomit technique of *Sanzhan*, the Old Man would lean over and spit into the wayward practitioner's hand as he passed. The logic of this threatened behaviour was that the incorrect, curved palm resembled the shape of a Chinese spittoon. 'No,' Sifu said. 'Old Man did not do this.' For one thing, to waste saliva contravenes the guidance of Chinese medicine. For another, Master Chee was not a coarse type who spat, hence Sifu was mildly offended when I suggested otherwise. Thirdly, the Old Man tended simply to ignore students who made mistakes, which I identify now as a fatal flaw in his group. Therefore the spitting anecdote contradicts several of Master Chee's most important traits.

It matters to *me:* what is true and false, what the Old Man was really like. If I don't record the fate of Chee Kim Thong and his club, nobody else will. I imagine all that will be left fifty years from now will be an idiotic anecdote about spitting, and that Sifu's vaunted lineage-exclusivity will leave the training hall empty.

* * *

It's nearly three o'clock; time to leave the café. I emerge into Orchard on a weekday afternoon. Trees and shopping malls mark Singapore's constant shifts between urbanity and jungle. The buildings evoke durians, Tang-dynasty palaces, the Great Wall of China and gemstones. The glacial architecture is insistently modern, a self-fulfilling prophecy of an Asian century. Yet on the billboards and in shop windows, aspiration so often has a Caucasian face. Intermingled with upmarket *feng shui* statues and boutique tea selections is a Coca-Colony of American fast food and European fashion-chains. Past the Goodwood Park Hotel – where we took Sifu for a Christmas dinner – past the Thai Embassy, past the Embassy of

Peru, past the Four Floors of Whores and Muddy Murphy's Irish Pub, I walk under the shade of trees wherever I can. The last pedestrian crossing is tortuous; the lights by Delfi Orchard are slow to change and the junction is horribly bare to the sun.

Dominic is one of my indulgences in Singapore. When I arrived here I searched online for a good barber and was chilled by some of the accounts I read. Expatriates wrote that Caucasian hair is different from Asian hair and should be cut differently. Contributors shared their horror stories. One description – 'like it was done in a Chinese orphanage' – remains lodged in my mind. Dominic came strongly endorsed as an expert in Caucasian hair. Most of his clients are well-to-do expat women, which gives me assurance.

When Dominic starts to cut my hair he asks whether I've any plans to travel.

'I need to go,' I say with a voice wearied by my recent difficulties in researching Master Chee's life, 'to an obscure village in Malaysia, although I've no idea how to get there. In June I'm going to China. How about you?'

'I'm just back from the Grave-Sweeping Ceremony in my ancestral village,' Dominic replies.

'Where's that?'

'It's this tiny little village in Malaysia.'

'Really? Whereabouts?'

'In Terengganu, right on the east coast.'

'That's a coincidence; it's the same state I need to get to.'

'The village is called Dungun.'

'You're *kidd*ing.'

As surprised as I am that we have been talking about the same place, Dominic is equally taken aback that a Caucasian has heard of Dungun and wants to visit. I tell him about Chee Kim Thong, how Sifu first encountered the master in Dungun, and the problems researching the Old Man, for whom we're not entirely certain we have the right name.

'I can believe that,' Dominic comments on the possibility that 'Chee' was a pseudonym. 'The Japanese had a lot of business in that part of Malaysia, even into the 1950s. Mostly they came for iron ore.'

The main problem with the journey to Dungun, I say, is that there is no train line on the east coast of peninsular Malaysia.

'You need to fly to Kuantan, then take a taxi,' Dominic answers. 'The taxi will take two-and-a-half hours. But it's the easiest way.'

It happens that Dominic's cousin still lives in Dungun, where he owns a pet store. Dominic pauses to send an SMS, which is answered shortly after.

'My cousin knows the old master,' Dominic says.

Fifteen minutes later I emerge onto Orchard Road with a highly presentable hairstyle, and plans to visit a pet store.

IV

MIST

22

BIG TENT, SMALL TENT

'Did I ever tell you I was supposed to make a movie with Bruce Lee?'

'You may have mentioned it once or twice.'

'Busy! All this is reserved. Come, let's sit here. Fried beef noodles tonight, ah? The movie was *Northern Fist and Southern Leg*. I was Southern Leg; Bruce Lee was Northern Fist. I was due to have a screen test, but – you know how things go, always delay, delay – then he died.'

'Very inconsiderate of him. Sifu, why do Wing Chun people always boast about how Bruce Lee studied Wing Chun? If he thought Wing Chun was so great, why did he go off and learn a bunch of different arts, and then invent his own?'

'If Wing Chun wants to say Bruce Lee is Wing Chun, it's just advertising. And the same thing: Bruce Lee was a brawler, a born fighter, but if he says that is some new art, it's just to get people into his school. Maybe some day *you'll* go back to the UK and call your school Murray Fist.'

'I doubt that. In the West we always want a wise, old Chinaman involved for credibility. "Murray Fist" wouldn't sound Oriental enough.'

'Alex, why are you laughing?'

'Because it's the opposite situation in Singapore. Here, people will take a martial-arts club or a book more seriously if there is a Caucasian involved.'

'You and all your DVD's and books! I can't believe you got rid of them. You had so many books on *Taijiquan*. Once you thought these are all treasures.'

'Then I realized they're actually trash.'

'You spent a lot on them. They were worth some money.'

'They were taking up space in our apartment.'

'Can you really learn anything from books?'

'No, *lah*. All this stuff about secret *gongfu* manuals is just old stories. You need to learn it from the master, because you need to *feel*.'

'If you are learning martial arts, maybe you can write things down to help you remember.'

'For memory, I can understand how that would work, but I don't think someone who hasn't seen certain movements before could learn them from a book.'

'These books are also a form of advertising for the master and the school.'

'Because the master becomes more strongly associated with the art. Hey, here's our girlfriend. Hello darling. Big party here tonight, ah? One Guinness and one Tiger, the large size.'

Happy birthday to you—

'Ah, when you two drink, you talk *on* and *on*.'

Happy birthday to you—

'Should join us, ah?'

Happy birthday, Esmeralda—

'Even if you can't learn new techniques from the books, are they good for other things, like martial-arts culture and philosophy?'

May the Buddha bless you.

'The quality is usually low. The problem is they all cut and paste from the same sources.'

'You don't need to go off and learn all of this philosophy. If someone says you need to be Buddhist or Taoist, it's all nonsense. All you need is to use your common sense. Be sincere and open-minded. If you are not open-minded, you will have problems.'

'Has it happened?'

'Recently I was teaching a breathing exercise, *The Virgin Prays to Guan Yin*. Like this, ah? You've seen statues of Guan Yin, the Goddess of Mercy? There are always the two figures beside her, praying with hands clasped like this. Anyway, one man protested when I taught. He said, "I don't want to learn this, it's Buddhism." He himself was a Christian and he thought because the technique has this name, he cannot learn. It will convert him to Buddhism, or his church will disapprove. Which is nonsense, you cannot think like this. If you ask me what religion I have, I have none. If you talk about God, to me it's Nature. But I respect all sages.'

'So what happened, did the guy quit?'

'No; I told him to think of the Virgin Mary, and he was happy.'

'So everyone's content.'

'You must be open-minded, like Mr Chee. There's no need to be rigid in your beliefs. You must never say, "Cannot learn." Ah, Alex?'

'Yes, Sifu.'

'I'm always scared this guy will say his church forbids him from *gongfu*. Thank you, no need to pour. We're going to mix it.'

'I'll do it.'

'50 per cent stout, then add the beer.'

'There was a guy in the UK who did quit because his church told him he might be possessed by demons during practice. Another person told me *Luohan Ruyiquan* can induce insanity.'

'Why does London have so much superstition? Guys who say things like this are always a bit crazy themselves. OK, help yourselves, no need for ceremony here. I can eat all I like, this new tea I'm having is supposed to be slimming.'

'Magic tea; magic, ionic mattresses; magic, oxygen-treated water. *Anything* except a diet.'

'No magic! All science.'

'Quite.'

'Sifu, there must have been *some* crazy people in KL.'

'OK, I'll give you another story. One day one of the students was talking to Mr Chee. He said when he practices he can feel the *qi* circling this way and that way, around this part of his chest, and so on. When he left, I said, "Huh? Sifu, I don't get any of this feeling." Old Man said, "Never mind, he's just imagining it." Then I realized that when people say this kind of thing, Mr Chee just humours them, he doesn't argue.' [*Narrows eyes, clasps hands over navel and tilts head to imitate Chee Kim Thong pretending to listen: nod, nod, nod; nod, nod nod.*] 'It's important that you do not imagine things. You think if you believe all this rubbish, you can learn? That's why I always tell you guys to let me know what feeling you are having from practice. Luckily you have some sense.'

'Usually the feelings are just pain.'

'Sifu, why did Master Chee not correct this man?'

'Old Man is not easy to learn from. You need to get him interested, ask intelligent questions. Some refer to him as The Cockle. When he closes up, he won't talk to you; if he thinks you can't get it, he won't waste his time. I used to get mad when one of the guys said something stupid instead of letting Old Man speak. Mr Chee would go and sit down, and I knew he wouldn't get up again for a long time. This is the traditional Chinese style. If you talk nonsense, he doesn't see the point correcting you.'

'Not like you, Sifu.'

'No; I give you guys hell. You've seen the scolding I give poor Travis. And you two this evening! Frankly, it's a good thing I wore my red shirt today, so people can't notice all the blood I have vomited. But Mr Chee kept quiet. Mr Dong Ying Jie also was like this. In our *Taijiquan* class, one of my classmates said the old poems talk about a concave back. Following him, all the students started to walk around like this.' [*Pushes shoulders forwards and hunches his back.*] 'So, once I saw these older guys doing it, I thought I must do the same, until Mr Dong pulled me aside to ask what the *hell* I am doing with this terrible posture. I said, "What about this *Taiji* poem?" He said, "That's not what it means." You can see the old poem was useless in the wrong hands.'

'So he corrected you, but didn't correct everyone?'

'He may have thought he was wasting his time. Maybe. Mr Dong spoke of the Big Tent and the Small Tent. In the Big Tent is the public class, but the Small Tent is for the select few, who get the real details.'

'Like having disciples?'

'Similar. But it may be that Mr Dong said it to those others already, and they didn't listen.'

'So it's their own fault.'

'Yes. And like I said, Mr Chee complained that when he did give advice, the students didn't listen. Old Man is very angry when he sees them. You can tell when he does this.' [*Shakes head steadily and chops upturned left palm with edge of right hand repeatedly.*] 'But they never notice how mad he is. Most of the time, he hides it. Old Man always looks like he's half asleep, eyes nearly closed.'

'You mean he was *pretend*ing?'

'Of course! When Mr Chee comes out to perform his eyes are very fierce. But he doesn't want people to see. This is old tradition; the master wants to disguise how strong his spirit is. For this reason, many masters will avoid people taking their photo. If they do allow it, they won't look at the camera. You'll see them stare at the ground or off to the side, or narrowing their eyes.'

'You're saying the Old Man was an *act*?'

'Like I just told you! When I drive Mr Chee around, he gets out of the car and hangs on to me; like he needs help, you know? Then he goes into the clubhouse and shows me a set. I say, "Sifu, why do you need my help walking? You can roll around like a monkey!" And we both laugh a lot.'

'In some ways it's all very secretive, but in others it's not.'

'How do you mean?'

'I mean that in popular belief we might think there is some magical practice that the master withholds from students. It's more like anyone can *learn* the exercise, the shell, but the real secrets are *within* that exercise, and only the Small Tent people will get them, or know that there's a difference. And similarly Master Chee is in front of people all the time, but they may not listen to him, or they don't know he puts on an act.'

'The art is *within* all of us. We only need to realize it. Like I always say, whether or not the student can get it is another matter.'

'But Sifu has also said some training is not for everyone.'

'It depends. When I started as instructor, Cheng Hai scolded me for teaching the Arhat training. All this,' [*lifts hands and circles wrists*]. 'All this. Cheng Hai said, "This is for lineage disciples, so we always have an advantage over the students; not for teaching to everyone." To me this is selfish, so I impart. Maybe when you guys teach you should hold it back at first, until you know and trust the student. Other training, Old Man won't ever allow people to learn. For example, the two soft arts Old Man has are *Wujiquan* and *Luohan Ruyiquan*. He allows every Tom, Dick and Harry to learn *Wujiquan*, but he told me not to waste my time on it, to focus on *Luohan Ruyiquan*. This *Ruyi* is not magic but unless you have a certain foundation in *gongfu*, there's no damn point. *Ruyi* is to do with intention, all internal. You can't get it just by trying to copy.'

'Some only care about saying they have learned.'

'There are people like this. Look at Travis: his Taiwan *Bagua*, *Xingyi*, White Crane, don't-know-what; cannot apply. He asks me to teach *Luohan Ruyiquan* because he wants to learn a high art. I refuse to teach him. I say, "There's no point. Already you have a body full of knives, all blunt." What can you do with a guy like that? What an idiot!'

'He will not be remembered with the Greek thinkers.'

'Plenty of people like this in KL, Long-Arm Lum especially: they say they have it, but the real art is lost. Overall, I will say that Mr Chee was unlucky not to have more good disciples. When I moved to Hong Kong, Cheng Hai was very happy. He said to Old Man, "We found one Chan See-meng, we can find another." But they couldn't find a talent. Old Man gets fed up.'

'So people want to claim the art or the master, but that might not include an effort to learn well.'

'We should not try to own the art or the master. If the master teaches us, we are lucky.'

'And it's up to us to work hard.'

'Sifu, initiation gives you some entitlement, doesn't it?'

'Initiation is like an adoption. The disciples are closest to the master and they are – this word in quotation marks, ah? – *supposed* to be the best, and they should learn most. But even initiates do not *own* the art. According to our rules, they cannot keep it to themselves, or only teach their sons. Unfortunately, there are always bad apples. Many arts have been lost this way.'

'Surely all that should count is the practice you put in?'

'Whoever you are, you must practice. Even I must practice: if I do not, I am giving back what Mr Chee gave to me.'

'If initiation involves a kind of adoption, can the link be broken?'

'Cannot break. That is why it did not matter when Cheng Hai tried to have me expelled the first time. Old Man handed me a membership card. I said, "What's this? Life Membership? These cost $500!" Old Man said, "Never mind, just take it." Mr Chee had paid the $500 out of his own pocket to reinstate me. This was just so people cannot cause trouble within the club. But like I say, if they try, it's nothing to do with being Mr Chee's disciple.'

'Since you were a disciple, it seems pointless to kick you out of the club; kind of a hollow gesture.'

'Once the master takes disciples, they are considered part of the family. If I was really a bad guy, the master would send his disciples to destroy me. They would cut my tendons so I would lose my *gongfu*. Even so, a parent cannot divorce a child. In my case, I was always with the father. Who can dispute that? I attended all the family occasions. You must understand this. When Sneaky Snake was rude to you in KL, it was because I criticized him years ago. I said, "Your father would be ashamed of you." To a Chinese this is a very bold statement. Because I am part of the family, I am permitted to make this sort of comment. But Sneaky Snake did not receive it well.'

'Let's hope the other sons give me a better reception.'

23

DUNGUN

Grey above and grey below. The fishermen have dragged their boats along the sand and overturned them for the late afternoon, leaving tracks that crisscross the smaller trails of crabs and driftwood. My map alleges that a small island lies off the Dungun coast but today it is obscured by mist. Impossible for me to imagine anything beyond, the prospect resembles the edge of a video-game universe: I might wade out to sea for hours, then turn to find myself only a few steps from shore. The character's legs continue to move, but no spatial advancement is possible. I feel that I have pursued Ah-Thong to the end of the earth. In *gongfu* I will advance as far as talent and opportunity allow; with this excursion and my imminent visit to Fujian province, I can do no more to follow the master's literal footsteps. I don't believe that Fujian will preserve much that is tangible of Chee Kim Thong's China, so Dungun feels like an ending. *Here and no further*, says the master, and the horizon echoes.

'A calendar is more useful than a clock in the Rip van Winkle town of Kuala Terengganu,' begins an old *Straits Times* article on Dungun. 'A calendar to tell whether this is 1831 or even 1901. There is little to insist that the year is 1951.' The air of changelessness reassures me that there is authentic experience here of the Dungun that compelled the Old Man to settle. The place offers answers.

The *Straits Times* journalist found Dungun dead even by the standards of this 'most backward of the East Coast States,' and a hostile home for Chinese ethnicities, which the Malays considered to be 'without rights'. These tensions continue, I have learned. The Chinese make up around two per cent of the present population.

'Only had one road back then,' Sifu said of his early visits to Dungun. 'Maybe has two roads now.'

Two roads plus an arrow to Mecca on the hotel-room ceiling.

On my walk along Dungun's main road, I was nearly killed when a van spun onto the pavement and tipped over on the spot where I had stood until the screech of tyres caused me to stagger backwards. I fell over outside Weng Hoe Auto and Parts Supply. A dazed Malay emerged from the van and regarded it from a safe distance, with a suspicion it might explode.

'Should someone call an ambulance?' I asked some spectators, who regarded me as though I said something stupid. A young couple – potentially Mr and Mrs Weng – gave me a seat and a drink of water outside the garage. The driver limped back to his vehicle and siphoned petrol from the tank.

By evening a mosquito buffet as I explored sandy lanes inhabited by chickens, indolent goats and a single bull. Many of the houses are wooden, with corrugated-iron roofs, although there are modern homes too that integrate arched porches, balconies and balustrades, and steep gables with intricate decoration in complex, Terengganu architecture. Master Chee's functional-looking grocery store survives on Jalan Nibong under a son's name – Chee Boon Jeng Enterprise – but was shuttered up for the Hari Raya holiday. Sporadically came the sound of excited car horns as drivers leaned out of their windows to greet the exotic Caucasian. The stillness recalls me to my first visit to Malaysia, when I took the train to Kuala Lumpur and reflected, as it rattled through endless jungle, how *emphatically* Master Chee fled China. I turn away from the sea to face the coastal road overseen by coconut, palm and Dungun trees. Why Dungun, in a world of possibilities?

* * *

A silver sky over an iron sea; one regards the other like past and present. This is a delusory punctuation of chronology, the arbitrary division of an ignorant past from a supposedly knowledgeable now. In memory I am sixteen years old, meeting Chee Kim Thong for the first time. For several years the instructor of our secondary school's *gongfu* group – affiliated with a club in London – has told us about the enigmatic Chinaman in Malaysia. Imagine our excitement when we heard that the master was to visit Ireland, of all places.

Putian, Xiamen, Singapore, Dungun. Now Ah-Thong journeys across the world to a musty church-hall in Dun Laoghaire, Co. Dublin, a seaside town of my childhood. Some participants have travelled from America and the UK. The seminar takes place daily for a week, but in retrospect it has assumed the continuity of a single occurrence, one extended rehearsal of the art. They say that by night the Old Man demonstrates, but the younger students are not invited. By day the London instructor teaches a routine while Master Chee watches. Occasionally the Old Man offers general commentary on the group's efforts, which the London instructor translates.

More focus required.

We practise primarily for health.

Mostly Chee Kim Thong is still.

Old Man just sat there drinking his tea, ah?

On concluding the routine I feel the master's eyes on me. He raises his hand and forms a tiger-claw in allusion to movements I omitted: two clockwise circles, one counter-clockwise. This is the extent of my interaction with the great Chee Kim Thong.

The silver sky and iron sea, like *yin-yang* writ into the horizon to represent the hard and soft, the male and female, the substantial and insubstantial. I have learned that there are two kinds of practise among Chee Kim Thong's adherents; one a vacuous dance of aerobic novelties, the other an agent of self-transformation. My mind's eye contemplates the students in the church hall and wishes my straight-talking Sifu was there to set them right: *Stance all wrong; breath-control all wrong; push hands all wrong.* The principles that should populate the motions are entirely absent; the imprecise gestures could never act as vessels for the major concepts. To say that that the movements are incorrect is not merely structuralist pedantry. The greatest worth of correct technique lies in its ability to alter the practitioner. Each part must be forged in accordance with the mould or the machine will not cohere. Without foundations, these enthusiasts can only hope for magical leaps of advancement. Perhaps the practice is so wrong that the Old Man doesn't recognise his arts, and attributes the more extravagant errors to different *gongfu* the students have learned elsewhere.

The Old Man will never tell you your mistake.

I resent this silence as I gaze into the South China Sea. Could Master Chee not have devoted the visit to the fundamentals of *Wuzuquan*, so that the Westerners would do *something* right?

As though the clouds have rolled away and sunlight bursts through, it hits me that part of the fault for my impatience with Master Chee's club, and the standard of his practitioners, is mine. It occurs to me now that few people *care* enough to question whether the techniques they practise are authentic, or will lead to mastery. It's the *idea* of a thing that captures the imagination, not the minutiae of its reality. The same is true of *gongfu* for most students. *I'm practising Chinese martial-arts! With a real, Chinese master!* Who am I to say that people shouldn't enjoy it, that they should have higher goals? I may as well tell teenagers playing football in the park to quit on the grounds that they would already have professional contracts if they were ever likely to play for Real Madrid. It's probably a harmless fantasy for hobbyists to say they practice top-level *gongfu*, provided they don't start fights with strangers. It's a fallacy to think that *gongfu* tradition placed these arts solely in the hands of committed monks in specialized temples. There were Shaolin monks who didn't study *gongfu*, and fighters in residence with no interest in Zen Buddhism. The art makes room for all such practitioners. Over the years I've considered *gongfu* in relation to Zen Buddhism, Taoism and Confucianism. Now I conclude that the only philosophy that matters is that if you enjoy something healthy, you are lucky and should persist.

* * *

In the morning I walk to the pet store and wait amidst the rabbits and kittens and fish tanks while the person at the till, possibly Wei Sin's wife, summons Wei Sin over the phone. Soon he arrives in a jeep, a moustache and a spirit of welcome, and says he's arranged for us to meet Master Chee's third son, Boon Tiong. We walk the narrow lanes between buildings. For such a small town – with no space constraint in evidence – the buildings huddle close together. Wei Sin indicates two old hotels that have closed down. I assume they attracted business when the Japanese came for iron ore and rubber. The town dwindled after the government closed the mines in the 1970s.

Wei Sin says that he played with Master Chee's son James when they were children. James, or Ah-Seng, has long since moved to Australia, where he teaches *Wuzuquan*. It was on a return visit to Kuala Lumpur that he contested the *Taijiquan* master, Koh Ah Tee. As a boy, Wei Sin studied *gongfu* under the eldest Chee boy, Ah-Liang, who held classes in a hall attached to a local Buddhist temple. The class ceased after a few months due, Wei Sin believes, to a lack of local interest. Master Chee was focussed on his disciples in Kuala Lumpur at that time. Momentarily I wonder why Wei Sin gives so much time to help me today. He assists me without reflection just because I'm here, and I asked, and I'm interested in one of Dungun's heroes.

Boon Tiong is waiting for us in the local *kopitiam*. In his sixties, he wears a short-sleeved silk shirt, spectacles and the obligatory Rolex. I recognise the features of Chee Kim Thong in him, relaxed into what Sifu calls the '*kampung* mentality' of rural Malaysia where Master Chee's face was made serious by war and want. Likewise Boon Tiong intimates the promise of his father's frame, but without the development of power by which the Old Man could seem twice his size. We exchange greetings and business cards:

CHEE KIM THONG & SONS REALTY SDN. BHD.
CHEE BOON TIONG
MANAGING DIRECTOR

This was the company set up to divide Master Chee's property among the family after his death.

Wei Sin sits with us. Occasionally he interprets, or asks for clarification on certain points because he knows a little about the family and the art. We order coffee and Boon Tiong asks who I practice with in Singapore.

'Chan See-meng is a good teacher,' he says in English. 'He gives it to you straight.'

'He is,' I say, 'the most blunt person I have ever met.'

Boon Tiong tells me he started to learn *Wuzuquan* in 1963, when he moved to study in Port Klang: 'Every Saturday morning I had to travel by bus to my father's house for training.' In the 1970s he assisted with classes in Kota Bharu.

Boon Tiong produces a folder from his satchel.

'I brought you some pictures.'

He displays several Ah-Thong-related treasures: souvenir programmes from club demonstrations and most surprisingly, a photo from 1952 of Master Chee's first *gongfu* group in Dungun, together with family members. Most of the students are boys in white shirts and shorts. The picture was taken some years before Master Chee took disciples. The waitress and a few elderly locals gather around the table for a moment to ask what we're looking at and why I'm in Dungun. Boon Tiong explains the photo to them.

'I didn't know there were so many students,' I say.

'This one is me,' says Boon Tiong of a baby on Chee Kim Thong's knee.

'Did these students learn *Wuzuquan*?' I ask.

'No; last-time my father was not teaching the *Wuzu*. He was teaching the Northern Style sets,' the external Shaolin style Chee Kim Thong learned as a pageboy from the bodyguard, Toh Yit Choon. 'It's not like *Wuzu*, where you study *Sanzhan* for one or two years. In the Northern Style, once you finish one set, straight away you learn another set.'

'Do you know what any of the sets were called?'

'One was *Kaishanquan*, "Opening the Mountain." Also these.' Boon

Tiong opens a martial-arts book and points at double broadswords, Chinese fans, staffs, butterfly knives, umbrellas and other household implements to be used as weapons.

'This one, this one; compulsory, compulsory, also compulsory.'

I recognise many weapons I learned years ago. At the time I didn't even know that these were not *Wuzuquan* sets. I'm amazed to realize that Master Chee encouraged this kind of superficial study. Only with the initiation of disciples did he teach *gongfu* in depth, and start to share *Wuzuquan* at all.

'People knew he had *gongfu*, but they didn't know how good until the Malay incident.' He points at Master Chee's hand on a photo. 'Do you know about my father's finger?'

'Excuse me?'

'At Nanputuo the Abbot noticed this finger—'

'The index finger?'

'The index finger is longer than the middle finger. He said it's not good for him to have this long finger, one finger only. So the Abbot bent it.'

'And it was normal length after that?'

'Normal. This is my father's story. What is the meaning, I don't know.'

'Were you close to your father?' I ask.

'We were all afraid of him.' Boon Tiong gazes at the group photo. 'Look at how stern he was!'

Wei Sin tells Boon Tiong that I'm writing about Master Chee and his initiates. Boon Tiong enthuses and says he'll send on more pictures.

'It's a shame the disciples argued,' I say. 'I'll have to record all this.'

Boon Tiong doesn't respond.

At midday Wei Sin drives me around the area. The clouds have dispersed. The primary colours of the Malayan peninsula burst forth from the trees, sand, water and sky. In this light the place resembles the wholesome Malaysia Sifu speaks of, where a child can climb trees, swim in lakes and torment turtles. But I have seen no children at play. Dungun is silent like a ghost town.

'What do young people *do* here?' I ask one of Wei Sin's teenage sons when we return to park by the pet store. He glances up and down the street and shrugs. Then he says he's moving to Kuala Lumpur soon to study.

Before I left the *kopitiam* I asked Boon Tiong, 'Why did your father come here, so far away from home?'

'My grandfather heard there are Hokkien people here,' he said. 'There is rubber, and the iron mine needs workers.'

Rubber plantations and iron mines chimed with the Chinese sense of opportunity. The obvious explanation eluded me because it is so alien to European culture. Opportunism always has negative connotations in Western usage. To the Chinese it's sensible to identify the advantages of going with the flow. I see now that for Master Chee's purposes, Dungun sufficed. 'It'll do,' was the wisdom of a great master and his father. Chee Kim Thong wanted anonymity and chances to provide for his family. To be a bus conductor, stationmaster, grocer, scrap merchant, traditional doctor and *gongfu* teacher brought success because they were opportunism in the most classically philosophical sense of harmony with the options available. He had struggled enough against circumstance in the war with Japan. Confluence with opportunity was not submission to fate – languid flotation on the river of life – but the endeavour associated with fulfilment of destiny.

The apparent contradictions are that Master Chee would retire to obscurity, and then allow himself to be coaxed into renown in the capital city; that he would establish a *gongfu* club without subsequently ensuring that the students studied by the correct methods. Officially, I know, the master's responsibility was only to teach his disciples, who should impart the art to the instructors, who gave public classes in turn. Between them they should have been able to secure the future of the club, I think; why this was not so is still irritatingly unclear to me. The *semi*-fatalism perplexes me: I can't pin down Master Chee's sense of what is ordained and what must be contested.

Before leaving Dungun I return to the coast and attempt to photograph the state flag, which has been hoisted over the beach. I believe it depicts a white circle on a green background. The wind puffs and the flag twitches. It is not even half-unfurled by the force. Now the breeze subsides entirely. The flag droops. Its design remains stubbornly concealed.

24

CONTEMPLATION

In a flurry of bad English dappled with Mandarin, Travis asks Sifu about the Macrocosmic Orbit, a system of energy circulation theorized in Taoism which is supposed to replicate the revolution of celestial bodies. For a moment Sifu is silent. From his pillar he looks beyond Travis, over the rooftop to the building opposite. Then he shakes his head.

'Not in my experience,' he says.

It's not the answer Travis wants. The celestial bodies overhead hang still, as though waiting for Travis's response.

'Sifu, I think, not wrong,' Travis says. 'Ever mention *kundalini*,' the yogic conception of the serpent in the spine.

'Different,' Sifu says.

'I think—'

'Don't think! Leave the thinking to me. I'm the Commander-in-Chief; when I say "Go forward and die," you go. *Aiya*! You always have to bring in other things, without practising the exercise we are talking about.'

The merciless putdown has two functions. First, Sifu knows that Travis won't take any instruction on board unless it is put very bluntly; even in this case he is likely to forget quickly. Secondly, the reduction of Travis to saturnine silence is the only way to prevent him from interrupting the class continuously with his observations and recommendations.

Still, I can sympathise with Travis's confusion. To learn *gongfu* we assemble a mosaic at the master's instruction. We have only a vague notion of the overall design, while Sifu knows the purpose of each segment. With little awareness of our true progress, we persist. Perhaps this necessitates affinity, manifesting in that sense that the art exerts a magnetic pull that compels us to go further and further. Mutual trust is vital between master and student. Sifu wants intelligent students, but at times this entails the paradox of being smart enough *not* to think, to follow the method in the confidence that it must be so; 'The technique is this way for a reason'. Sifu's response is a way of telling Travis to trust the process. The point of what Sifu has said tonight, as I understand it, is that the contemplation practice helps to 'go in deeper' and develop coordination of mind, body and breath.

'Most exercises I have seen have no benefit,' Sifu says. 'A load of BS. Many teachers bluff, and the students do not notice. For example, if you're an old guy you can say it is good exercise simply to sit in the stance for half an hour with deep breathing, but it does not improve your art without the correct technique.'

I attempt to suggest it's similar for meditation, but I have made a cardinal error by use of the word 'meditation,' onto which Sifu seizes.

'Do not say "meditation!" We say "contemplation."'

'What's the difference?' I say, a little too impatiently, because I *know* that Sifu distinguishes between 'meditation' and 'contemplation', but I'm not sure why it's important to uphold the distinction so pedantically.

'As I have told you, it's because we must *prepare* ourselves to meditate,' he says, and explains by reference to Bodhidharma, the Indian monk who originated Zen when he travelled to Shaolin temple in the sixth century.

'When Bodhidharma went to China, the abbot heard he was coming and arranged to meet him at the port in Guangdong, with all the monks and officials. But when they saw Bodhidharma coming, in tatters, the monks looked at one another. "*That's* Bodhidharma?" Immediately in their mind, they looked down on him.

'Bodhidharma said, "Let me give my presentation now." So all the monks sat down, cross-legged, waiting for the sermon to be delivered. They said, "When's he going to start to talk? He's closed his eyes." Then they started fidgeting. Scratch here, scratch there. So the story says. "Why is he not delivering his lesson?" After another half an hour, Bodhidharma got up, told the abbot, "Thank you very much," and he left. The abbot asked,

"Why are you leaving?" Bodhidharma answered him, "All of you are not ready for me yet." The abbot protested, "We're all waiting for you to deliver your lesson!" Bodhidharma said to him, "While I was with you, everyone down there was fidgeting. Your minds are not even calm. How can you listen to me talk?" Later, in Shaolin-*si*, Bodhidharma knew he needed a way to prepare the monks. He sat in a cave for nine years and meditated. When he returned to them, he devised the Stretching of the Sinews and the Changing of the Bones to help the monks become ready for meditation.'

Thereafter 'Zen Buddhism,' which means 'Sitting Buddhism'.

'Bodhidharma professes a calm mind,' Sifu continues, 'so you can ask, "Who am I, what am I doing here?" So you can *think*. What does it do to you? It does nothing. Do you see my point? *Contemplation without contemplation*: you hear some of this Chinese philosophy and you think, "What the bloody *shit* is that supposed to mean?" It simply means calming yourself down, to understand what you are doing. But you must be ready, you must have the technique.'

'*Hmmmmm*,' Alex muses as Sifu concludes the story. 'All of this Buddhism …'

'I knew it!' Sifu laughs. 'You think your church will not like it. But Buddhism is not a religion; this is a fallacy. Buddhism comes from Hinduism; it's a fact. *Bodhi* is just a Hindu word for our "intuition." And Buddha is not a god, he merely acquired the technique of meditation.'

'Why do people worship Buddha as a god?' Alex asks.

'Occasional devotion is easier than practising tenets,' I suggest.

'If you say there is a god, we are *all* sons of god,' Sifu says. 'Buddha is not even such a great guy. He grew up a prince and never saw all the sorrow in the world. While he's off having his experiences – learning when he sees all the people who suffer, getting enlightenment under the tree – do you know what his wife is doing? She's at home, caring for the family. If you ask me, the wife is the better person.'

Alex and Travis are silent. I'm not sure 'we are all sons of god' appeases Alex's fears of blasphemy. Travis doesn't understand a lot of what is said, but refuses to ask for clarification. My own interest in contemplation, or meditation, is relatively new. It arose gradually as I perceived that when Sifu uses the word 'spiritual,' his meaning is very different from what the respective Christian Brothers who taught us would intend. To Sifu, 'spiritual' appears to relate to a tangible, if not immediately obvious, aspect of consciousness. Therefore, spiritual development is simply a progressively deeper comprehension of the physical universe. The practice appeals to me as the next step on the journey into unknown realms. This must be the purest art of all, lacking even outward movement.

Now my thoughts turn on the benefits of seclusion to self-cultivation. Chee Kim Thong's ability suggests that a monastic lifestyle is not essential to attainment in *gongfu*. Formally he worshipped the pantheon of gods in Chinese folk tradition; privately he remarked to Sifu that the benefits of prayer were primarily psychological. He went from a wartime city to a rural retreat, but he was no monk. I ask Sifu about the benefits of ascetic isolation.

'In a way, we are yogi,' Sifu says. 'But some yogi will live in the desert and practice the same thing for fifty years, like circling the stomach.' He stands and demonstrates the abdominal rotation. 'I think they're idiots! Who wants to live like that? Maybe if you want to meditate all the time. It's not necessary for our purposes.'

'So they live in seclusion,' I ask, 'because it's easier?'

'Easier.'

Easier to listen to the music of the spheres away from the hum of traffic, and to look for enlightenment far from the glare of street lamps. The monastic retirement of a *gongfu* monk can appear attractive to an aspirant. Part of this, I suspect, is that the paradigm of absolution from worldly responsibilities provides an excuse when we feel our own efforts are inadequate by contrast. A great deal of simplification occurs to visualize this cliché, since so much of a monk's time in reality is consumed by chores associated with the everyday function of a monastery.

'But we don't need to continue to that level,' I say.

'No. It's just avoiding distraction. Not everyone must be a monk. We have our duties, we have career and family.'

There was a practical dimension to Sifu's deepening interest in meditation. At first he would only undertake contemplation under duress: *Old Man would point to the corner and make me sit there to calm myself down.* Maybe Sifu's turnaround related to the onset of middle age, but it was also a means to navigate tensions within Master Chee's club.

Despite his lifetime membership, Sifu kept a low profile on his reinstatement in the Chee Kim Thong Pugilistic and Health Society. He no longer taught classes in the club, and would not let the headquarters display his photo to trade on the champion fighter. As such, Sifu left Cheng Hai to enjoy his status as the only initiate who was regularly involved with the group at that time. To Sifu, this was not a desirable prize.

Sifu directed his energies in two new directions. The first was an exchange of martial-arts traditions with Japanese visitors, a product of a larger project to share Japanese culture globally that was commenced in cooperation with the US Peace Corps. From these efforts Sifu became acquainted with Donn. F. Draeger, Robert Smith, the Aikido expert Nakamura Abe Sensei and the champion swordsman Toshima Sensei in 1971. The second new departure was dedicated practice of meditation, a phase which appears to have resulted from one of Sifu's characteristic Coincidences.

A friend persuaded Sifu to attend a lecture on Buddhism, delivered by a prestigious speaker who was visiting Malaysia.

'The speaker flew into a rage,' Sifu recalls, 'because he could not answer my question.'

'What was the question?' I ask.

'I cannot remember.'

I imagine Sifu informing the lecturer that Buddha was domestically irresponsible, or that Buddhism is only an offshoot of Hinduism. Despite this disappointment, Sifu agreed to accompany his friend the next time a significant lecture was announced.

'Soon after, a top *Svami* came down to KL. *Svami* is the Indian name for a monk, ah? Ah. It seems that the house where this *Svami* was staying belonged to Ramachandra, a senior officer in Bank Negara. Once again, my friend persuaded me to go along. At Ramachandra's house was a crowd, all Indian. Each had to register with his name and address.

'The name of the *Svami* was Yogacharya, known as the Yoga Monk. He was a very handsome and majestic-looking old man. He made this statement to me: "I visited US, and I'm on my way back to India, to Ranchi, and I cannot understand why I need to stop in KL, which is out of the way. I want to meditate to find out the purpose of my coming to KL."'

'You mean,' I suggest, 'he's a fatalist, so there must be some reason for him to be there?'

'*Must* be a reason. Yogacharya dismissed the group to attend to his own meditation. I was horrified because he told us to be back at 6 am the next morning, which meant I had to pick up Mr Wong at 4 am. But since I promised Mr Wong, I had to do it. At about 6:15, Yogacharya came out, and all paid their respects, kowtowed and so on. Yogacharya said, "I have to take five black sheep back into the fold." He called out five names; my name was one of the five. The Indians were shocked. Some said, "I have been reading scriptures for years and am not chosen. This Chinese boy does not even know who is Master."'

Sifu loves any opportunity to affect an Indian accent.

'Yogacharya taught and demonstrated all day to the five of us,' he continues. 'There was a complex ceremony.'

'What did it involve?'

'*Aiya*! Too long to explain. Something like my initiation with Mr Chee. But what Yogacharya taught me was way beyond what Mr Chee showed me. This is why, when I went back to Old Man, I said, "This Kriya technique works far quicker than our Shaolin Diamond Mudras." This is when Mr Chee said, "If you find it more effective, you'd better practise it." See why I have so much respect for this Old Man? Mr Chee was proud that I had become so interested in meditation.'

For Sifu to become enthusiastic about meditation demonstrated, I suppose, that the champion fighter also had depth, even if these efforts led him away from day-to-day activities at the Chee Kim Thong Pugilistic and Health Society. Sifu began to attract the notice of other meditation experts.

'Around 1971, '72, I received another visitor. A neighbour called to my door. This man lived five or six doors down, but we had never spoken. He said' – the Indian accent again – '"I am looking for a Mr Mung. Is Mr Mung here?" Daphne told him, "There is no Mr *Mung* here. There is Chan See-*meng*." The neighbour explained that there was a yogi in his house who asked to see me. This was *Svami* Natarajan.

'As soon as he saw me, Natarajan embraced me. He said, "You are my disciple. Your name is Gurudas Ananda." Ah-Chris, you must remember these names, ah?'

'I have trouble with the long, Indian names,' I protest.

'Write it down. Natarajan said he will come to my house at 4 am. He lives in Ipoh Road, at the Elephant God Temple. As soon as he said this, my heart sank. If he wants to see me at 4 am, I must get up at 2 am! But he said, "Never mind. I will come to you in my spiritual aspect."

'At this time, Daphne's sister was staying with us. Around 4 am, she woke us with her screaming: she said she saw a ghost in the house. It was Natarajan, chanting and striking a bell – *ding, ding, ding* – to cleanse the house.'

Whatever Natarajan meant by his 'spiritual aspect,' it caused the Chan household to think his untimely intrusion the work of a wandering spirit.

'Thereafter,' Sifu continues, 'I went to the Elephant God temple every Tuesday and Thursday to meditate with him. When I started, the Indians complained to the *Svami* that I didn't know the customs. We had to walk around the temple in a certain way. We ate banana and honey. Then we would sit and meditate.'

Within a year, Natarajan returned to India. Sifu started a meditation group in his home.

'But quickly, it was getting like a cult,' he says. 'People asked if they could kiss my feet. Girls would kneel before me, with all the boobs hanging out.' He makes a circular gesture to convey a bosom. 'This is temptation; you may start to think you are a god. I didn't want to lead a cult. I sure as *hell* don't want people kissing my feet. We risk becoming like the fallen angels.'

Sifu discontinued the meditation group and practised alone.

* * *

'Duties, even if everything is illusory?' I say, in reference to the Zen philosophy that our perception of reality is arbitrary. 'We would still attend to the requirements of an illusory world?'

'It's a contradiction,' Sifu says, and I infer from his terseness that he will not be drawn on the subject any more; at least not before I have caught up with him further perceptually. Until then, Sifu leaves us with the contrarieties of banality and transcendence.

The practical manifestation of this paradox is that at a point every afternoon I rise from my desk, lock the door to my office, and sit on a rug. Then I must forget about students, publications and meetings, and focus entirely on the contemplation exercises. Sometimes there is cheerleading practise beneath my window. Initially I found it ridiculous to make these efforts in the incongruous setting of a buzzing, twenty-first century university campus rather than the monastic idyll of my imagination. Now I have reversed that opinion; the whole point of contemplation and meditation is surely that they belong to all places. The contemplative mind-set must be brought into the rush of the everyday. On a cosmic scale we flicker in and out of existence. *The substantial into the insubstantial.* In everyday life we contend with the *yin-yang* revolutions of mundanity, with little idea how the petty manifests or redoubles the grand. Sifu too is bound to these vicissitudes, at one point a master above commonplace concerns, the next a *gongfu* disciple beleaguered by political power struggles, in and out of Chee Kim Thong's organisation even still.

25

THE SECOND EXPULSION

It is *not* Chee Kim Thong's birthday, I think. In 1960, Cheng Hai and Sifu visited the master for the occasion on 18 April, but the Chinese chart important dates by the lunar calendar, which changes every year in the Gregorian system. Damned if I'm going to start calculating Chinese calendars, I've decided that 18 April is the best I will do. Today – as on the same date last year – I have invited Sifu to dinner in celebration of Master Chee and the anniversary of Sifu's initiation.

The venue is a Japanese restaurant in a hotel. Our return to the scene of last year's dinner evokes painful memories of *sake* and a three-day hangover. I kept offering toasts with the chef, who came in and out of the kitchen in his apron to chat with Sifu. Now as Sifu orders a bottle of *sake* I protest that I'm teaching tomorrow. He bellows with laughter.

'Ha, ha! He's learned. Maybe you will not disgrace me this time.'

'I do like a little warm *sake*.'

'We say the *sake* that is heated is never the high quality.'

'Crude and Rough, eh?'

We sit at a bar that fronts the kitchen, so that Sifu can chat with passing staff. He explains that he knows the chef from his previous restaurant.

'Because I supported him in the early days, he always remembers me.'

The chef's gratitude amounts to what I call the Chan Menu. Beginning with sushi, we are treated to a procession of the best cuts of fish for a sum that is nominal in the scheme of fine Japanese food. The second benefit is that this kind of occasion often makes Sifu reflect on the past and bring up details I haven't heard before.

A waiter emerges with an enormous bottle of *sake*, some of which he decants into a small carafe with a niche in the front that holds ice-cubes. Sifu fills my glass to the top and I blanche.

'Come,' he says, raising his glass. 'No need for ceremony,' he adds as I attempt, in accordance with etiquette, to clink with my glass held at a lower level than Sifu's. He indicates the first food to arrive. 'This prawn with mayonnaise was the favourite of the Americans in Japan. Try.'

While we eat we discuss one of the final upheavals in Sifu's relations with the Chee Kim Thong Pugilistic and Health Society. In 2003 Sifu was invited to meet a couple of journalists in Kuala Lumpur. One wrote for the *The Star*, the other for the Chinese-language *Nanyang Business Daily*. Naturally, disaster ensued. When the resultant articles were published, the *Nanyang Business Daily* journalist referred to Sifu as Master Chee's successor.

'Cheng Hai got very angry. He *demanded* that I retract what I said because I hadn't been confirmed Old Man's successor, had never had a succession ceremony. I told him, "There's nothing for me to retract." In the interview I showed them the fan stamped by the Shaolin Abbot, and the certificate from Mr Chee which names me as Old Man's "most precious disciple." *I* never said I was successor. If other people say I am, it's not my fault.'

Cheng Hai seized, litigiously, on the distinction between 'precious disciple' and ordained 'successor,' faulting Sifu with the content of the article. Once more he enlisted a bureaucratically-minded friend to deal with the younger disciple. They composed a letter that expelled Sifu from the club all over again.

'I thought they couldn't expel you as a life member?' I say.

'Once Old Man is gone, who can stop them?' Sifu answers. 'Maybe I should have moved to KL. It was difficult to see the situation from Singapore. Here, try this octopus.'

Ironically, Cheng Hai was subsequently removed from the club's committee.

'It was when he tried to acquire the building for himself and turn it into a *feng shui* academy. He brought a load of guys he knew onto the committee who would vote in favour.'

'Yes Men.'

'Ah. But at the last minute, when they saw what was going on, the board had an emergency meeting. They passed a motion to restore the *old* committee. *Then* the committee voted to eject Cheng Hai from the board.'

'So he's out? Who's left in this damn club?'

'Only off the *board* so he can't do any mischief; he's not out completely. Here's your favourite, the yellowtail,' Sifu says as a sliced, raw fish appears alongside tuna, swordfish and salmon. Already I feel dangerously engorged.

'Wasn't Cheng Hai the chairman of the International *Wuzu* Federation?' I ask. The IWF is a China-based organisation that unites different *Wuzuquan* lineages for events. 'Doesn't that mean he has influence, traction?'

'So what? Do you know what it takes to be chairman? A red packet, RMB100,000. *You* could be chairman, if you could be bothered. And look at all the stupid things the *Wuzu* Federation does. They call themselves *dan* grades, the Japanese ranking system! After he's dead, they say they rank Mr Chee a tenth *dan*. Who are they to assess Mr Chee? They're nowhere near his ability. Then they say *they* are all tenth *dan* too. So they put themselves on the same level as Old Man!'

'I thought grading systems weren't traditional,' I say.

'They are not,' Sifu answers. 'Really, the sash doesn't have a knot in it. It's worn under the clothing. You can't even *see* it! Our sash is only there to protect the spinal column and prevent hernia, like a weight-lifter's belt. But we don't have all this black-belt rubbish.'

'So why would the *Wuzu* crowd adopt it?'

'To commercialize.'

I think back to Travis's criticism of martial-arts festivals: *Everyone clap, everyone happy, everyone get a medal. Westerners pay a lot of money.* I imagine a succession of banquets, toasts, group photographs and demonstrations.

'They exalt themselves,' Sifu continues, 'by saying they are as good as Mr Chee. Certain people want me to come back to the club in KL. I told

Mak Tian Meng I will do it if they send me a letter of invitation. I said also that I'll put an end to all of this *dan* grades rubbish; I'll make people send them back and stop making claims.'

'And?' I say.

He shrugs.

'And nothing.'

'It sounds like the whole club is rotten,' I say.

'That's what I said to Tian Meng. It seems there are people like Lim Chee Wah, Lian Ah Chaun and David Yap, who learned a lot from me but aren't allowed to teach in KL by the committee. I told Tian Meng to get hold of them and start again with a new school.'

'Is Tian Meng close to Cheng Hai?'

'Ha! I will not say he is *close*. But he tries to keep the peace. Cheng Hai told Tian Meng he would not go to the last *Wuzu* Federation event in Quanzhou. But then he did go with fifteen students. In effect, he bypassed the club.'

'It sounds like Cheng Hai's unsure whether he wants to be in the club himself. He's only certain he doesn't want *you* in it.'

* * *

Even the club committee-members who value Sifu's expertise from afar might be reluctant to yield their *gongfu* titles in exchange for his characteristically blunt advice. He is aware of this possibility, I think.

Occasionally Sifu tells of an episode late in his banking career, when he was deputy director of a major bank's operation in the Asia-Pacific region. The company sent Sifu on a training course at the University of Pennyvania's business academy, the Wharton School. The other attendants – to Sifu's chagrin – boasted glittering qualifications, but far less distinguished experience than he possessed. Additionally, the Americanized HR principles espoused in the seminar were at odds with Sifu's *modus operandi*. In their critiques of each other's methods, bankers called attention to Sifu's tyrannical manner. Fortunately, the course convenor came to Sifu's rescue.

'He said, "Mr Chan *has* to be assertive, he is the deputy director of the bank." His only suggestion,' Sifu goes on when he tells this story, 'was that I could be a little less direct. Instead of saying, "Chris, get me coffee," I should say, "Chris, would you mind getting me coffee, please?"'

This anecdote is one of Sifu's favourites for its supply of the word 'assertive,' one of his primary self-definitions. He understands that it's problematic to order people around, but can fall back on an incident in which a third party deems it acceptable for *Chan See-meng* to do so, and in which the practice is handsomely repackaged as 'assertive' behaviour. Yet to recount this episode does not necessarily – as he intends – convince the audience that special rules apply to Sifu. Certainly I can think of other ways to interpret the anecdote, and don't think assertiveness would be accepted as a prelude for a reign of terror at the Chee Kim Thong Pugilistic and Health Society. It is true that the *gongfu* club, like the bank, is a hierarchy. In the club, as at the bank, most committee members are vastly below Sifu's level. However, many on the committee are elderly and accomplished businessmen, who are not used to subjection. To tell them that they must now fall into line would ignore a truth of human nature.

That conflict may never arise. In years of discussion, Sifu's status as exile has not changed, despite strong support for him among committee members, both old-timers and younger practitioners who appreciate his depth of knowledge. Yet Sifu's vocal supporters are outnumbered; not most problematically by a few of Cheng Hai's allies, but by a deluge of club members who don't know or care about his level of expertise, and hence see no reason to rock the boat. It's one thing for me to gaze into the sea near Dungun and say that people should be left to their harmless fun, but quite another when the fate of the art requires informed assessment of potential leaders. Even people close to Master Chee fail to appreciate true comprehension, from Mak Tian Meng telling me to learn as many sets as possible, to Chee Boon Tiong naming Long-Arm Lum the exemplar of the comprehensive repertoire. Everyone in the club knows that Master Chee rated Sifu highly, but few apprehend what that *means*; consequently the attitude to Sifu's prospective management is, widely, indifference. The exhortation to return that Sifu craves is improbable. Therefore, an impasse: the club won't beg Sifu's services, and he won't volunteer. If Sifu's distance from the Society was externally effected at first, it is a matter of principle by now.

* * *

To expel Sifu again in 2003 didn't satisfy Cheng Hai. Shortly after the letter came, Sifu heard further reports from Malaysia.

'Cheng Hai had got a sixth *dan karateka* who was going to challenge me.'

Among serious martial artists, it's poor form to issue combat challenges. A traditional *gongfu* challenge progresses through the stages of push hands, demonstration and tests of sets, and free sparring. Either party can halt the process early if a clear difference of standards is evident between the contestants. To ask for combat outright is unconventional.

'What does a karate guy have to do with Master Chee's group?' I ask. 'You mean he was a sword for hire?'

'Yes.'

'But isn't it a humiliation for a martial artist to say he needs another fighter – from another *art* – to do his dirty work for him? What does that say about Cheng Hai's belief in himself, and his own students?'

For an alleged *gongfu* master to enlist a champion from another school appears an admission of total failure. Not only did he fail to attain a sufficient standard to compete for himself, but Cheng Hai's tuition yielded not a single worthwhile student to fight his corner. Louder than his expulsions of Sifu, this challenge by proxy screams, 'I cannot'. No wonder he attempted to convert the clubhouse from a place of martial arts, in which he encountered disappointment, to an academy of *feng shui*, the discipline to which he had diverted his reputation.

Perhaps hatred blinded Cheng Hai to the logic that a sword for hire signals weakness. To enlist a strongman is not the gesture of someone who cares about his own reputation or that of his organisation. In fact, the triumph of a *karateka* over the Old Man's Most Precious Disciple could finish off the reputation of Master Chee and his Society entirely. Cheng Hai was willing to bring the whole club crashing down. His desire to obliterate Chan See-meng consumed him even after their master's death. But there was no evidence that this *karateka* would be a match for Sifu.

'What do I care about this Karate sixth *dan*?' Sifu says. 'Karate is a hard art. In this kind of training the body deteriorates quickly. When a guy reaches sixth *dan* he's old, already finished as a fighter. Anyway, at this time I was coaching Singapore's Security Command, the VIP bodyguards.'

After he retired from the bank, Sifu spent several years as instructor of a group of bodyguards within Singapore's governmental Security Command. Every evening the Police Superintendent collected Sifu from home to lead the classes. Sifu taught the bodyguards a distillation of *Wuzuquan*'s most important techniques, including Swallow-Vomit, the Whip Punch and *Tiaoqie*. His own combat mentality changed during this period.

'Old Man was still alive when I started teaching the bodyguards. He said, "You can no longer hesitate in combat. If someone attacks you, you must put him down at all costs." I was shocked. In my younger days, Mr Chee was always telling me to be less aggressive. But now he said, "This is for the government, you can't play around."'

'One day, Old Man comes to watch and is so proud! He saw how good the students had become by specialization in just a few techniques.'

Inspired by this class, Master Chee phrased the 'Most Precious Disciple' document to specify that Sifu was allowed to teach the arts according to whatever method he wished. If Sifu had discovered a more modern and effective approach, the Old Man wished him to integrate it to tuition at the Society.

'Coming back,' Sifu says. 'When I was first asked to teach at the Security Command, they sent nine guys to test me, all second *dan karateka* at their physical peak. Young guys, in their thirties. So why should I worry about some old sixth *dan*?'

'What was the outcome?'

'This *karateka* decided not to get involved. That was the end of it. Then

I also challenged Yap Cheng Hai to meet me, not for a contest, but to air his grievances. I said since he is supposed to be such a devout Buddhist, he should meet me in the temple. Then he can swear before the statue of Buddha and Guan Yin and repeat all the bad things he says about me behind my back.'

Like the physical contest, the showdown in the temple never happened. Thus Sifu's last meaningful interaction with his sworn brother-initiate Yap Chang Hai was a wet squib. Even these final exchanges did not occur directly. The threats, retorts and rumours were relayed by third parties such as Mak Tian Meng and Tony Wong, the Tibetan lama's erstwhile navigator.

For dessert a waitress serves us green-tea flavoured ice cream.

'You see how I enjoy my life,' Sifu says after the first spoonful. 'You think I want all this trouble with Yap Cheng Hai? It's a waste of time.'

I agree that it is a waste of time, while reflecting that it's nonetheless unusual for Sifu to relinquish his commitment to *gongfu* and Chee Kim Thong so easily. Yet I don't feel entitled to raise the issue of Sifu's duty to the art. Having recounted his struggles with the club, Sifu should be allowed to enjoy his dinner.

'You know,' I say, steady-footed as we get up to leave, 'I think I may survive this time.'

26

NATURE

In the haze it looks more like Hong Kong than Singapore. The smoke has blown to us across the sea, from Indonesian forest-fires. *The fires are illegal*, choking Singaporeans have complained. *The fires are the work of Singaporean-owned companies*, others have retorted. At its worst the streets were deserted, the government issued hourly updates on the concentration of pollutants in the air, and the pharmacies sold out of protective masks. Sifu cancelled training sessions, concerned that deep breathing would be harmful to us in this atmosphere.

This morning the haze is less dense. The tower blocks stand shadowy in the gloom. I take the journey across Singapore by taxi. Still the roads are quiet. Vehicles are dotted so sparsely that I arrive very early for class. I emerge slightly queasy, a combination of the haze in my lungs and the Taxi Uncle's insistence on using an on-off, wah-pedal technique on the accelerator rather than applying steady pressure.

I see no-one as I linger a few minutes in the void deck of Sifu's building. Invisible in the grey half-light, a bypasser whistles – flawlessly – the riff from 'Gorky Park'. I ascend to the rooftop and warm up with the Eight Brocades exercise we learned last month. Now Sifu materialises from the obscurity. Order is restored.

'Most is blowing towards Malaysia now,' he says of a development that pleases many Singaporeans.

It's a Tuesday morning. Until recently only Sifu and Alex met at this time for a lesson on *Taijiquan*. A few weeks ago Alex invited me to join them. The official reason, he said, was that it would be easier to practice push hands with me than with Sifu, because the gulf in their standards was too great. I was glad for the chance of exposure to a different art. So far I have learned some of the *Taijiquan* partner-work and a few, isolated techniques. Alex can't attend class today, but I rose at six to make the usual time.

'What do you hope to learn today?'

'Whatever you say, Sifu.'

'Good. To me, *Taiji* is shit. Mr Chee's *Wuzu* is much more refined. *Luohan Ruyiquan*? Better still.'

'Why teach *Taiji*, Sifu?'

'*Aiya*! Alex makes me. He devoted years to *Taiji*. In a way this is good, because Mr Dong's techniques will not be lost.'

After a few moments' reflection, Sifu says, 'You are still a bit too hard. I want you to have more experience of soft arts. I will teach you Dong's short form, only thirteen movements. If you are interested, you can go back later and learn the whole form of 108 movements. Start this way.'

Usually we face lengthwise from the shaded end of the car park. For *Taiji* we position ourselves in the centre of the area and look across the rooftop into the haze.

'Today I will teach you Grasping the Sparrow's Tail. Watch.'

We Grasp the Sparrow's Tail up and down the car park, with one step for every set of hand techniques. I prolong my respiration to inhale and exhale once in each repetition. Sifu chants Mr Dong's favourite verse on coordinating the breath and motions:

> *When the sun goes down, the moon goes up;*
> *When the moon goes down, the sun goes up.*

We continue in silence, then Sifu sits and I seize the phantom bird alone.

'Still it is not done well,' Sifu says. 'There are three ways to perform. In *Taiji* we talk of the tiger, the crane and the snake. Not the same way we talk about these things elsewhere, ah? Ah. The tiger is the worst, the most stiff. Many clench their buttocks and ruin the whole set. At the moment you are a crane. For this art, you must learn to move the torso like a snake.'

Where he sits, Sifu coils his torso back and forth and repeats the hand motions.

'See? I come out like a dragon. When we practised in front of Mr Dong he would move this way in his chair, only his stomach area. I wondered, "What is this guy doing?" Then I saw that he followed the form mentally. His body moved along with us. Isn't it hypnotic?'

'I can feel it when I practice over and over.'

'Yes, you get into the rhythm. But this also is a very good fighting technique. You see when you attack with both hands' – Sifu motions for me to attack him, and parries, twists my arm, and pushes me back – 'I counter like this. You will vomit blood on the spot! Isn't this like our *Wuzu*'s Swallow-Vomit? You see what I mean when I say all arts are the same when they are done well?'

'I can see that the two techniques are similar solutions to one problem.'

'*Mmmmm*. To me, *Taiji* is quite flawed. It only became prominent because Yang taught at the Qing court. This also is why the art is done slowly. The opium addicts couldn't do the *Taiji* fast. In reality, I can do it slow or fast, or any damn way I want. This is why I sent on the old video of Cheung Gee Kwon. He does it fast, like Shaolin art.'

Sifu stands.

'See one more time.'

He demonstrates the entire thirteen-move set.

'I am no longer myself,' he says, still playing the pattern, 'I am now *Taijiquan*.'

'What do you mean,' I ask as Sifu sits once more, 'that you are "now *Taijiquan*?"'

'You must expand your consciousness, become magnanimous. Ask yourself: do you know who you are?'

Do I know who I am? It doesn't sound like a question to preoccupy the average sparrow-grasper. 'Magnanimous' is a word that Sifu uses in a beguilingly literal-minded way, to mean that the consciousness might expand from the restrictions of the self, outward into physical space.

'What does *Taijiquan* mean?' Sifu asks after a time.

'I've heard it translated as "Ultimate Fist."'

'OK. Forget about the "fist" part. Fighting is simple; *anyone* can learn to fight. When we say "ultimate," we mean the universe, all creation. To me, *Taiji* simply means "Nature."'

'So when you perform the set… You express a force of Nature, or *become* Nature?'

'Yes. This is why we talk of unity: *tian-di-ren*, Heaven, Earth and Man.'

Tian-di-ren refers to the harmony between humanity, material nature and the processes of nature. Sifu's use of 'Nature' with a capital *N* refers to this union. If we must succumb – if that is what Sifu is saying – to the fluctuations of universal energies, it sounds to me as though our actions are arbitrary expressions, with allegorical qualities. The act of turning this page satisfies a cosmic impulse that might equally be fulfilled by a breeze dragging a leaf along the pavement. If we unite *tian-di-ren* we can correctly perform Shaolin *gongfu*, but we may as well sit in meditation, or cultivate rock gardens. There are grounds to doubt our agency, and to wonder whether, when we perform certain actions, we have not done something else entirely that is, in Sifu's slippery cosmology, a karmic equivalent.

'And that's why,' I say, 'you can credit the art, or the masters, but not yourself?'

'In a way.'

The dissolution of self into universe underscores the paradox that to set oneself up as a master is an unwitting acknowledgement of incomprehension. Personality disintegrates at a certain point of expertise. A surge in my mind as though the broken lines that join the dots are appearing at last. A picture begins to reveal itself in which I see that the relationship of the practitioner to the world through the art also hints at the answer to a persistent question. Why does the tournament-winning Chan See-meng, his teacher's favourite, stand detached from Chee Kim Thong's club, when he could justifiably assert his authority and take charge?

'I don't want to run a *gongfu* club,' Sifu says.

'But Master Chee wanted you to,' I answer. 'And isn't the best kind of leader one who doesn't want that status?'

Furthermore, I try to explain, to me being director of the club, as an agent of the art rather than entirely self-interested, sounds similar to being one with Nature.

'I have told you what happened. The succession never occurred.'

'Aren't you afraid the art will be lost?'

'It will be lost. I don't know when.'

'But that doesn't – necessarily – have to do with whether or not there's an organisation? Is that what you mean, that martial-arts clubs just don't work? I've started to believe that.'

'They *can* work.'

I'm not getting the answers I expected. I feel close to the truth, but unable to grasp it. Sifu studies my expression.

'Paramahansa Yogananda tells a story,' he says. 'When he is running a school in India, a young deer comes to stay on the grounds. It grazes on the grass and drinks from the stream. All the schoolboys love this fawn, and Paramahansa Yogananda too comes to love it very much.

'Then one morning, the schoolboys come to him crying. The deer is very sick. They plead with the teacher to help. So the master takes the deer into the house and they tend to it. Its health improves a little bit and it appears that the deer may live.

'But then that night, the fawn appears in Yogananda's dream. It says, "I am destined to die. Why are you impeding my progress?" Yogananda realizes he should not interfere. He gathers the boys together and explains it to them. They cease tending to the deer, and in a short while it dies.'

'What the hell is that supposed to mean?'

'What must be, must be.'

Again he has switched abruptly between the metaphysical and banality: 'Come, let's have our breakfast.' As I put my sodden T-shirt into the rucksack he sets off a few paces ahead of me, inscrutable, now disappeared entirely into the fog.

Sifu cannot teach me this exercise. Bodhidharma is the teacher, he says. Therefore we set out today to perform an invocation. Will it succeed? 'If you have the affinity,' Sifu says. 'When I learned, my hands began to move, and I said to Old Man, "What's going on?" Mr Chee replied, "Bodhidharma is teaching you the technique."'

We are in Sifu's apartment. After practice I showered and changed into fresh clothes, because I must be clean to perform the ritual. We sit on the couch. Sifu has brewed us a pot of *The Guan Yin* and chopped a melon for us to eat, both of which are considered cleansing.

'Have you memorized the words I gave you?'

'Yes, Sifu.'

There is an altar by the window in the rear corner of Sifu's apartment. He has placed an offering of oranges in a bowl, and a glass of water to symbolise purity. Smoke emanates from an incense burner; I recall Sifu said that he always uses the 'high-quality incense'. Just like him to say something like that. All is ready to begin at noon, an auspicious time.

As we wait for Sifu's grandfather clock to strike midday I become apprehensive. If the invocation succeeds, what would that *mean*? 'You must merge into that plane,' Sifu said, but the referent of that instruction is unclear to me. Our fundamental *gongfu* practice is so worldly, so *physical*. Contemplation elaborates certain aspects of *gongfu*, such as energy and spirit, but Sifu explains these ideas in ways that makes them tangible. Now, though, we are set to plunge off a precipice into an abyss, from what little I understand. Unknown experience awaits in whatever bodily occurrence it is that constitutes Bodhidharma's Palm, which does not, Sifu says, conform to normal *gongfu* movements. Or, nothing awaits at all. I may stand there talking nonsense, to no effect.

Sifu said previously, 'If you ask me to explain how it works, I cannot.' If I have evidence that some external agent, unseen and unheard, teaches me Bodhidharma's Palm, does that compel me to believe in a world of invisible spirits, or that the Shaolin patriarch's wisdom can be retrieved from a cosmic consciousness that pervades the universe? Sifu has also said of *gongfu* practice that 'it is within us all,' buried, waiting to be discovered. If that kind of essentialism applied in this situation, it would mean that Bodhidharma's Palm would make itself known from *within* rather than without, or that the fulfilment of the inner potential is to connect with the cosmic consciousness. I decide simply that the rite is worth attempting. Sifu told me that he approached Bodhidharma's Palm from the disinterested position of cultural investigation. If this sort of procedure is possible – I have to find out, don't I?

Still a couple of minutes to go. I stand before the altar. I swallow saliva. What if the invocation doesn't work, and nothing happens? Sifu would shrug and say I lacked affinity with the art. I would begin to doubt him a little if tantalizing avenues of experience were closed to me on the unsatisfactory grounds of 'affinity'. There would be no reason for me *not* to conclude that Sifu was bluffing, talking nonsense with recourse to mysticism. I want to dodge this bullet, not to test our relationship in this way. But there's no getting out of it now.

The clock chimes. I look to Sifu. He nods.

'*I* ...'

There is a statue of Bodhidharma in a corner of the room, but Sifu told me to concentrate on a Buddha figure on the altar. This Buddha is seated in the lotus position.

'*Request you, Bodhidharma Svamiji* ...'

I close my eyes, but the silhouette of the seated Buddha remains in my vision like an after-image of the sun behind closed eyelids.

'*To teach...*'

And my hands begin to circle through the smoke in movements I haven't seen before.

27

BIG DOOR, SMALL DOOR

Five minutes from Sifu's building the light-rail system reaches Sengkang, where it connects with the purple line MRT. As I exit the carriage a man pushes against me to board ahead of the queue. With a subtle muscular contraction I apply the bouncing technique. He is confused to be pushed back, as it were, by his own shove, although I don't appear to have moved. It serves him right. *Please give way to alighting passengers* is essentially all that is asked of public-transport commuters, along with *No Durians, No Spitting* and *No Assault on Bus Captain*.

Down the escalator, through the station, across the motorway flyover, down the steps, I wait for the bus. There are seats upstairs. The air conditioning is arctic. No one assaults the Bus Captain. Half an hour along the Seletar Expressway the bus joins the red line MRT at Woodlands for the final stage of my journey. The train isn't busy so I get a seat without jostling.

Damen, xiaomen; the 'big door' and the small. All evening we practised footwork to step around an opponent. Footwork is strategic. The goal is to achieve a more favourable angle in relation to the antagonist. When the front door is closed, I try the side door. To adapt – *bian*, 'change' – is among the advanced four of the Eight Essences. This can refer to a minute wrist movement on contact, or a bigger shift in position, entire changes of tack to achieve an advantage.

'The front is the big door,' Sifu said, and used his index fingers to indicate a rectangle around Alex's torso. 'Let's say now the front door is shut. This means the guy is tough, or well-defended. So what? I won't hit him where he is strong; I'll go around to the side door and attack where he is soft.'

He jabbed Alex in the ribs to demonstrate.

I changed into a clean T-shirt after class, but my leggings are pungent. A preened young woman a few empty seats away looks at me incredulously when the odour wafts across the carriage. I make an apologetic face and she snaps her head away.

Don't jump, but *push* yourself sideways. Then two steps forward, each with an outward-circular motion of the rear foot, which becomes the front foot. Inhale as the feet move. The circles can test the terrain, sweep an opponent's feet, or deflect kicks. The complete drill is an evasive spring sideways, two steps forward, a spring to the opposite side, and one step back. Repeat.

'Your stance is too wide and too narrow,' Sifu said, confusing me.

I hope I don't leave a sweat patch behind me on the seat.

Tonight's emphasis was to cover ground and effect strategic positional adjustments.

I remove the towel from my rucksack and half-stand momentarily to place it beneath me.

The story, for the thousandth time, of how, as a teenager, he took dance lessons to impress local girls, and realized that the precise footwork was comparable to *gongfu*. Our steps look like a crane too, of course. A crane will lift its leg and step carefully, 'gingerly'.

In the masters' footsteps, so to speak.

The station names sound over the intercom.

'You can tell if the guy is a fighter from the way he covers distance.'

Chan See-meng's students must cover distance.

Marsiling. Kranji. Yew Tee.

Gradually Sifu complicated the exercise with turns. At times we all ended up facing in the wrong direction. Surprising that we didn't collide.

The carriage has filled up. The girl who glanced at me feigns sleep in case she is expected to yield her seat to the elderly.

Drag the feet against the ground. This is why the soles of our trainers go in holes.

But there was more than footwork at stake, wasn't there? The way he spoke?

'Not everything must be done in a straightforward way, in the obvious way,' Sifu said with an exasperated tone. 'This is the meaning of the big and small door.'

He was not merely frustrated by our performance. There are other ways to do things: it's a fairly obvious point. Often Sifu gives a vague prompt and expects a very specific response. It's rare for him to bother with subtext, so I knew that he was getting at something.

Too tired to consider the lesson in depth, for a few minutes I nod off where I sit, my feet still twitching in circles.

28

THE CHANGING
OF THE BONES

Fury when you attempt the corrected movement and still can't get it right. One hand blocks in a low arc while the other cuts high, simultaneous with a step forward, all impelled by the power of rotation at the waist. You notice that Sifu has ceased correcting you, and has focussed on Alex's attempt instead. He sees that the difficulty irritates you. At this stage you're not fearful of offending him. It's probable that you can't take any advice on board in this mood. Besides, Sifu seems to enjoy it when you're annoyed, possibly because he was much the same as a young man.

'When I was hot-headed, Old Man would say, "Let See-meng alone, he will calm." Sometimes he would make me sit down and meditate. When he didn't want to look at me any more, he would send me off to make tea, even though this is the job of the juniors.'

Meditation! Or *contemplation*. A whole other area of practice in which you feel, likewise, that you have made no advancement, and might continue in that way if you sat in the lotus position until the end of time. Despite mysterious invocations of Bodhidharma, and peculiar sensations during contemplation – which might lead you to conclude that you have reached an inner realm of *gongfu* practice – you feel that you continue to struggle with the same, old things.

Lately it has been like this. In addition to the perceived lack of progress, you have experienced almost continuous discomfort. Your shoulders have been tender for months on end, the cumulative effect of the daily 'specializations' that tug at your tendons. On the MRT home this week your joints burned. After your last session with Sifu you collapsed into bed feeling like acid corroded your body.

Tonight's practice makes your blood boil. Awareness that this emotion is irrational only causes it to increase by contrariety. As your relationship with Sifu has deepened, he has acquired the ability to irritate you like a relative would. You want to be able to perform the technique; you don't want to be told that you are doing it wrongly; you don't want to *tell* yourself it is right when it is probably not. The dire feeling that the technique hasn't improved despite your close attention, intensified by the unwelcome remembrance of finger-wagging Zen wisdom which tells you that you should not hope for progress. You reflect on the character flaw that leaves you unable to simply enjoy a hobby. Instead, this pursuit of an enigmatic and impossible paradigm of mastery. Would it be better to live in happy oblivion under a coloured-belt system, with achievement doled out regularly on a fixed and unambitious scale?

At the end of class, you apologize to Sifu for being moody. The anger settles down – not disappears – deep within your centre. You tell Sifu about your recent practice.

'This pain is the Changing of the Bones,' he says. 'You will feel like your whole body is having a fever.'

'So pain can be a kind of milestone?'

'If it is the correct sensation.'

There's more to it. You describe the dissatisfaction you have experienced in recent practice. The techniques, you say, seem inadequate in ways you can't specify or rectify. Simply, they *feel* wrong.

'I'm glad you are having this feeling,' Sifu answers. 'This is a sign you are trying to burst through to the next level. Hey, this is not me being so smart, this is Mr Chee! All it means is that you are ready for the next stage, the higher art. About time. I've been waiting for you two; now I'm ready to impart.'

The Changing of the Bones: into what?

V

RAIN

29

TOO MANY SIFUS

There's a mix-up on my arrival in China, so the hotel manager upgrades me to an immense suite that overlooks Xiamen and its neighbour, the smaller island of Gulangyu. The city is prosperous once more and the waterfront under my window teems with tourists on their summer holidays. They linger near street performers, and queue for ferries that make the short trip across to Gulangyu, 'Drum Wave Island,' where the waves pound against the cliffs. They cycle by the sea. They gather to watch games of chess at stone, street-side tables that have boards embedded in their surfaces. Some spectators place bets on which Chess Uncle will win. It is a Special Economic Zone, a pocket in which Socialism with Chinese Characteristics amounts to rampant capitalism. This is modern Xiamen, suggestive to my mind of an urbanized Cornwall, half-encircled by low mountains. I imagine that as a beauty spot the city remains like it was when the young Ah-Thong moved here in the 1920s; at least so the green-blue appears in my viewpoint, which allows me to look back in time and disregard modernity, distant beneath my window. However, historic Xiamen was a dangerous slum, and Chee Kim Thong had little time to appreciate scenery.

The hotel manager invites me to have dinner and see Xiamen's nightlife. I have a free afternoon on this first day in Fujian province, and explore the coast. Twice, on different pretexts – passports and foreignness – I am refused entry as a visitor to Xiamen University. While I stand aside to plan my next move, I notice that those who get past the security guards call them 'Sifu'. Several taxi journeys teach me that local drivers too expect to be addressed as 'Sifu'. The only formality I expected in the service industry was that I might have to call a manager *laoban*, 'boss'. Now I suspect that, had I addressed the first guard as 'Sifu,' I would have been ushered in to stroll through Xiamen University, with sunshine above and government-approved ice cream in hand.

By the time I meet the hotel manager for dinner, I'm impressed that there must be a great many Sifus in Xiamen. I intend to ask Roger about local nomenclature, but it transpires that he has his own term for the city's tireless public-servants. He has lived in Asia for thirty years and, in addition to Mandarin, speaks fluent English with a Swiss-German accent. Roger carries a faint smile and a man-of-the-world air. I get the sense that nothing ever surprises him.

After dinner at the hotel, we decide to visit some bars uptown. We wait for a taxi outside the hotel, but none will drive up to the rank by the door.

'These bastards,' Roger says through closed teeth, as the nth passengerless taxi sails by on the main road in front of the hotel.

'They can see us waiting here.'

We walk to the main road to improve our chances of finding a willing taxi driver. After a few minutes a car stops for us. As I close the door a bypasser flicks flyers for prostitutes in to land on the seat. The man turns away with satisfaction when the business card he tosses for one pimp lands upright, wedged between two seat cushions. The car begins to move. A vomit-proof cover on the upholstery prevents use of the seatbelts.

Although our destination is a short distance along the coast, the driver turns in the wrong direction so he can circumnavigate the island and run up a high fare.

'These bastards,' Roger exclaims again after he corrects the driver, who is soon engrossed in a phone call through a wireless headset, which he conducts with deliberate, languid mumble. It's a kind of double bluff, as though he wants to appear casual through negotiations of an important matter, but is keen that we should notice the pretence.

'They're all from Henan province,' Roger says. 'They come down here to drive taxis, the bastards.' To the driver: 'You're from Henan, aren't you, you bastard? Hey! *Ni cong Henan lai, ma?*'

222

The driver smirks and turns his attention away from his phone call momentarily.

'*Shi.*'

He mutters on the phone again. Triumphant, Roger continues:

'Heh, heh. You bastard.'

The driver blasts his horn at a woman who pushes an old man in a wheelchair over a pedestrian crossing. Roger raises his eyebrows as if to say, 'This guy is some bastard'.

We step out of the car at another of Xiamen's luxury hotels. Roger pauses to light a cigarette, and tells me he opened this hotel. The taxi jerks away down the road, the still-conversant driver concerned with more important matters than road safety. Inside we order a beer at the hotel's German microbrewery, a relatively new luxury in the area. Loud drinkers occupy one large table, but the cavernous bar is otherwise empty.

'When he opened it the owner charged 100 renmibi for a half-litre, and no-one came,' Roger says. 'He's cut his prices, but it's still too expensive for these bastards.'

'It looks like they're not quite used to German beer,' I say as two revellers collide en route to the men's room.

We move on to Haiwan Park and drink at a few of the bars that overlook the bay. The establishments are stylish but too Westernized. Alleys off Xiamen's main, coastal road held more promise on my earlier explorations: shadowy food-markets, street-side restaurants and peculiar antique–stores. But Moneyed Xiamen is too much like Moneyed Everywhere Else for my taste, even if the beer is cheaper than in Singapore.

I am reluctant to reveal that the purpose of my visit is a *gongfu* pilgrimage. Instead I tell Roger about Sifu's wish to open a traditional English pub in China.

'Although this man has a lot of schemes,' I conclude.

'He'll be alright if he knows how things are done here,' Roger responds. 'One of my European friends got shut down because he didn't understand how it works. It's the same with that microbrewery. This isn't Germany. The owner needs to figure out how things work here.'

'You mean greasing the wheel?' I say. Roger nods.

'It's the officials. The bastards all want bribes.'

We finish our drinks and walk out to the main road, where we flag down another taxi to drive us back to the hotel. This time Roger smokes out the window and chats with the driver, while I reflect that mastery to one man is illegitimacy to another.

30

WHAT COMES FROM SHAOLIN RETURNS TO SHAOLIN

The Abbot is taking his nap. Come back in two hours.

To kill time we explore the grounds. There are so few monks and visitors to be seen that our arrival – although by the front gate – had the air of infiltration. The atmosphere impresses dog day rather than diligence. Most of the *gongfu* tourism takes place in nearby Quanzhou, in short-term residences for wide-eyed enthusiasts who believe they will absorb the magic of their location. The city is populated by various schools that claim allegiance with South Shaolin, with many gradations of entitlement. Quanzhou is primarily an industrial place. The journey between train station and temple is all I intend to see of it.

Sabrina insists that we pause in the Great Buddhist Hall so she can make a wish for her birthday, which is today; I reckon it's her twenty-eighth. She lights a joss stick and kneels silently before an immense Buddha. Yesterday she told me she wasn't religious, and said immediately afterward that she hopes she will be a man in her next incarnation.

After the birthday wish – details of which remain secret – we explore the temple complex. Sabrina takes some photos on her phone, which she promises to relay to me by e-mail. While she takes pictures, I contemplate the slogan on her T-shirt, which reads:

Love

Not
Missiles

The style of architecture in the temple complex – red lacquer on the wooden supports; tiled roofs that slope down then curl up lazily, like the tail of a reclined dragon – is a gathering of familiar friends, since Singapore is so heavily indebted to Fujian culture. Three temples in Fujian province claim to be the site of the historic South Shaolin Temple, based on archaeological discoveries. Fuqing appears to have a strong case, but Quanzhou has seized the initiative. Construction began here in the 1980s and is ongoing. Placards describe projected additions to the monastery and offer opportunities to sponsor roof slates or donate larger sums. There are photos of the mayor, the Chinese premier and dignitaries in hard-hats as they lay keystones and shovel symbolic, inaugural cuts of earth.

Our progress has the creeping quality of guerrilla warfare; in and out of buildings based on how long we can tolerate the sun.

Amituofo …

'Do you hear something?' I say.

Amituofo …

'Oh yeah …' Sabrina says.

Amituofo …

We follow the sound to a tree on the Meditation Pavilion. There are several lotus-flowers made of pink plastic attached to the branches. We find that, amidst its plastic petals, the anther of each lotus has an inbuilt speaker that emits the Buddhist salutation at regular intervals.

Something strikes me as off key when Sabrina exchanges pleasantries with a gardener, who snips at a bush with shears. Historically, Shaolin monks were assigned the chores of cooking, cleaning and gardening. I'm surprised to encounter paid helpers such as this gardener and the janitor we spoke to earlier, a kindly old woman who warned us against the expensive tearoom upstairs.

Sabrina – who goes as Yu Lan in Chinese – is the interpreter I hired in case the Abbot offers a scintillating interview. By SMS, Sifu says he doesn't think he knows this 'young 'un'. First of all, the personnel at South Shaolin have changed since his last visit. Secondly, the Abbot who stamped the fan and certificate that Master Chee gave Sifu was the Internal Abbot, who didn't usually have any contact with outsiders. While the northern Shaolin focuses on demonstration *wushu*, the southern temple has adopted *Wuzuquan* as its primary art. My hope is that the present External Abbot might have studied at this temple on one of the occasions when Chee Kim Thong or Sifu visited to teach *gongfu*. There is, at least, the written record of the *Wuzuquan* lineage that the Internal Abbot amended on Master Chee's final visit.

We sit on a bench shaded by trees. A group of boys assembles in the courtyard before the Main Shrine Hall. A burly instructor lines them up. He wears yellow robes yet – his head unshaven – is not a monk. Evidently the boys are summer-campers on their first day. The teacher devotes considerable time to making them stand up straight and form neat rows. The boys prove resistant material to this process, which exhausts its fascination as a spectacle quite quickly. On the adjacent bench, one man nudges another and nods towards me. My posture is conspicuously straight, so in this context it's reasonable to infer that I study *gongfu*. Sabrina notices too and adjusts her posture.

In the gift shop I ask to inspect a silver statuette of Guan Yin, but in my hand I see that it is plastic. It stands on a base of transparent plastic flecked with small, white squares.

'It's all crap.'

I don't mean to say that the entire *temple* is ill-advised. The buildings and greenery are beautiful; it's just that unusual decisions have made to flesh out this skeleton. The temple reminds me of the Chee Kim Thong Pugilistic and Health Society headquarters. While I find this an impressive facility, I wonder what goes on within these walls nowadays. My curiosity about the personnel at South Shaolin deepens.

'What time is it now?'

* * *

The Abbot will not see you.

We're talking to two monks with shaved heads and mustard-yellow robes, whom we found slouched in a corner over their mobile phones. One referred me proudly to his elder, considered an authority on *gongfu* history. They are loud and have twitchy eyes. They tend to let their mouths hang open, a habit that always irritates me for a reason I can't identify. With relish the elder monk gives me the *nobody-sees-the-Abbot* line.

'I come from Chee Kim Thong's school,' I say.

He snorts.

'Chee Kim Thong is dead.'

'I study with his disciple, Chan See-meng.'

He squints.

'I haven't heard of Chan See-meng.'

'Chan See-meng taught at this temple in 2003 and 2007. He lives in Singapore.'

Agape, he scratches.

'There is no *Wuzuquan* in Singapore,' the monk says, jerking his head when he speaks. 'Chee Kim Thong's son in Malaysia inherited all his arts. He came to a meeting here,' one of the *gongfu* festivals the temple hosts with performances, photo opportunities and medals. The last statement had an air of finality, and I decide to leave.

'From what you saw of those monks,' I say to Sabrina as we amble downhill towards the exit, 'do you think their *gongfu* is likely to be any good?'

'No,' Sabrina replies. 'They were typical Quanzhou types. They're probably not real monks. People get grants from the government to study Buddhism here.'

Crude and rough.

Silently I chide myself for having indulged the notion that there might be experts at Shaolin, despite learning long ago that there is little in a name or a declared affiliation. North Shaolin is a notorious tourist-trap. Should a declared allegiance to *Wuzuquan* make the South any better?

On our way out of the temple complex I linger to inspect the Stone Archway. In relief are carved illustrations of Shaolin practice and historical incidents. The most famous is the episode in the seventh century when the thirteen monks supposedly helped the prince defeat the last Sui emperor. Thus Shaolin became nationally heroic. It was redeemed from the suspicion once afforded to its imported Buddhism. A millennium later, Shaolin *gongfu* would be considered quintessentially Chinese, a symbol of resistance to foreign oppression. Yet to communicate Shaolin's nationalist credentials, the arch portrays a legend of monks fighting alongside the future emperor. In reality, the monks did no more than eject a common enemy from their own territory; a feat undertaken in the temple's own interests.

I don't feel any connection to this place. Sifu's opinion is ambivalent. While he is the globe-trotting investigator of masters, detector of frauds, he also likes the idea of affiliation. He refers to A-Levels – the school leavers' exams – as 'my *Cambridge* A-Levels'. His talk is decorated with the names of illustrious financial institutions and government bodies and, indeed, allusions to the British Empire when that rhetoric suits. Sifu speaks of Shaolin tradition as an abstract concept, a set of ideals such as heroism, justice and discipline. The difference between us, I suppose, is that I find the ideals of Shaolin too greatly displaced by the Quanzhou temple, while Sifu endorses the association by, for example, returning the art to Shaolin. This requires a person to overlook the reality for the sake of the paradigm. Perhaps Sifu did so only out of duty to the Old Man. At the conclusion of his stay in 2007, the Abbot asked him to return and teach for several months. At first, Sifu was excited by the invitation, which might lead him to find a successor. The bad news was that Sifu was expected to pay his own expenses for travel, food and accommodation.

'That's not an honour,' I said. 'That's an invoice.'

In the taxi to Quanzhou Station, Sabrina asks me about the monk's declaration that Sneaky Snake is heir to Chee Kim Thong's arts.

'Is the master's son always the best?'

'A master's son is hardly *ever* the best,' I say, mystified at the way people suspend normal logic in *gongfu* discussions, as though the eternal precepts of talent and effort don't apply, and the art is imparted solely by supernatural transference.

Quanzhou's inter-city train station shines with metallic newness and unkept promises. For what seems eternity, we queue to collect our seat reservations, and then proceed to the platform. The escalators have, inexplicably, been turned off permanently. Notices announce that completion of the elevators has been relegated to an indeterminate future. Old women struggle up the stairs with loads strapped onto their backs. The train is punctual. The first-class carriages look impressive but feel fragile beneath us, a floating IKEA of veneered crappiness.

'Can you fly?' Sabrina asks when we're seated on the train for Xiamen. It's the latest in a series of questions about my abilities.

'No,' I say. Then I add: 'Maybe in another month or so.'

The train speeds between the two coastal cities. Taiwan lies nearby. One of Master Chee's *gongfu* brothers, a monk, fled to Taiwan during the Japanese occupation. *That* would have been a monk worth meeting. Perhaps he is there still, ancient, in retirement.

Back in Xiamen, the sun sets over Yundangnei Lake. Finally I give in to Sabrina's pestering and agree to teach her some *gongfu* in the park, amurmur now that the heat subsides with joggers, dog walkers and a group of *Taijiquan* players whose leader smiles as we pass.

'I'll show you our Heavy Hand technique,' I say when we find a quiet spot. I demonstrate the motion with the edge of my palm, and then offer my forearm.

'Chop my arm,' I say. Sabrina cuts at my limb cautiously, then with greater enthusiasm. When I'm satisfied, I add more detail.

'Do it in a relaxed way, so you're deadweight. You don't need to use much force, just make sure it's the right kind of strength.'

Sabrina complies. I feel greater power in her strokes. Momentarily a loose dog investigates us.

'Now,' I add, 'instead of aiming for *here*, the top of my arm, aim *here*: out the other side, as though your hand will go through me.'

She bites her lower lip and shakes her head. She's afraid she'll hurt me. I teach her the final two movements to complete the technique: *cut, parry, retaliate*.

'That's fast,' Sabrina says.

'The more relaxed and heavy it is, the faster it becomes.'

It's nearly dark, time for me to return to my hotel and recuperate for tomorrow's expedition. Sabrina runs a few paces ahead, mildly hysterical from the day's caffeine.

'Do you think it's strange that a Westerner is in China teaching *gongfu* to a Chinese girl?' I ask.

She giggles and swipes at imaginary arms.

I have enjoyed today. In different circumstances, the encounter at Shaolin could have been a significant disappointment. Whatever paradigm I associate with the place is not threatened by its fluctuations of personnel, who have no greater claim to the tradition than I, nor by its building projects, nor the wares of its gift shop. However, the emotional effects of the visit to Shaolin are nullified, above all, by its minor consequence to my purpose in China. The real pilgrimage in Fujian concerns another temple entirely, and another art, the Old Man's greatest treasure.

31

YOUR HEART'S DESIRE

'For the first couple of years we didn't know Mr Chee had this other art,' Sifu told me. 'Then one year at the annual performance for our ancestors, on the anniversary of our initiation, he demonstrated *Luohan Ruyiquan*. We asked each other, "What is this?"'

Sifu had a chance to learn the mysterious *gongfu* in 1963 when two businessmen approached Chee Kim Thong for assistance. They had a considerable background in *Taijiquan*, but asked Master Chee whether he knew any exercise that offered greater medical benefit. The master replied that he could help them. He recommended that the pair learn *Luohan Ruyiquan*.

'But everyone can't just learn direct from Old Man,' Sifu said. Master Chee decided that he would teach the soft art to Sifu, who would pass it on in turn to the elderly students, 'a Mr Ng and a Mr Chong'. Master Chee supervised the classes and answered questions, but did not perform the techniques himself.

The financial incentive must have been exceptional; nonetheless, the two businessmen acquired only a familiarity with *Luohan Ruyiquan*'s first section, certainly not mastery. The Old Man's motives are difficult to fathom. *Gongfu* and commerce do not mix well. The encounter with the businessmen inspires Sifu to cite the story of the *Taijiquan* patriarchs Yang Chengfu and Chen Chanxing: 'You think your money can *buy* my art?' However, Sifu came from a rich family, and reached the lucrative heights of banking; Chee Kim Thong was a peasant whose livelihood depended on the uncertain market-value of his skills. I have no doubt that the businessmen must have possessed good *Taijiquan*; lacking this base, they would not have benefitted from study of *Luohan Ruyiquan*. Thus, the art was not simply for sale to any buyer at the right price. Yet I wonder whether Master Chee might have given the callers a different answer on another day.

Sifu's knowledge of *Luohan Ruyiquan* was relatively superficial at this time, 'only the shell'. He learned the set quickly from the Old Man and taught what he knew over the course of a few months at one of the businessmen's houses. Typically, Master Chee volunteered little. For his part, Sifu did as he was told. I suspect he assumed that the soft art was chosen simply because *Wuzuquan* was too rigorous for these students. It's probable that this apparently gentle practice had less appeal for the young and combative Chan See-meng. Others in Chee Kim Thong's circle felt differently. Although Master Chee didn't intend for his terseness to entice, *Luohan Ruyiquan* became a subject of fascination among his followers. They referred to the practice as the 'Elderly Set' because of the circumstances in which the unknown *gongfu* came to light in Kuala Lumpur.

Meanwhile, Master Chee was equally enigmatic about the medical needs of Ng and Chong. In the Old Man's plan, Sifu was to supply the treatment, but was not to know of the ailment.

'When I had taught them their new movements,' Sifu explained, 'Old Man told me to go off and practice my *Wuzuquan*.'

Sifu heard snippets of conversation as Master Chee answered the businessmen's questions. Occasionally there were unexplained titters.

'I tried to sneak over and hear. They mentioned something called the "White Crane Shoots into the Sky,"' Sifu recalled. 'But if I tried to listen, Mr Chee would send me away to stand in the corner, and start whispering. He said, "He's too young to hear these things." You know, an old-fashioned type. But the two guys said, "Let him listen."'

'"White Crane Shoots into the Sky,"' I repeated. 'Is that some kind of technique in *Ruyi*?'

'These two rich men,' Sifu answered, 'each kept a number of wives, like traditional Chinamen. Showing off. But they were getting old. They needed help to service all these wives. This is why they went to Mr Chee.

I discovered that "White Crane Shoots into the Sky" means having an erection.'

Within a few months the businessmen learned the first section of *Luohan Ruyiquan* and were satisfied. Sifu continued to concentrate on *Wuzuquan*. In later years, Master Chee conjured sequences for students who demanded new routines, but he did not offer them *Ruyi*, and refused outright those who requested it. Students heard legends of an art called 'Elderly Set' and reasoned why it was so.

Because it rejuvenates an ancient master for combat, they said.

Because it requires the wisdom of age, they said.

In time, club members accepted those speculations as truth. Master Chee's performance for the ancestors, and the two elderly men who needed to pleasure their wives, faded from memory.

Nearly two decades passed before Sifu had cause to think of the soft art. It did not occur to him in that interval that in all of his *gongfu*, *Luohan Ruyiquan* would be his greatest pursuit. At the heart of the story a statue on the altar in Sifu's living room, where the incense burns.

32

THE GODDESS OF MERCY

In 1980, Master Chee announced suddenly that he would visit Sifu in Hong Kong. The Old Man was increasingly frustrated with the club in Kuala Lumpur. Hong Kong offered escape and an opportunity to discuss martial arts with someone who understood. Additionally, Chee Kim Thong came with agenda.

'Whenever we talked about the low standards in KL, I would get myself into trouble,' Sifu said. 'Old Man would always say, "You must come back and teach them." But he knew I don't want to run a *gongfu* club. So Mr Chee wants to know, who *will* run the club when he's gone? This is a real concern for Old Man. When I moved to Hong Kong, Cheng Hai was very happy. He told Old Man, "We found one Chan See-meng, we can find another," but they couldn't find a talent.

'So I went to collect Old Man from the airport. All the way in the car he gave me hell, scolding me for playing squash. He said, "It does nothing for you, for your health."'

Squash, rather than *gongfu*, injured Sifu's knees. The Old Man berated him for neglecting martial arts.

'I said to him, "Nearly forty years old already; what do I want more *gongfu* for? I don't want to do all those silly things they learn in KL: Beggar's Art, and Dog-Hitting Stick, and 108-Drunken-Don't-Know-What."

'Then the Old Man referred to himself in the third person. He said, "Sifu only has a few bits of treasure for you." I told him, "I don't want to learn!" But Old Man answered, "Sifu wants you to learn." With this I knew he had me; I could not argue.'

Master Chee phrased his wish to evoke Sifu's oath of obedience two decades previously. While Sifu grumbled, he knew he would have to concede to his teacher's wishes. As they negotiated the traffic to his home in Repulse Bay, Sifu wondered what the Old Man had in store. But when Chee Kim Thong entered Sifu's apartment and saw the Goddess of Mercy, he froze.

The statue of Guan Yin with a Thousand Hands was a recent arrival in Sifu's home. Years later he brought it to Singapore, where it stands next to a bowl of oranges, an incense burner and various Buddhist and Hindu artefacts. Guan Yin joins two hands before her chest in prayer. In front of her abdomen, two further hands support a small pagoda. Many additional arms reach down, up and to her side, forming a flame shape of hands around her body. Some hands hold implements; most reach out empty. The Thousand Hands enable Guan Yin – the one who hears the complaints of the world – to assist the needy. The tip of her crown forms the tiny figure of a seated Buddha. Sifu's acquisition of the statue was a charity of sorts.

'One day in 1980,' Sifu said, 'I received a call to ask if I was interested in a statue of Guan Yin from China. It had been ordered specially by my friend Rosalyn. Then the statue was carried all the way from China by a nun, because it had to be treated in a certain way, according to the people in the temple. This is the belief, ah? She would not let it touch the ground, or put it on seats used by other people. This would degrade the statue, so to speak. So, this nun tied it to her back. When she sat down, she rested the statue on her lap, never on the floor. Can you imagine? All the way from Fujian to Hong Kong like this.

'But by the time the nun reached Hong Kong, Rosalyn's father had died. "In these circumstances," my friend explained, "the deity cannot enter the house." So the nun had come all the way from China, and Rosalyn could not accept the statue. Over the phone my friend said to me, "I know you like to collect these things." He explained to me that this was something special; a replica of the Guan Yin with a Thousand Arms statue in a temple called Nanputuo. I told him, "Sure." The requested donation for the statue was HK$1,200, but I offered $2,000 as a donation. So Daphne and I drove all the way to North Point in Hong Kong to pick it up from a nunnery.'

When Master Chee's trance broke, he busied himself about the statue wordlessly. Sifu watched in bemusement as the Old Man searched the room until he found a yellow cloth, which he placed under Guan Yin. Next he fetched Sifu's statues of the Shaolin figures Bodhidharma and Bai Yu Feng to rest on either side of the Goddess of Mercy. He lit joss sticks, prostrated himself before the statue, and prayed.

'Then after some time, the Old Man said, "You are ready to learn the higher arts."'

Master Chee asked if Sifu was aware where the statue was from.

'I said, "Nanputuo." Old Man said, "Your ancestor is from Nanputuo."'

He referred neither to Lim Hian nor Yong Yeuk, but the Zen master who taught him *Luohan Ruyiquan* and, according to Boon Tiong, adjusted the Old Man's index finger. The two met in the late 1930s.

'When he was in Xiamen,' Sifu said, 'Mr Chee became tri-state *gongfu* champion. Soon after, he received a challenge from a monk. This monk was sent to test whether Mr Chee's *gongfu* was as good as his reputation.'

As a result of the challenge, Master Chee was invited to meet the monk's master, known as Yi Chan Chan Shuai. This title, which means 'a great Zen master,' designated an Abbot.

'Was he based at Nanputuo itself?' I asked.

'I don't know,' Sifu answered. An ascetic and a renunciate, Yi Chan Chan Shuai lived among the immense boulders above Nanputuo, the temple that sprawls along the southern base of Wulao Peak. We speculated that the Abbot might have fled the northern Shaolin temple in Henan province at the time of its most recent incineration in 1928, or one of the affiliate temples burned by order of the same warlord, but other than the art there is little evidence of his existence. Whenever Ah-Thong arrived at this master's home, he found Yi Chan Chan Shuai seated on a high table, deep in meditation. It would take half an hour, the Old Man told Sifu, for the master to return to the mundane world from this state, gradually restoring the feeling in his limbs. In turn, he appears to have slipped out of this world almost without trace.

With more pedestrian concerns, Sifu was relieved that he did not have to learn the same 'silly things' as the students in Malaysia, but remained cautious about Master Chee's plans.

'Mr Chee said, "The whole world has asked me to teach this and I turned them down. Now I'm asking you to learn. Will you learn?"

'I asked him, "What are the prerequisites of this training? Do I have to give up alcohol, or red meat, or sex? I mean to say, what's the point in being alive if I can't drink, or womanize?"

'Old Man said, "You don't have to give up those things. The only requirement is that you have good character. If your character is not good you will vomit blood, and the blood will be black in colour."

'So I answered, "Sifu, I don't think I can learn. I don't have a good character." Old Man said, "Of course you do!" I told him, "No, my character is bad. I'm very bad-tempered. I can't stand being around idiots."'

Master Chee reassured Sifu that his character sufficed. Red meat and alcohol were not under theat. The Old Man persuaded his disciple to undertake the new practice for deeper comprehension of *Luohan Ruyiquan*. On this occasion at least, Sifu did not vomit blood.

Chee Kim Thong began to visit Hong Kong monthly for intense sessions on the soft art. Sometimes he brought his son Boon Teck, and a few senior club members such as Mak Tian Meng, but he sent them away on errands during the secretive *Ruyi* practice. The Old Man corrected movements and performed Mother and Child practice with Sifu. When they rested, they discussed *gongfu* theory. Their conversations led Master Chee to demonstrate wonderful techniques that are now lost. On one occasion the Old Man misheard Sifu make a comment about energy. In the belief that Sifu had asked about the effect of mantras on the body, Master Chee demonstrated a breathing technique that incorporated chanting in a manner that none present had ever witnessed. On Master Chee's invitation, the students found themselves powerless to attack him, according to Sifu. Some speculated that the Old Man must have repelled the Malay mob with this technique.

They were happy. As Sifu and Master Chee practised together privately and discussed theory in detail, it was like the old days in KL.

'Early in the morning, Daphne would wake me. She said, "You need to get up. Your Sifu is waiting." *Click, click, click,* Mr Chee went around our training room and turned on all the lights. I would find him standing there in his black suit, so impressive! I wish I had a photo of him like this.'

The visits to Hong Kong were doubly significant for Master Chee's legacy. While the Old Man ensured the survival of his treasure, he also acquired material to appease his club members' appetite for novelty.

'People were always asking Old Man for new arts,' Sifu said. 'Beggar's Art, the legendary doctor Hua Tuo's exercises, anything they had heard of, they imagine is some wonderful art, they want to learn. Anything except work at the real training! When I was at work, Mr Chee went off to the bookstores. He would find all the old books on these arts.'

Provided the books were authoritative, Master Chee could perceive the essential characteristics of the arts, which he used to devise new exercises for those who pressed him in KL.

Perhaps he did the right thing. The students were oblivious to Master Chee's exhortations to specialize, to excel in a small selection of techniques. With this attitude, they could never become good at *gongfu*. In the Old Man's position, I think I would turn such students away and hope for more dedicated practitioners. By humouring their fascination with new sequences, Chee Kim Thong could at least attend to the flexibility and aerobic fitness of the club members, a kindness towards their dilettantism. To acquire superficial knowledge of many techniques is to manifest the same mediocrity over and over, but most participants didn't know the difference. Even in modest efforts, most students would only persist if the material enticed them as new. I feel now that – in his reticent way – the Old Man did his best.

Luohan Ruyiquan is not a light undertaking. A student who studied in a weekly class, without a good foundation in *gongfu*, would struggle even to remember the opening sequence, and the details would be lost. These problems would be magnified in a group setting: at best, that *Ruyi* would be a flowery dance. As such, the Old Man was correct to withhold *Ruyi* from popular consumption. When Sifu returned to live in Singapore, he taught *Ruyi* to a group whenever he visited KL. The class, which continued for two years, included such luminaries as Long-Arm Lum and Peter Seow. Sifu says their attainment was slight. I suspect Master Chee approved of the class only as it compelled Sifu to think even more about his own *Ruyi*.

There was much more of *Luohan Ruyiquan* for Sifu to learn than what he imparted to the businessmen in the 1960s. The first section laid the energetic groundwork. Later stages of the art develop *fajin* – explosive power – and more direct combat applications. Twenty years later, Master Chee's most talented disciple had still not explored the full possibilities of this art. What sufficed the sexual health of two elderly men merely scratched the surface of *Ruyi*, the Old Man said. *Luohan Ruyiquan* would dominate their time together from the first meeting in Hong Kong to the secretive sessions in Master Chee's clinic twenty years later. The Old Man exerted himself with Mother and Child practice to boost Sifu's ability. Because of these efforts, some club members say that my Sifu killed Chee Kim Thong.

* * *

Among the boulders on Wulao Peak – of the Five Old Men Hills – I look down on Nanputuo Temple and the adjacent Xiamen University's Lotus Lake. A complex of more than a dozen buildings, Nanputuo is crowded with tourists, as it was when I walked through the grounds an hour earlier. In the Mahakaruna Hall, a woman prostrated herself before the statue of Guan Yin with a Thousand Hands. Physically the Hall is a constrained space, in which the eight-sided building narrowly encloses the statue. It has an air of spiritual intimacy ill served by the heavy traffic Nanputuo attracts. To watch a religious display felt intrusive. To me Guan Yin can only be an avatar, a personification of benevolence. There's more to it than that, Sifu tells me. He says that the sacred places and statues help to focus the mind on the underlying ideas better than would, say, prayers to a telephone box, or a coat stand. As such the Guan Yin statue can be a point of communication between the devotee and the abstract notion of compassion. To Sifu this is an all-pervasive force, but to channel it requires deep knowledge or external assistance. Hence the temples, statues and holy places that vibrate in the key of this force, like the setting of Nanputuo, by the sea and under the hills. As for what part of this place resonated with *Ruyi*, I cannot say.

'I went all over the mountain,' Sifu said. 'I tried to find the exact spot where they practised.'

He found no evidence of the *Ruyi* Abbot and his disciples. Mak Tian Meng too made inquiries around Xiamen to no avail.

'Nobody had heard of *Luohan Ruyiquan*,' he said.

It is unlikely that an elderly monk will leap out of the foliage to reveal himself as one of the Abbot's disciples. In the late 1960s, Master Chee travelled to Penang in Malaysia, where one of the *Ruyi* disciples fled during the Japanese invasion. He settled near Kek Lok Temple, where Master Chee visited him. Cheng Hai and Sifu accompanied the Old Man to Penang, but the monk – like Lim Hian's daughter in a similar episode – declined to see the young initiates. Another *Ruyi* monk fled to Taiwan, but we don't know where precisely. It appears that the history of *Luohan Ruyiquan*, and its master, Yi Chan Chan Shuai, is irretrievable.

It doesn't matter: I didn't expect to dig up the bones of the Abbot, or uncover *Ruyi* history where Sifu and Tian Meng could not. The disappointment at Shaolin underscored the pattern that all revelations have come to me on rooftops and in food courts rather than the places that brag of status. The Taoists say that the sage can understand the universe without leaving his hut. *Luohan Ruyiquan* does not belong to this place any more than Shaolin *gongfu* belongs to Shaolin Temple. Not to say that the effort was worthless. A pilgrimage might work like a statue, and bring me closer to Chee Kim Thong by sharing the places he visited.

From a carpenter's roadside stall, I purchase a Guan Yin statue in sanders wood, wrapped in a yellow cloth. I like that she represents compassion, and Nanputuo, and – by the story of how Sifu returned to the art – *Ruyi*. Strictly, of course, no souvenir should be necessary, because the art itself is most important of all. To perform *gongfu* pays tribute to all of the associated concepts, people and places. From arrival in Singapore airport tonight, I will go directly to Sifu's home to learn. Like Sifu many years ago, I am caught up in the profound possibilities of *Luohan Ruyiquan*.

33

LUOHAN RUYIQUAN

Imagine that you lift a mountain, push the clouds away, and pull the stars towards you. Fill your lungs in stages as you perform the Five Elements, in this iteration called Metal, Wood, Water, Fire and Earth. Inhale, hold; inhale, hold; inhale. The edges of the hands sweep in, the heels press down, the outer wrists bear up like a wave, the palms screw outward like paper twisting in a flame and then rotate inward to overturn soil. The fingers join before the solar plexus. Sifu always intones '*Amituofo*' at this movement. If the Five Elements constitute the universe, how can there be this sixth, conclusive movement? It may be that the Boundless Light of *Amituofo*, all-pervasive, informs each of the phases and finally displays itself independent of them. The combination of Elements also achieves this totality. Remember that Sifu translates *Ruyi* as 'your heart's desire': if this is what you wish the movement to mean, be it so, this is your *Luohan Ruyiquan*.

By turns you are a yogi, a fighter, a gymnast; slow, fast, utterly still. The spine stretches to awaken the *kundalini*, the hands move through treacle, the feet kick low under monastic robes. You are a staggering drunkard, now a white crane, the Crippled Immortal from death returned and – not just *any* monkey – the Monkey King, snatching fruit from the orchard of the gods. Breathe short and sharp, jump and kick twice in the air. Protract the respiration. This movement makes your hands hot; this one turns your palms white in the centre. Sit on the ground in the Guan Yin pose; there is a moment's rest here before the sway resumes, back and forth like waves of the ocean.

Walk the pentagon, the hexagon and the octagon. You give the techniques names of your own, and remember them by certain associations. This circle is like stroking a fat woman. Sifu resembles a dance partner when he performs the Mother and Child with this downward arc of the arms and turn at the waist. Here, the palms should feel like the suckers of a squid on an attacker's forearm. The tricksy, Cristiano Ronaldo footwork. This sequence you call 'Death by Kicking' for its potential fatality to the fatigued practitioner. Last night, at a drowsy outpost between sleep and wakefulness, you twitched your limbs in this movement, to which you devoted a solid hour that evening. This stroke you thought was the conclusion to Part II until Sifu revealed, 'I only said it to make you happy'. Then he demonstrated the ensuing techniques while you despaired, mutinous and exhausted.

Luohan Ruyiquan is difficult to learn. If you don't plant your feet and use the correct kind of strength, you will push yourself over at the very first movement during Mother and Child practice. Power proceeds from intention; you apprehend the principle mentally, but it must flow through your limbs to manifest in your execution. The art makes demands on your strength, balance, breath control and flexibility. It coaxes you ever deeper into fineries of skill. You don't know when advancements will come. Sifu cannot guarantee that they ever will; 'Whether you can get it, I don't know.' Yet you must set aside any doubts. Play the set like a beautiful piece of music, always at the correct cadence. Savour *Ruyi* as though you enjoy a priceless wine. At times the set will play you; then the nuances of the motions suggest themselves, as you become like lovers who know each other's secrets. Refine until you touch infinity.

Sifu says, 'You are merging into the plane.'

You perform our heritage, the history of our lineage. This too is an invocation. When you gain new insight to the movements, Sifu says it is because the lineage masters have come to help you. The set re-enacts the lives of your predecessors. With this movement, Chee Kim Thong escaped his manacles in the Japanese prison. On the night Sifu first met the Old Man, the master used this technique to bounce Yap Cheng Hai up into the air. With the following motion, he intercepted Sifu's punch and blasted him backwards through a fence. These breathing techniques helped two elderly men shoot the White Crane into the Sky. After an hour of struggle you performed this movement correctly, and Sifu said, '*Can*'. This elbow-strike Cheng Hai extracted as a static meditation-pose for hobbyists. The next stroke will acquire a story of its own just because it is, inexplicably, your favourite. This segment of fine wrist movements, like a mudra, Sifu will omit from a public demonstration. In old video footage from a performance on the anniversary of initiation, Master Chee stretches one leg out straight in this way, and squats slowly down to the ground. His students marvel at the feat and wonder, 'What is this art?' You can answer, 'I know this art; it is *Luohan Ruyiquan*.'

Join your hands again in the *Amituofo* pose.

Sifu says, 'I give you 35 marks out of 100.'

* * *

On a break in my drills I look over to see what Claire is doing. She stands with feet together, then takes two circling strides forward. She ends up on one leg, with her left foot hooked behind her right knee. Simultaneously she hits out with the backs of both hands, right over left.

'*Aiya*,' Sifu says. 'You told me you had studied some White Crane, but then, when I saw the Crane! It needs to be a double hit, like *this*.'

He demonstrates. Claire attempts it and gradually achieves the desired effect: a relaxed hit with the backs of the wrists causes the fingers to whip forwards in an involuntary, second attack.

'Don't look down! This is shyness.'

Sifu tells Claire to begin again. She proceeds further into the sequence this time, turning left from the one-legged position and using the waist rotation to whip her hands downward. Then she turns 180° right and repeats the technique the other way, so that her right palm faces up and her left is down. This art – whatever it is – looks difficult for a beginner. Soon Sifu notices that I'm eavesdropping on the lesson.

'Hey, stop playing truant! Concentrate on your own training,' he says.

In a few minutes, he will leave Claire to practise and offer me advice on the exercises he set this morning. But I'm not to know what Claire studies. Sometimes Alex meets Sifu to learn the principles of investment, and sometimes Travis takes Sifu to Johor Bahru to dine with the masters there. This too is another story, one I don't know.

34

MASTER AND DISCIPLE

'Alex, grab my butt. *Aiya*, he's shy. Lower! I promise not to fart. Come on, this is your chance for some free sexual harassment.'

Alex hesitates, then moves his hands further down Sifu's buttocks. After his latest, devastating assessment of our *Ruyi* performance, Sifu wants to correct some of the yoga-like tension exercises. Briefly a janitor appears on the rooftop to collect a few scraps of rubbish from the drain. Alex snatches his hands away from Sifu. We exchange pleasantries, but the janitor doesn't comment on the spectacle, and descends the ramp to progress downward through the levels of the car park.

'This should cause the testicles to lift,' Sifu continues. 'Do you remember checking that each other's testicles were moving?'

'We have sworn never to speak of that incident,' I say.

'Touch is important,' he says. 'Like I always say, you need to *feel*. Old Man would grab my hand and put it on his torso to show me. "Put your hand here, here." This is the lineage training, the real art. Without this detail, forever you can never get it. See how close we are to Kriya yoga, this kind of meditation: also physical, very tiring. Our *Ruyi* is only a step to the left of this kind of meditation. That's why I'm happy you are so interested, Chris. You must work until you can expand your consciousness, become magnanimous.'

Again, Sifu uses the word 'magnanimous' in a very literal way, as though the mind might transcend the limits of an individual to inform and be informed by the rest of existence. Previously he said that Nature acts through the practitioner; today he advances that concept with the suggestion that it's a two-way street.

'You two are always talking about meditation,' Alex says.

Sifu laughs.

'Well, I don't mean to leave you out,' he says. 'I keep telling you, I'm afraid to offend you. You'll say your church don't like this, don't like that.'

'But I'm *interested*,' Alex says, and Sifu is greatly pleased.

It's not necessarily that Sifu wants us to agree with his perspective on existence. I think he'd actually be disappointed if we signed up fully, accepting without question his anecdotes contingent upon far-fetched coincidences, and his sweeping rejection of all religious systems. The examined life is of paramount importance to Sifu. A reflective student will progress, although, 'How far? This one I cannot answer you.'

It will be up to Alex to reconcile the natural philosophy of our meditation with church doctrine. His enthusiasm to do so marks a new phase of his training. Maybe the universal energies – impersonal to me – will occur to him as a form of pantheism, a god-in-all. Perhaps my own interpretation will change tomorrow. A new stage of practise awaits me too, although on different grounds from Alex's.

'Since we are talking,' Sifu says, 'let us review the contemplation.'

'I've brought my cushion,' I say, and retrieve a *zafu* from my rucksack.

My meditation cushion was handmade by Zen monks at a monastery. I ordered it especially. Sifu inspects the cushion and hands it back to me.

'This one no good,' he says. 'Not firm enough.'

Alex sits cross-legged on the concrete, while I place the cushion beneath me to help straighten my spine. Sifu elaborates on the directions he gave previously. The exercise is not to sit vacantly, endlessly, but to follow a method of breath control and concentration. When this takes effect – discernable in physical sensations – Sifu will 'go in deeper' with additional instructions. To Watch the Breath requires detached observation of one's own respiration. The trick is to remain aware of the breath without controlling it. Achievement of this foundational skill brings the practitioner across a perceptual threshold: all day long we could theorise that body and mind are separate, but by watching the breath we *feel* the division.

It's a Thursday morning. For around fifteen minutes we attempt our practice amid the birdsong of the rooftop and, occasionally, Sifu's voice. Finally, Sifu ends the session and tells us to walk around a little. We reconvene to report our experiences.

'I have the physical sensations,' I say, 'but nothing else.'

'Nothing yet,' Alex says, whose interest in this practice is much newer.

'See how hard it is to concentrate?' Sifu says. 'This will also help your *gongfu* by developing *yi*, your intention. This is why we say *Ru-yi*: your heart's desire comes from your intention. Travis tells me he gets up at 2 am and meditates for three hours. Since it's so hard to do fifteen minutes starting off, you can understand why I never believe him.'

'Have you heard from him recently?' I ask.

'He brought moon cakes for the Mid-Autumn Festival,' Sifu says.

Sifu discouraged Travis from learning *Luohan Ruyiquan*.

'You would waste your time,' he said. 'You cannot get it.'

'I *must* learn,' Travis replied.

To resolve the dispute with Travis, Sifu announced that he would have to pay fees like everyone else in order to attend the *Ruyi* classes. For some time Travis avoided the fees we all contribute to Sifu with exaggerated tales of how little he was paid. When Sifu told him he would have to pay to study *Ruyi*, he ended Travis's interest. I haven't seen Travis for around eight months. Sifu hoped he might be free of his burden, but recently Travis has questioned him on when we will set *Ruyi* aside, so that he might attempt a return to study *Wuzuquan gratis*.

When Alex leaves to tutor a student, I perform *Luohan Ruyiquan* for the third time this morning. Sweat streams down my back and forehead. Usually, Sifu can't resist leaping in with corrections, or even narrating the movements, but this time he is silent. I know that watching someone perform this art is enough for Sifu to fire into life. I become aware that, internally, he plays the set with me.

'Chris, when you retire,' Sifu says as I conclude, 'teach this, and make sure you charge a lot of money.'

'A lot?' I repeat sceptically.

In Asia, many businessmen take an interest in *gongfu* for their health, and seek out good arts, but the West is a different world. I have a profession, an income, and am not interested to persuade strangers that my art differs from the *Taijiquan* in the local community centre. I assume *Ruyi* is for me alone and that if I ever teach, it will be to the few who are truly interested, and that it will not be a lucrative enterprise.

'I'm serious!' Sifu says. 'Years ago in Hong Kong, I taught for free. The students took advantage. If the weather was bad, they would not want to practise. I would call them up and the guys would say, "We didn't want to practise in the rain." Then if the weather was good, they would not come, and would not give me any notice. After, they would tell me, "Since it's sunny out, we decided to spend the day with the family." Others went off with their mistresses, and told their wives they were learning from me.'

'So they took you for granted,' I say, 'because they hadn't assigned any value to the training?'

'Yes. That's why I always say you must pay, must feel the pinch. You see, Chris, when you try to help people, it doesn't always work. Old Man also had trouble with this. He tries to help his sons, and they break his heart. Long-Arm Lum also gives Mr Chee a lot of stress. This Lum could only get work as a bill collector. He didn't even get promoted to clerk. Frankly, he's an idiot. He goes around to collect money, that's all he can do. But he loves to learn *gongfu*, and Mr Chee feels sorry for him. So the Old Man gives him a room in the clubhouse for free. Plus, an allowance of $600: Old Man is actually giving Lum pocket money!

'All Lum has to do is help grow herbs for medicine: put them out when it's sunny, take them in when it rains. But even this he cannot do properly. He kept leaving them out in the rain, so the herbs were all ruined. You'll ask him and he'll say, "Oh, I forgot." He drove Mr Chee crazy. If Old Man can't stand you, it must be something really bad. He complained to me about this Lum.'

'I feel less sympathy for Lum,' I say, 'when you mention that he always leaps in to criticize people when they train their *gongfu*.'

'Yes. Lum was also involved in gossip about me, although he does not know anything about me. He just wants to join in. This made Mr Chee very upset, but he kept it in his heart. It goes to show; when you try to help, often people will take advantage. Therefore, be selective who you teach.'

'I think you're in a stronger position for choosing students,' I say.

'If you have confidence, and remember the things I have taught you, you will be fine,' he says.

'But I mean that you have this claim to the lineage, the initiation—'

'Not necessary. I keep telling you: you have the lineage training. What more do you want? You don't need initiation. If you come to learn like this, and work hard, you are my disciple. That is enough.'

I say nothing. Sifu is telling me I'm his disciple, and my response is as though someone handed me a briefcase with a million dollars: if I was reasonably sure the money wasn't laundered, I would exit as quickly as possible, asking no questions, before the donor changed his mind. I'll share the good news with Alex later, although I suppose it shouldn't be a surprise; perhaps we've been neurotic not to have perceived what Sifu was telling us all along, and failed to identify his means of adjusting the terms of discipledom.

As for initiation itself, I'm satisfied that Sifu has made his call. I've never been able to imagine a day when we would set aside our usual mode of interaction to behave as though we were in China 200 years ago, kneeling before an altar and swearing sacred oaths. The implications of initiation already occur in our relationship; obedience, and the commitment on one side to teach sincerely, and the other to learn, is enacted if never promised ceremonially. Like the universe, the art and its practitioners are in constant flux. What matters most is that we retain what is best about the *gongfu*: the real techniques, and the most positive aspects of the relationship between the master and his followers. Late in life, Chee Kim Thong sold vacuous affiliations, which brought him only unhappiness. He didn't even want money for himself: 'There was $500,000 in the Old Man's safe when he died.' Sifu has learned from the Old Man's experience. I think Master Chee would have to accept that this lesson steered Sifu away from the role that the master wanted for his disciple, as head of a *gongfu* school. Sifu has retained the soul of the art and discarded the trappings. What he has given me I would not trade.

* * *

'"*That's* not my puppy," I read. '"Its tail is too fluffy." Here, you have to feel the fluffy ears, like this.'

'*Whoa!*' Jun Jie says, widening his eyes and spreading his hands out in amazement. Then he grabs his plastic cup and wanders off. Fortunately we've read the work twice in succession, so I'm not left in suspense over which is the correct puppy. I sip the *The Guan Yin* Sifu has brewed. Jun Jie returns with a toy car, which he offers to Claire. She accepts it graciously.

'How's it going?' I ask.

Sifu, looking grandfatherly in his spectacles, is at his table with a jar of red paste and a chop, his traditional Chinese seal.

'Doesn't it look good?' he says.

We look at the instructor certificate, which Eng Soon designed. The ghostly, background image is a reproduction of the Most Precious Disciple certificate, with a photo of Master Chee, his note of endorsement for Sifu, and his own seal. Over that are typed, in Chinese, the names of the arts I have studied; the *Wuzuquan* patterns and *Luohan Ruyiquan*. Sifu has insisted on certification in case anyone questions my entitlement to teach his arts.

'You can hang it up with your university certificates.'

'I'll give you $50 if you write "Most Precious Disciple" just there.'

'Hey look!' Sifu says.

'What's up?'

Jun Jie has snatched Claire's cup and is drinking from it.

'He's taken Claire's cup. Maybe that means Claire will have the next kid, ah?'

'Is this some crazy Chinese thing?'

Occasionally Sifu urges us to hurry up and have children. Sometimes I suspect he sees caring for a child as one way to prompt the necessary expansion of consciousness. Claire says nothing.

'Who's this handsome devil, standing here?' I say.

At the bottom of the certificate, in high quality, Eng Soon has reproduced my portrait photo with Sifu. We did our best to follow the format of Sifu's initiation-day photo with Chee Kim Thong and Seng Pang, so that Sifu sits while I stand behind his shoulder. As I inspect the picture I recall how anxious I was that the photo shoot would go well, as though – I reflect now with bemusement – there was much that could feasibly go wrong. True to what he says of *gongfu* portraiture, Sifu half-closes his eyes in the shot.

'OK,' Sifu says. 'Are we ready to go for our nasi biryani?'

Our next adventure will be to a restaurant in Little India that Sifu has raved about for some weeks, to the point that he has arranged to take us there for lunch today. It's always blazing in Little India, with hordes of labourers sitting around as you leave the MRT station. It's one of the few parts of Singapore that trundles along with little evidence of modernity: there are no sparkling malls, there are street vendors selling paraphernalia for Hindu rituals, and it's probably the area with the fewest air-con units in the whole country. A hardware store in Little India still bears the sign *Cheng Ho*, the name of Yap Cheng Hai's brother.

'I'm ready,' Claire says.

'Good,' Sifu says, as he puts on his shoes beside the front door. 'Hey, you know usually the master is not meant to pay, right?'

'But you're always bragging about how Master Chee insisted on getting your meals,' I say. 'I feel this keeps the tradition alive.'

'Old Man always treated me,' Sifu says. 'But don't be jealous of my life, ah?' and he's off towards the elevator.

35

TIME IS SHORT

When I first practised with Sifu he told me, *'Time is short'*. He explained that when he studied with Chee Kim Thong the master would often say, 'Time is short,' just as Lim Hian, the *Wuzuquan* master, said it to the young Ah-Thong.

Sifu first met Master Chee in 1960. He remained Chee Kim Thong's close disciple until the master's death in 2001. In youth, Sifu practised full-time with Master Chee: late nights, early mornings and any other opportunity they could find to practise *gongfu*. *'Time is short,'* Master Chee said all the while, despite the protests of the youngster who rubbed sleep from his eyes. In the video footage Sifu gave me from Master Chee's final months, they spend hours on end shut away in the Old Man's clinic, discussing the details of the art and training together. Yet when Sifu reflects on these last days with the master, after forty years together, he says, 'I didn't expect him to go so soon'.

Time *is* short.

Sifu goes through phases of telling the same anecdotes regularly so that, in a certain period, a favourite narrative becomes a refrain in our conversation. Over the last few weeks, he's often returned to the story of an old friend. He recounts it again on our way to breakfast after practice.

'This guy was in his fifties,' Sifu says. 'Very suddenly, a beautiful girl in her twenties fell in love with him. She was Chinese-American, visiting Malaysia at that time. After a while, she came to live with him in KL. None of us could understand how he got a girlfriend like this. He didn't have a lot of money. He smelled terrible; he smoked three packets of Lucky Strike a day. So when he was in my car I had to roll down the windows and leave the aircon on just so I could tolerate him. It didn't make any sense! Why would a beautiful, young girl choose a guy like this?

'Then, just as suddenly as she came, she left him and went back to America. My friend was heartbroken, he couldn't accept it. I went with him to all the different fortune-tellers. He asked them why she left, whether she would ever come back, and if there was anything he could do. They all said the same thing: "Your affinity has ended." Nothing he can do. They said this girl had some debt to my friend from a previous life, but now it was repaid.'

Instead of coffee I've taken Sifu's recommendation and started to drink *the si kau* recently, strong and black tea with a subtle, floral quality. I like it so much that I want to know where I can get some. It occurs to me to ask as we ascend the steps to the food court.

'I think it's called Pigeon Tea,' Sifu says. 'It's Indonesian. Hey, you want to go to the old side or new side?'

The collection of local shops has edged ever nearer being a modern mall, and more than ever the wet market is an outpost of yesterday's Singapore. A few metres away, the building makes an abrupt transition to newness, and there stands another food-court that has recently been renovated. Novelty and different varieties of food have attracted us there recently, although we've griped about high prices and small portions. This morning the new side seems the enemy.

'The drinks are better on the old side,' I say.

'That's good,' Sifu says. 'Today I feel like eating *prata*,' Indian bread served with a dish of lamb curry sauce. *Prata* is only available on the Old Side.

When I queue up for drinks, Sifu asks the Tea Auntie in Mandarin where the tea comes from.

'She says it's just ordinary tea, the same as in all the food courts,' Sifu tells me. Then, to the Tea Auntie: 'But he's going back to UK.'

The Tea Auntie reaches under the counter and takes a pack of tealeaves, which she hands to me as a gift. I thank her, and wonder if it's right to bring the tealeaves to England, whether they should be left as part of the magic in this place. However, I decide it's enough of a sacrifice to forego hawker-centre food.

'Alex should visit with you,' I say. 'The food in the UK is very bland, he'd like it.'

'Ah, not so bad,' Sifu says, who was sent to the best London restaurants by the bank. 'All the roast beef. Remember, if you go to a Chinese restaurant in London, you must tell them you have standards. Say, "Hey, tell the chef there's a Human Being here."'

'The chocolate is good too,' I say. 'Much better. Not like the terrible Mars bars you get here, made in Malaysia.'

I carry the tray with drinks back to our table and hand Sifu his cup of tea. Although I've never served tea to him in a formal initiation ceremony, I've done so hundreds of times because we enjoy each other's company. I find this version preferable. Over the last few weeks we've had numerous farewell dinners – Peking Duck in Orchard with my classmates, biryani in Little India, Beef Wellington at the Cricket Club – but I'm glad that the last time I see Sifu, for now, brings us to our regular haunt.

We've argued recently, which seems to be some way of dealing with my departure. When Sifu says 'you are like a son to me' it's usually the precursor to an advisory narrative that I receive with ill grace, such as the interminable discourses on how I should sign up for a life-insurance policy.

'I'm not happy with you moving to the UK,' he says. 'Their economy is very bad.'

I knew I wouldn't stay in Singapore forever. Even if I accepted a long-term position here – overlooking Claire's reluctance – I couldn't imagine that my life would continue the same way. When I add up the time I spend practising, commuting across Singapore to Sifu's house, and learning about the old days in food courts, I can see that it is a special effort, unsustainable. These pursuits are haunted by a guilty sense of truancy. Whether or not I attain enlightenment this afternoon, I will nonetheless have a pile of essays to grade tomorrow. I can repeat the mysterious Bodhidharma invocation whenever I like, but that doesn't alter my interaction with people in the tangible here-and-now. These Shaolin practices are important to me, but it's vital that they enrich my life rather than provide an escape from it. I think Sifu knows this too: if Claire and I had a child, for example, he must know that I wouldn't spend every recreational moment on *gongfu*. A permanent appointment at the university would also entail a more rigid timetable. But above all, while Claire and I enjoy a comfortable lifestyle, the sheer distance from home counts against Singapore, and the feeling that we would always be foreign here. Change appears inevitable. That time was short gave urgency to my practice. The prospect of me bringing the art to the West encouraged Sifu too.

Some weeks after I accepted a job in the UK, the university in Singapore offered me a permanent position. By this time Claire and I had our hearts set on the cobbled streets and ales and brooding landscapes of northern England. Sifu asks what I think of this sequence of events. I say that Asia has made a fatalist of me. There's no point wondering 'what if,' because 'if' didn't happen. Sifu agrees.

If Sifu preaches fatalism, it's also clear that he lives by it. He is still wealthy, but spends cautiously. Sifu's current lifestyle is a world apart from his experiences as a high-flying banker in Hong Kong. The developments in my career lead him to reflect on his own trajectory.

'I lost a lot of money through investments,' he says. 'When I invest, all that hatches is worms. I must accept that I will never be a multi-millionaire.'

It sounds like Sifu has come to terms with his financial destiny in a way that Yap Cheng Hai never has. Yet I know that Sifu suspects there may be further twists in his favour. But it's pointless to dwell on unpredictable vicissitudes, so he takes what he gets for now.

Likewise, I've realized it's futile to speculate on the possible, alternate histories of Chee Kim Thong and his disciples. It may have been better for the Old Man if Cheng Hai had left him as a grocer in Dungun. A more authoritative attitude from Master Chee towards the club might have prevented argument between the initiates and the degradation of his arts. The permutations and possibilities are dazzling. If Sifu's friend had not offered him the Guan Yin statue, would the Old Man have taught him something else entirely? Had Travis not pestered him to accept students in the Botanic Gardens, would Sifu teach me years later? None of the variant histories occurred, and speculation on the could-have-beens underestimates, from Sifu's perspective, the importance of an unseen magnetism that drew us all together. *It's just our affinity.* Many years ago, a man met an orphan and treated him as a son. Decades later, a man meets an older one in a strange country and, although the newcomer is neither a teenager nor an orphan, a version of the tradition persists, centring on *gongfu* practice. Maybe Sifu is right; it would be wrongheaded to pick apart the machinations by which that situation arose.

'I won't go to the airport tomorrow. I will be all teary.'

Presumably this is humour, and he is simply too lazy to go the airport.

'There's no point in going all the way out to the airport,' I say. 'It's a waste of time. When I visit my family in Dublin, we never see each other off at the airport either.'

Besides, a departure-lounge send-off isn't our style.

'Mak Tian Meng told me he prays for me,' Sifu says. 'He told me, "See-meng, because I care for you, I ask Lord Buddha to help you."'

'That's nice, I suppose,' I answer.

'But I mean to say, we're *grown men*: he doesn't need to tell me things like that, right?'

'No, it's not necessary to say things like that.'

We eat our *prata* in silence. After a while, Sifu starts to complain about my *Ruyi*: 'Still a bit too hard; work on your softness.'

Finally Sifu mentions return visits. We discuss the necessity of Mother and Child practice at certain intervals, and when it would be feasible or advisable to learn new sets. We decide to progress with meditation instructions over Skype, as this area of instruction requires little physical contact.

'The fruit is on the tree,' Sifu says. 'You need to reach out and take it. Better do it! It will be intense when you visit, because there will be so little time.'

I say that's OK, but I don't make any promises about returning. Those declarations are for people who never come back.

BOUNDLESS LIGHT

36

THUNDER

Some say that bells originated in India. The metal sang out with sacred sounds in allusion to the vibrational energies behind all existence. The people too must resonate in those keys, like pitchforks, when they breathe and meditate, until they are in tune with Nature.

Overhead peal the bells of an English cathedral at midday. Once there was a monastic community in this place. *It's all interrelated.* Bells, temples, monks. You find it almost impossible to speculate on a common origin for the monastic traditions you have encountered, and then account for the extent of their divergence.

By a grove near a river, you experience a murmur of apprehension. You wonder whether the art can survive in this world. You remember the precepts, but can they manifest in this new environment? Although you are aware that these anxieties contradict fundamental principles of the art, you feel that those lessons are – with the teacher – very far away.

Finally, it is too cold to stand around in procrastination. It is in part to warm up that you begin. Immediately, the familiar electricity courses through your limbs. Metal, Wood, Water, Fire, Earth, *Amituofo.* Universal. Placeless. The Old Man used to rap his knuckles against the table, knocking to set the rhythm for Sifu's performance. You discern a pattern to the bells and time your practice in unison. Now you understand that what is within you cannot be taken away. Inhibition disintegrates, and the dance of elements emerges into daylight. Irresistible and intoxicating, the art rushes down your arms and out your fingertips.

* * *

An e-mail came from Sifu with the subject line, 'Need your assistance to unify the Club.'

Long-Arm Lum has died and, a week later, Yap Cheng Hai. Lum passed peacefully at the Chee Kim Thong Pugilistic and Health Society headquarters, where Sneaky Snake found him, but the eldest disciple's end was terrible. For months Cheng Hai was unable to sit up in bed. He was blind in one eye. Eventually he succumbed to liver cancer. It was a protracted decline as an embittered invalid.

Mah Chai Soon, Lum Koon Hoong, Mah Ping Kwong, Yap Cheng Hai. The older practitioners in Kuala Lumpur watch as their generation passes. Some say that the Old Man watches his initiates from beyond the grave, and punished Cheng Hai.

'A few weeks ago,' Sifu said over Skype, 'Mak Tian Meng called and asked me to pray for Cheng Hai. I told him I could not be a hypocrite. What has happened to Cheng Hai is very sad, but I am not Jesus Christ; I cannot simply forget. I tell you, Chris, Bai Yu Feng, our *Wuzu* founder, is looking in *consternation* on the loss of his heritage.

'I told Tian Meng, "Mr Chee wants us to get the club back together. *You* are the person who can clear the air. You must explain that I instructed you to remove my photo from the clubhouse in 2001. It doesn't mean Mr Chee sacked me from the club. With this truth known, the club members and committee can reunite."'

What must be, must be. Where is the line drawn to determine that the destined state has been attained? How can we verify that what *must be* has been correctly identified, and now *is*? I thought that Sifu adopted a *laissez-faire* attitude to the club. Now, what 'must be' is revaluated in light of Cheng Hai's death. A man with steadfast belief in his own myth, Sifu may well have determined that, with Cheng Hai out of the way, Chan See-meng – Man of Destiny – would revive the fortunes of the Chee Kim Thong Pugilistic and Health Society. For a time, I thought it would be so.

Tantalizingly, the idea of reformation lingers in the air. On one

262

week, off the next, a debate fascinating to a spectator but infuriating to an advisor. For me, fresh impetus has emerged from an unexpected source. In Durham I showed the Most Precious Disciple document to a calligraphy expert and got new insights to Master Chee's intentions. Sifu himself, of limited education in the Chinese language, would make little headway with traditional characters hand-written in mirrored script. He accepts the wording as it was translated for him. The text mentions particular arts that the Old Man taught Sifu and how he cared for the young disciple by cooking special meals to help him grow strong. The document also endorses Sifu's modern teaching-methods explicitly. The characters Sifu dwells upon say 思明 宝徒 惠存, 'presented to my precious disciple See-meng'. *Bao* (宝), 'precious', speaks for itself, but it isn't *exclusive*; other disciples could likewise be 'precious'. There is no such superlative as 'most' in Master Chee's words, although one might consider uniqueness as implicit if nobody else holds a similar document. On the other hand, I've come to believe that establishing Sifu's status isn't the primary purpose of the document at all.

The calligraphy expert, from China, was struck that Master Chee backdated the document, composed around April 2001, to correspond to Mid-Autumn Festival in 2000. Mid-Autumn Festival is traditionally a time for families to reunite. By this interpretation, the *text* of Master Chee's document explains his close relationship with Sifu, but its *meaning* as encoded in the date is an instruction: *reunite the family*. The club needs a leader, but it has never been about one person, but a family. The Old Man's repertoire was so immense that even the best disciple only attained a portion. I imagine that Chee Kim Thong hoped different people, from Sifu to the durian-farmer Mr Ho, practising only his running-on-the-spot meditation, would inherit his assorted arts. He wanted a show of unity from his disciples that proved beyond them.

While aware that the question was reductive – *crude*, even – I asked Sifu to evaluate Chee Kim Thong's gifts. Sifu, who was asked, but declined, to succeed two great masters who were more famous than Master Chee but, in Sifu's opinion, inferior. Sifu who, for all his arrogance, plays down the ease with which the Old Man's tuition equipped him to win an international martial-arts tournament. Sifu, sought out by *gongfu* masters, yogi and Tibetan lamas to learn their arts, but who remained devoted to one above all.

'You told me once,' I began, 'about a saying in *gongfu*, that only once every 500 years will come a practitioner so talented that he can learn all the arts. Was Master Chee that good?'

'Yes,' Sifu said. 'He was very good.'

How could any organisation survive such a loss? The Chee Kim Thong Pugilistic and Health Society is no longer a *gongfu* club. It is mainly a dispute over real estate.

Thus Chee Kim Thong: doubtless a reasonable bus conductor, a conscientious grocer. He was a bad organiser, a stern and remote father in the Chinese tradition. But the energies of the universe were child's play to Master Chee. We worldly beings can only theorise and practise, and hope to capture a glimpse of his vision. Through the stories and arts, we aspire to derive the wisdom of the Old Man's experience. Was Chee Kim Thong the greatest? I do not know, and he would not care. He was an artist, and art is not a competition.

* * *

Of the rebel leaders who achieved prominence in the seventeenth century, former soldier Li Zicheng was the most famous, and he hated Shaolin. The civil unrest that swelled in the early decades of the century resulted from famine. Many in central China resorted to eating grass and tree bark. It is thought that Li Zicheng mutinied over unsatisfactory army rations. Hundreds of thousands turned to banditry, and individual gangs could number ten thousand. The nature of authority at the time was such that law-abiding citizens found little to differentiate the marauding bandits from the unruly soldiers sent to restore order. The pursuit of the army usually just compelled bandits to move from one rural hideout to the next, hide-and-seek with machetes on an enormous scale.

By the mid-1630s, thirteen major gangs had agreed to cooperate against the imperial forces. Brutal punishments prescribed by the Emperor's eunuch officials failed to dissuade the bandits, who acted from desperation against a corrupt regime. Meanwhile, the Emperor appeared powerless to remedy either the corrupt regime itself or the widespread unrest. Various divisions of the imperial army recruited Shaolin monks to help quell the rebels with their famous staff technique. Because of this military participation, or to gain the temple's agricultural produce, Li Zicheng resolved to massacre the monks who remained at Shaolin.

He tricked them. Li Zicheng sent one of his generals, Li Juyi, who persuaded the monks still in residence to perform the Thousand Buddhas Supplication for his benefit. As the Shaolin initiates beat drums, burned incense, recited sutras and meditated in the course of this ritual, Li Juyi led his troops in quietly and slaughtered the monks where they sat.

Li Zicheng marched on Beijing, where he defeated the imperial forces quickly. Watching from the Forbidden City – the imperial stronghold – the Chongzhen Emperor was paralysed by indecision. He did not know whether to flee or attempt to hold Beijing. But Du Zhizhi, a eunuch official, opened the city gates to Li Zicheng's troops, who sacked Beijing. The Chongzhen Emperor left his palace for Coal Hill, where he stood on the boulders and surveyed the siege of the Forbidden City. For identification he left a note inscribed simply *Tianzi*, 'Son of Heaven'. The Emperor hanged himself from the branches of a pagoda tree, and the Ming Dynasty ended.

Li Zicheng declared himself King of the Shun dynasty. He warred against the surviving nobles and was killed within a year. The Manchurians benefitted most from this situation. They exploited the chaos of the peasant rebellion, and captured China easily. Ostensibly the new, foreign rule was disastrous for Shaolin. The Qing dynasty paid lip service to the temple as a spiritual landmark, but for fear that skilled rebels might emerge, they outlawed martial arts on pain of death. For three centuries there was no abbot at Shaolin, and the temple fell into disrepair.

But Shaolin *gongfu* survived. The arts were transmitted secretly. The *qing* salutation of Chinese arts, because of the *yin-yang* symbolism of its open palm paired with closed fist, became a symbol for the *yin-yang* motif of the Ming dynasty, that had 'ruled by night and day'. Shaolin *gongfu* was rebellion: *Overthrow the Qing and restore the Ming*. The perception that Shaolin monks had fought foreigners in aid of Chinese emperors became more important than the particular circumstances attendant upon those collaborations. Shaolin was suppressed, but in its suppression it was embraced as quintessentially Chinese by a population that resented its conquerors.

So *Wuzuquan* can survive without the Chee Kim Thong Pugilistic and Health Society. The desolate clubhouse need not signify the death of the art. Even if our *gongfu* is disadvantaged by the lack of leadership and our want of a communal space, those are inconveniences, not terminal illnesses. Bodhidharma meditated in a cave for nine years to think of a new way to teach the *dharma*, and Zen Buddhism was born. To Adapt is one of *Wuzuquan*'s more advanced principles, for when our initial attempts reveal the need for another tactic. These arts evolved in contexts of difficulty, to address challenges. *Gongfu* is not an organisation, or a building, and it can survive without that infrastructure.

How to adapt? Shaolin took the practices of the yogi and the Shaman and altered them to suit the monks' needs. Now I must determine a new context for my *gongfu*, be it in words or in new teaching opportunities that avoid the pitfalls of the Chee Kim Thong Pugilistic and Health Society. Certainly I am not a once-in-500-years *gongfu* talent, but I can be less avaricious than Master Chee and less arrogant than Sifu. He is right, my master, to criticize forbears occasionally, where tradition guides us to idolize them. We must humanize our predecessors in order to comprehend their experiences, and we must identify their faults – if sympathetically – to find our own paths, knowing that we are not doomed to measure ourselves against flawless immortals. What matters most is that there is an authentic art to pass on.

* * *

'So, why did you come back so soon?' Alex asks as we walk along the car park. In the months since I left, Sifu noticed the strolls of respite had become more protracted, so he has limited us again to the painted word *SLOW.*

Why? Because my practice needed fresh impetus. Because I wanted to see the old devil. Because I wanted to set a precedent and prove to myself that it was possible to return. Because I didn't want to feel that I was cut adrift.

'It's not so soon,' I say.

'Hey!' Sifu yells as we dawdle by the ramp. 'Stop playing truant.'

We quicken our pace.

'Now,' Sifu goes on as we return, 'you must practise this Thunder Fist for at least 100 days continuously. That's the only way a new art will get into you.'

Thunder Fist belongs to *Wuxingzhang*, the Five Elements Palm that Master Chee learned after he studied *Wuzuquan*. Since both are White Crane arts, there is considerable overlap. Sifu says that 'the power is slightly more refined' in *Wuxingzhang*. This will deepen our comprehension of how power can be expressed, and hopefully result in improvement to all our arts, including *Luohan Ruyiquan*. As such, a journey continues that is more complex than chronological advancement from basic arts to difficult ones. Our initial *gongfu* prepared us for contemplation, and later meditation; in turn this made us ready to learn higher *gongfu*. But the higher *gongfu* revealed subtleties within the supposedly basic techniques. Already I feel a difference in my quality of movement after ten days of intense concentration on Thunder Fist. The cost has come in several varieties of pain, some of which have kept me awake at night. One Thunder injury prevented me from forming the correct hand positions until Sifu found some medicine to massage into my wrists.

'Just imagine you are chopping wood,' Sifu repeats of the eponymous Thunder Fist stroke; a back-fist that drops onto a target like an axe deployed with deadweight strength. The loose, wood-chopping visualization gives a bouncy cadence to the technique. And then, one of Sifu's abrupt changes of subject:

'Hey, where is Travis? He said he would be here this morning.'

In spite of himself, Sifu intimates that the picture isn't complete without Travis. It's not solely that he wishes to criticize Travis's attempt at Thunder Fist. There's a game-like quality to their relationship, I see now. Sifu would never admit it, but he enjoys scolding Travis. In turn, Travis, as long-suffering victim of Sifu's tirades, has a niche in a close *gongfu* group under a true expert.

'Look at us,' Sifu says. For a moment I wonder whether he intends to continue these thoughts, or criticize our performance again. 'Aren't we lucky to be here, enjoying this friendship? Is this not enlightened?'

Is this not enlightened: typical of Sifu to push aside the esoteric definitions of that word with an interpretation both simplistic and profound. We came together to share this interest; this is enlightened behaviour, which can relegate transient hardships and organisational politics to the shadows.

'What time is your flight?' Sifu asks.

'Not until this evening,' I say.

'Have you had enough yet?'

I look upwards, over my shoulder at the sun and clouds and apartment blocks.

'Not quite.'

'Good. One more round.'

At times this week I had the old, mutinous feeling of being too tired to continue, reversed utterly now. Time is short, but there is opportunity yet, before the blaze of the midday sun, to practise and review, practise and review. Although we're tired from the morning's session, the art will provide a firm footstep, an assured strike and the life-giving breath. The craftsman and his apprentices can continue a while longer.

ACKNOWLEDGEMENTS

Many who helped with the composition of this book appear in its pages; I won't repeat those names here, hoping their contributions are self-evident. Thanks to everyone who has helped me advance my interest in martial arts, and to the allies I've made on this adventure, from the Hairy Friends of UCD – Dave, Gordon, JJ and Mike – to the *wuxia* on the Malayan peninsula.

In the early stages of composition, the creative writing community at Nanyang Technological University helped me decide what kind of book this should be. Appreciative noises towards Tash Aw, Barrie Sherwood, John Tangney and above all to Jen Crawford for allowing me to burst into her office with asinine queries.

For assistance with aspects of Chinese history, culture and places, my gratitude goes to Rana Mitter, Hu Yunhan and – Caucasiandom's ambassador to Fujian Province – Amoy Bill.

The first draft prompted exceptionally useful commentaries from Sarah Castleton and Paul Murray, likewise the second draft from Christine Chong. I hope I've made it better and not worse.

At Durham University, Simon Litchfield identified a place for me to practise. Simon, I miss our lunches! Love to Jenny Holden and Vidyan Ravinthiran, who encouraged me to stick with it when the writing process was arduous. Ali Alizadeh and Ant Howell offered valuable insights as the text lumbered towards publication.

Maddy and Pearse: behold what your parents' life was like before you provided new diversions.

Although this is what my mother would call 'a very odd kind of book,' it's dedicated to my parents.

Lightning Source UK Ltd.
Milton Keynes UK
UKHW01f1812100918
328669UK00001B/60/P